At the ALTAR
of the
BOTTOM LINE

At the ALTAR
of the
BOTTOM LINE

The Degradation of Work
in the 21st Century

Tom Juravich

University of Massachusetts Press   AMHERST AND BOSTON

LC 2009034658
ISBN 978-1-55849-725-2 (paper); 724-5 (library cloth)

Designed by Dennis Anderson
Set in Dante by Westchester Book Group
Printed and bound by Hamilton Printing Company.

Library of Congress Cataloging-in-Publication Data

Juravich, Tom.
    At the altar of the bottom line : the degradation of work in the twenty-first
century / Tom Juravich.
        p.   cm.
    Includes bibliographical references and index.
    ISBN 978-1-55849-725-2 (pbk. : alk. paper)—ISBN 978-1-55849-724-5
(library cloth : alk. paper)
    1. Labor—Social aspects—United States.   2. Working class—United
States.   3. Quality of work life—United States.   4. Work environment—
United States.   5. Industrial sociology—United States.   I. Title.
    HD8072.5.J87 2009
    306.3'60973—dc22
                                                                        2009034658

British Library Cataloguing in Publication data are available.

For all the workers whose voices still cry out for bread and roses

CONTENTS

At the ALTAR
of the
BOTTOM LINE

INTRODUCTION

The Degradation of Work in the 21st Century

It's so regimented. You can't go to the bathroom. You can't get up and get a drink. They technically say that you can do this, but you really can't. You can only go within your appointed time. They're very inflexible. It reminds me of a hospital environment. Everybody eats at the same time. Everybody drinks at the same time. It's the same type of thing. You have 600 to 700 people in this building. Everybody does what they're supposed to do within their appointed time. But we have families, we have issues, we have things going on outside of this company that impact what goes on within the company. But that doesn't matter. You can't be late no matter what. You can't be out. It's very regimented and doesn't allow for you to be a human being. Ellen (2003, 1)

AT FIRST glance one might think that this is a historical account of women working in the garment industry in the early part of the twentieth century. Or perhaps it's a description of work in a sweatshop somewhere in the global South where young women make clothing for designer labels or fashion expensive athletic shoes. It is neither. Nor is it a report of work in a small, marginal U.S. firm or a low-wage retail store such as Wal-Mart.

Ellen, whom I interviewed several times for this book, works as a customer service representative for Verizon, one of the largest telecommunications companies in the United States. Her description of her work—the regimentation, the narrow scripts she must follow, the constant monitoring, and the tremendous pressure to sell, all happening within a rigid, inflexible schedule—is harrowing. This is not the way work was supposed to be at a major U.S. firm in the twenty-first century—in the postindustrial "new" economy. What happened to flextime, telecommuting, and self-managed work teams? What happened to the family-friendly workplace?

And it's not just Ellen's particular job, or just work at Verizon. Something is not right in the American workplace. We can feel it every time we talk to the next-door neighbor, a brother-in-law, or a woman we work with. For any of us lucky enough still to have a job, the workday has gotten longer, harder, and more stressful. And part of the stress is worrying that if we don't keep up, we might not hold on to our jobs. As unemployment skyrockets in the wake of the economic meltdown of the fall of 2008, the pressure is on.

The American workplace has become a crucible, fueled by the outsourcing and offshoring of work, new work systems, and an economy that grew slowly for a long time and then went into free fall. Employers have turned up the heat on American workers. Like Ellen, too many Americans find it harder and harder to settle in and just do their jobs. Instead they feel they have to prove themselves day in and day out—prove their skills, their dedication, and most importantly their economic value to their employers.

At the end of the work week, as Americans stagger into the precious few hours they have left for themselves or their families after finishing the errands and the chores, the laundry and the dishes, too many feel stressed, exploited, exhausted, and abandoned. With little job security, and dignity and respect in short supply, it is no wonder they feel as though they're being sacrificed at the altar of the bottom line.[1]

There are important economic roots to this crisis in the American workplace. For much of the postwar era, as productivity rose, so did workers' wages (Kuttner 2007, 192). With strong unions and governmental regulation of the economy, American workers got something for all their hard work. By the end of the 1980s, however, this link between productivity and wages was broken. For example, while productivity in the United States grew a whopping 33.4 percent from 1995 to 2005, wages for those with high school and college educations remained essentially flat (Mishel, Bernstein, and Allegretto 2006, 4).

American workers, Wolman and Colamosca point out, "have led the race to become competitive again, but they seemed fated to return to the starting line again and again. They are looking from the outside at a prosperity in which they have no part and working in a job market in which they can find no peace" (1997, 7). Because of this stagnation of wages for working people, income inequality in the United States is as high today as it was in the 1920s (Scheve and Slaughter 2007, 1).

Spiraling health care costs have eroded wages further. Nearly 47 million Americans are without health care coverage and pay the costs out of pocket, often having to choose among medical care, rent, and basic living expenses. Even for those covered by employer-based health care, the amount families spent on deductibles and out-of-pocket medical expenses increased 117 percent from 1999 to 2008. In 2008 it reached $3,354 a year, approaching one month's salary for the average American worker (Kaiser Family Foundation 2008).

Over two decades, many American families have compensated for the lack of wage increases by working more hours (Jacobs and Gerson 2004, 31). More women and other family members entered the workforce, just to stay even. Some economists suggest that there is no problem of overwork, that average weekly work hours for individuals have remained steady over this period (Rones, Ilg, and Gardner 1997). Jacobs and Gerson (2004, 5), however, unpack this average, suggesting a "growing time divide between those working especially long weeks, who would prefer to work less, and those working relatively short weeks, who would prefer to work more." There doesn't seem to be any middle ground in this economy: either you are not working or, if you are working, you are working far too much.

Chronic overwork has also been reflected in the growth of mandatory overtime. As employers cut permanent workforces to the bone, mandatory overtime became a standard practice in many workplaces. In 2005 over a quarter (26 percent) of American workers were subject to regular mandatory overtime that added, on average, almost ten hours a month to their work schedules (Golden and Wien-Tuers (2005, 6–7). When we consider that more family members are working and that overtime hours—for some voluntary but for others mandatory—are added to what for many were already long regular work weeks, it is no wonder Americans are exhausted and families have been pushed to the "fault line" (Rubin 1994).

After the 2008 financial collapse, workers faced a new set of insecurities. The most striking was the loss of equity in their homes. With wages remaining flat, many Americans had used their growing home equity, made available to them in a variety of new financial instruments, to purchase automobiles, pay for college, and even to cover medical expenses. But then the housing bubble burst, and in 2008 more than $2 trillion was lost in home equity in the United States, and 11.7 million homeowners owed more on their mortgages than their homes were worth (Wotapka 2008).

At the same time, many Americans felt a similar blow to their pensions. In 1980 approximately half of all Americans were covered by defined-benefit pension plans whose payouts were unaffected by fluctuations in the market. By 2008 the number of workers covered by defined-benefit programs had dropped to less than 20 percent (Silvers 2008, 24). The remaining 30 percent of pensions were shifted to 401(k) or other savings programs that were vulnerable to market variations, and many workers lost significant portions of their retirement savings when the stock market collapsed.

These statistics provide an important overview of the massive changes that affect work and workers across a wide swath of the economy. The fundamental changes we are seeing in workplaces across the United States are not reducible, however, to the economics of work. What we need to explore is how employers are responding to this economic context and fundamentally altering the way work is being done. We need to examine how workplace changes actually play out in what workers face every day in office cubicles, on factory floors, and at construction sites. This is not just the "invisible hand" of the economy working, but employers' purposive decisions on how to run their workplaces and treat their workers.

Neither do the economics of work tell us what these changes really mean to workers and their families as they sit around the kitchen table and try to make sense of their work and lives. As part of this project I interviewed Kathryn Peras and her husband, Pete, who had been laid off from his job of many years. Kathryn is frustrated that what her family is going through gets reported as just a statistic:

> [The unemployment rate] went up 3 percent, [and] people think that's not a lot. Try to walk in my shoes and see how it feels. I bet they wouldn't be too pleased. With unemployment [insurance], you get a little bit of money, it's not as much as you got before and it will tide you over, but what's going to happen to your home, your family, and all the other things that you've worked hard for? (Peras and Peras 2001, 30–31)

How can a number ever capture what a worker or a family goes through when a job of twenty-five years suddenly ends?

By looking only at the macro-level economics of work, one can also very easily see workers as simply passive victims of larger social processes. What the number of workers laid off or the number subjected to new work practices does not tell us is anything about *how* these changes have played out, often over many years. The truth lies in the details of this struggle, not just in how it ends. To understand what is happening in American workplaces today and to begin to envision alternatives, one must go inside and examine these struggles in real work situations with real people. What one finds is not as neat as quantitative charts and graphs, and is surely not as pretty. But it is out of the contradictions and complexity of these situations that insights emerge, allowing us both to understand what is happening and to be able to envision alternatives.

To learn more about the new reality American workers find themselves in and the lives they have had to make around it, I began in-depth interviews with workers in four very different kinds of workplaces: call center representatives, operating room nurses, undocumented workers in fish processing, and displaced industrial workers. I started in the fall of 2000 and spent the next eight years finishing the project. Although not by design, I ended up chronicling the dynamics of work in America during the presidency of George W. Bush.

In each workplace I was fortunate to find truly remarkable people who were able to reflect on their work with great insight. In the interviews I sought detailed descriptions of the everyday, but I also tried to create a space where workers could reflect on their work and their lives beyond the everyday. Here I was looking at workers not just as subjects of the interviews but as analysts of the situations they found themselves in.[2] When the interviews reached this level, they took on a life of their own. More than once we talked so long the room turned dark—we hadn't noticed that the sun had long since gone down. At other times I had to schedule another interview because there was too much to absorb in one sitting. In some ways the hardest thing to do was to call it quits. When I finally did, I had conducted eighty-five formal interviews.

In the pages that follow, the workers I interviewed tell their stories. I believe they have more to add to our understanding of the American workplace and the lives workers are making than my paraphrasing, summarizing, or trying to explain to the reader what they really mean. To ensure accuracy I made audio recordings of all interviews and had them transcribed verbatim. I didn't want just approximations of what workers told me. I wanted to capture their exact words and the cadence and rhythm of voices that the poets speak about. Somewhere in these voices—sometimes halting and other times impatiently staccato—I would find the story I was looking for, and the stories I found were far beyond what I could ever have imagined.

Stressed, Exploited, Exhausted, and Abandoned

I began my interviews in Andover, Massachusetts, with women and men who work as customer service representatives at a large Verizon call center. Working for the phone company has always been considered a good job. It's stable (everybody needs a phone, even in hard times); it provides decent pay and benefits; and it's free from the physicality of waiting on tables or working on an assembly line.

But I learned that what it's like to work for Verizon today is a long way from what it was like to work for the phone company in the days when it was a regulated monopoly in the United States. In a highly competitive industry that has gone through a series of mergers and acquisitions, Verizon has introduced a host of new technologies, work practices, and management systems that have intensified the work at every turn. As call center jobs have come under the constant threat of offshoring, the work has become more difficult and more stressful.

Ellen has already told us about the continual monitoring of her time and how she can't even leave her work station to use the bathroom as needed. But in addition to the monitoring, workers' frustrations at Verizon are also about the unrelenting pressure to make sales. Ellen's best friend at Verizon, Margaret, explains that "as many as five or six times a day an e-mail may pop up on your screen from your supervisor: 'You guys are making me look bad.'" She adds, "If things get really bad, there's actually a report that they can pull, the 'every breath you take' report is what they always called it. I don't know what it's really called, but they will show you exactly what you did every second of the day" (2001a, 15).

Margaret is hardly alone. The American Management Association reported that almost three-quarters of U.S. firms were "actively monitoring their employees with electronic surveillance tools of one kind or another" (Wallace 2004, 216). In his *New Ruthless Economy,* Simon Head reports that he found "again and again that information technology was being used to renew a long-established industrial culture whose values had supposedly been displaced by those of the 'new economy'" (2003, xv).

Instead of fulfilled, empowered workers or self-managed work teams, what emerged from my interviews at Verizon was a new form of hyper-Taylorism. The human resources practices allowed workers little flexibility and required large amounts of mandatory overtime. You cannot talk to Verizon workers without feeling their stress.

In New Bedford, Massachusetts, I explored the work and lives of the approximately 3,000 undocumented Guatemalans who work primarily in the fish-processing industry. It is impossible to write about work in the United States today without considering the role of the estimated 12 million undocumented workers. Chacón and Davis report that "they're a quarter of workers in the meat and poultry industry, 24 percent of dishwashers and 27 percent of drywall and ceiling tile installers. It is also believed that undocumented workers comprise up to 25% of the construction workforce, and about a third of garment workers" (2006:157). Segmented in this labor market with little chance of advancement, they are the new American underclass. What is happening in fish processing in New Bedford closely parallels what can be seen in meatpacking and food processing. As work has once again become nonunion, wages have plummeted, and the number of accidents and injuries has skyrocketed, and many of the jobs in fish processing have fallen out of the bottom of the domestic labor market. Employers rely largely on an immigrant workforce.

The fish processing plants in New Bedford seem a world away from the Verizon call center. There are no human resources policies and no sophisticated employee monitoring, just work as it was done throughout most of the nineteenth and twentieth centuries. Workers cutting fish in New Bedford are on their feet all day in the cold and the damp, working with very sharp knives at a blistering pace. They are fired if they don't work fast enough. Some are hurt, and others are mistreated by supervisors with whom they can barely communicate. One worker describes his experience in one of the most notorious fish houses in New Bedford:

> [My boss] doesn't know how to treat people—treats people like they aren't human. It's not right. He hits people. He has this magic marker and will paint people with it. On last Wednesday I was working and he grabbed the marker and painted me on the side of the face—for no reason at all. [My boss] has painted a mustache on me before. He put a paper tie on me and sent me to the office. He will say, "Go see the secretary, your girlfriend." (Kyler Workers 2000)

Guatemalan workers are routinely paid under the table, at rates below minimum wage, and cheated out of hours. One employer had workers punch out after eight hours, punch in again for another employer, and return to their same job, to avoid paying overtime rates. A major immigration raid by U.S. Immigration and Customs Enforcement in New Bedford

in 2007, coupled with the economic recession, has driven Guatemalan workers deeper into the underground economy. Without papers, in the shadows
of the American economy, theirs is a story of exploitation.

I also interviewed nurses in the operating rooms at Boston Medical Center, which was, until recently, the public hospital for the city. Health care is
central to the U.S. economy but an industry in turmoil for patients and
workers alike. The growing corporatization of Boston Medical, as in hospitals across the county, has had a dramatic impact on patient care. The operating nurses I interviewed describe a new assembly line approach to surgery
as the hospital forfeits its commitment to care in favor of increasing revenue. This drive for profits has pushed Boston Medical nurses to the brink.
With a growing shortage of nurses, largely exacerbated by the working conditions created by this new bottom-line approach, too few nurses are working too many hours. Union leader Celia Wcislo describes the effect of this
system:

> You've taken on two shifts of overtime above your regular one. Someone
> gets sick and they call you in to take a third shift. You get sick because
> you're exhausted by this, which causes someone else to work the over-
> time and you see the attendance problem starting to go up. You can see
> someone working several weeks at sixty hours and then have some
> weeks where they're sick because they've worn themselves out. And then
> management goes berserk because you're calling in sick. (2002, 10)

Nurses do their best to hold on to their commitment to their patients and
their colleagues. They go without meals, fill in for those who are out, and
work double shifts or on the weekend even when they shouldn't. But up
against bottom-line medicine, their culture of caring has left them
exhausted.

Finally, I interviewed industrial workers who had been employed at
Jones Beloit in Dalton, a small town in western Massachusetts. Jones Beloit
was an internationally known manufacturer of high-quality machinery for
the paper industry. The plant in Dalton, part of an extremely profitable division, was abruptly closed when the parent company filed for bankruptcy
following the failure of a dubious foreign investment to build paper mills
using their machinery in the Indonesian rain forest.

Glen Boden, a highly skilled machinist who crafted parts for Jones Beloit machinery over thirty-four years, recounts overhearing remarks made

by one of the managers from the plant that was going to take over their work:

> He was snickering. I happened to be up in the office doing some business and I was walking down the hallway and they were talking about their meeting and he was snickering like, "We're going to torpedo this place." They had such grand plans. They were going to close that place and move it up there and make more money than we made. Oh, my God. We told them, "There is a little bit more to this than you realize." "Oh, no, there can't be. Anybody can make a widget." That was a quote. "Anybody can make a widget." (2001a, 26)

Their bravado ultimately turned out to be little more than a fantasy. The company never recovered from bankruptcy, and like so many other American firms, it was broken up and sold in pieces.

This is not a story from the 1980s of the closing of an ancient plant that had outlived its productive capacity. Instead, it is a modern tale of workers getting caught between an irresponsible corporate decision and the hard realities of the global market. Despite their highly efficient production and the steady profits they had contributed to the parent firm, the workers at Jones Beloit were simply abandoned.

With the financial crisis of 2008, we have seen these kinds of plant closings grow exponentially. As with Jones Beloit, so many closings have absolutely nothing to do with the productivity of the workers or the quality of their products. Rather, plants are shuttered and workers sent packing, victims of corporate irresponsibility, the collapse of the stock market, frozen credit, and stalled consumption.

The Paradox of Work in the Twenty-first Century

In each of the four sites, employers and the industries they were part of adapted to growing competition, the globalization of production, and a crisis in profitmaking by expanding through mergers and acquisitions. Verizon gobbled up it competitors; Boston City Hospital merged with Boston University Hospital to become the Boston Medical Center; and Jones Beloit became part of the global firm Harnischfeger. Even the fish-processing industry in New Bedford went through no less consolidation. Such consolidation, driven by the search for increased profits, fundamentally altered the way work was done in the four sites. Each employer in a different way turned up the heat on its workers, leaving some workers feeling stressed and others exhausted, exploiting some and abandoning others.

As we step back from the specific details of the four case studies, it is clear that a series of paradoxes is emerging in the contemporary American workplace which are hard to reconcile within our postwar thinking about work. At some very basic level it is becoming difficult to distinguish between good jobs and bad jobs. For most of the postwar era, good jobs were the ones at major firms that provided decent wages, working conditions, and benefits in what economists called the primary labor market. Bad jobs were the ones in the secondary labor market at the periphery of the economy—jobs with little security, poor wages, and few benefits. The line between good jobs and bad ones is not so easy to draw anymore.

From the pay and benefits of the call center reps at Verizon or the nurses at Boston Medical, it would be difficult to conclude that they have anything but good, very good jobs. Yet do good jobs require employees to ask permission to go to the bathroom, or employers to discipline employees for being sick, as at Verizon? Or do good jobs require a professional worker with twenty-five years of experience to work weekends or overnight shifts, like nurses at Boston Medical?

It should be noted that the sixty-hour weeks and twelve-hour shifts at Verizon and Boston Medical Center are part of a trend among major employers—the kinds of firms we expected more from in past decades. After World War II, large, established employers such as General Motors and Ford were innovators in labor relations and employment policy, offering working conditions far removed from the cruelty encountered in jobs in the secondary market. Today, however, working conditions normally associated with small, marginal firms are becoming commonplace among some of the nation's largest and most respected companies. The historical link between large, profitable firms and the creation of good jobs in the United States has been broken.

There are no fewer contradictions in Dalton or New Bedford. In Dalton the workers at Jones Beloit had a series of record-breaking years in terms of productivity, excellent equipment, and a seasoned, highly trained workforce. The plant was abruptly closed nonetheless, and all efforts by the workers and their union to keep work going in Dalton were thwarted by the company and government regulations that were supposed to help them.

In New Bedford the Guatemalan workers, like most other workers there, punch time clocks, receive regular paychecks, and pay taxes, including Social Security. Like other workers in New Bedford they rent apartments for their families, pay the electric bill, and go to the grocery store—a life they could have hardly imagined back in the Guatemalan highlands. But it is not a life like that of their neighbors and coworkers. They cannot collect unemployment or Social Security, and they cannot use any state or federal programs for housing or to help their children, even though they contribute to them. At work, on the street, and in their homes they are subject to arrest and deportation—all in an instant.

Despite the hardships workers at these four sites have endured, in a fundamental way they have not given up. The call center representatives help out an elderly customer beyond what they are supposed to do or extend a conversation to grab a chance to sit back in their chair for a minute. The nurses at Boston Medical persist in their single-minded goal of advocating for their patients, including the poor and the homeless, in a system that seems not to care. And despite their exhaustion, they stay over to work a double or weekend shift so that another nurse can have time with the children.

The workers at Jones Beloit and their union provide a model of how to respond creatively to a plant closing, rather than simply collapsing under the weight of inevitability. The young Guatemalan Mayan men, even though they have been uprooted from their families and their homes and they work long, difficult shifts, hold onto the spark of life, priding themselves on their ability to make life better for their families both here and back home.

One of the threads running through the case studies is the dedication of the workers to their families. Verizon workers took their precious personal days to go to a school play or celebrate a kid's birthday even when they were desperate just for rest. Nurses at Boston Medical worked nights and weekends so that they could care for their children, even if their sleep patterns would never be the same. Wives of the men who were laid off at Jones Beloit, even those who had never worked outside the home before, found part-time, low-wage jobs in order to hold on to a bit of the dream they had built. One of the Guatemalans, Juan, worked two full-time jobs to send money back home. "A lot of people are doing the same thing," he said, "working two jobs, maybe sleep four hours and get up. I am thinking about what we do for love of our family" (Juan 2001b, 7).

Although the love of family and children are powerful motivators, we have seen the harsh new realities that workers are facing in today's workplaces. In the short run, many have figured out how to survive, but they have done so at great cost to their own health and well-being. It is incredible what the human body and spirit can endure and still function.

The four sites where I conducted interviews represent professional workers, skilled workers, and low-wage workers in the service economy and in manufacturing. They include workers in a major metropolitan area, a small town, and the suburbs. The four sites include firms and industries that are growing and those that are under attack. And they represent workplaces where women or men or people of color make up the majority of the workers. The four sites allowed me to dig in deeply enough to get a sense of the complexity of what is happening in the American workplace but provided enough variety to give me useful points of comparison.

It should be noted that although all of these research sites are in Massachusetts, this book is not just about work and workers in Massachusetts. Every state has hospitals and call centers. Most have growing immigrant populations and some industrial workers. And because of the homogenization of the American culture, the differences between states are less important than they once were. This is an American story.

Factory of Broken Dreams

TOM JURAVICH

I wanted to be a teacher, I thought that I'd be good
Working with children, at least my momma thought I could
So I started off at college, but it was all too big and new
I was back in Southie, before the year was through

My aunt Helen said, I should try
Down at the phone company
She said I think they're hiring, sometimes they'll pay your college fees
So I've been at Verizon, now going on five years
I earn a decent living, but sometimes I can't stop the tears

As I sit here, sometimes it seems
For all of us in here . . .

It's not some kind of office job, I can't believe the pace
I'm hardly done with one call, they send me another case
They time my every motion, it's all about the speed
Selling stuff to people, I'm not sure they need

As I sit here, sometimes it seems
For all of us in here
It's just a factory of broken dreams

Sometimes I think of college, teaching's on my mind
But I never do get started, with the commute and the overtime
Then I had my little Joey, a sweeter boy you'll never know
But when his dad left me to raise him, this job was all she wrote

I sometimes think of quitting, setting myself free
But I'd start at half of what I make here, and where would that get me?
So I guess they've really got me, at least that's what it seems
I just don't know where to put them, where to put my dreams

As I sit here, sometimes it seems
For all of us in here
It's just a factory of broken dreams

I wanted to be a teacher

1

STRESSED

Customer Service Representatives at Verizon

I take the calls, do what they need, resolve their problems—fine. To talk to customers all day—fine. It's not a big deal. But when you have random people listening all the time going, "Well, that wasn't perfect." Well, I'm not always perfect. But you know what—it wasn't bad. If it's not bad, leave me alone. . . . I'm not used to being treated like a five-year-old. Which I get a lot of that. The verbal spankings. I'm not used to being told, "This is what you need to do every second of the day." The way the job is set up, you actually have to, if you get up to go to the bathroom, you have let to them know that's where you went. That's crazy. If I'm going to the bathroom, I'm going to the bathroom. And don't ask me at the end of the day why I was missing for ten minutes. . . . I do what I'm supposed to 99 percent of the time. Margaret (2001a, 2–3)

MARGARET IS a customer service representative at the Verizon call center in Andover, Massachusetts. At thirty-three, she's been with Verizon a little more than five years, after working in a number of positions in hospitals. She left hospital work because of the inflexibility of the scheduling. The single parent of an eleven-year-old, Margaret needed more time to raise her daughter. Ironically, as she will readily tell you, she has less flexibility now. With her open face and easy laugh you can imagine a kind and caring mother, yet there is an edge to Margaret. As she describes her workdays and the life she has had to build around them, she gets very hard very fast. She struggles to fight it off, but the stress is getting to her.

Verizon's Andover Call Center

Verizon's call center in Andover, Massachusetts, is right off Route 93, a few miles north of its intersection with Route 495, Boston's outer beltway, twenty-five miles or so northwest of Boston. At the confluence of two of the major arteries heading into and around Boston, it's the kind of place you would expect a truck depot or perhaps a warehouse. As you exit the highway onto

River Road, it's obvious that the corporate world has come to this suburban, in some ways almost rural, part of Andover. The modest country roads, with a few major entrances and exits cobbled on, are dotted with a variety of corporate buildings and company headquarters, including Minuteman Park, an upscale collection of corporate buildings in the flatlands of the Merrimack River, just across from the old industrial city of Lawrence.

Two generations ago, the counterparts of the women at the call center worked in the textile mills of Lawrence. They lived in Lawrence and walked or took trolley cars to work. Today, call center reps careen in their cars along the interstates from all over the eastern part of Massachusetts and southern New Hampshire to work in Andover. Virtually no one lives in the immediate area—there really isn't much housing available. As you drive down River Road a mile or two past the corporate park, you see how rural the area is. Older colonial houses mix with modest houses from the 1960s and 1970s. An occasional McMansion intrudes, too, too big, too boxy for the neighborhood. As with many of these suburban/rural corporate parks, not much else is around. No stores or places to get a quick lunch or have your shoes fixed— just a gas station and a mini-mart, a roadside motel and its large family restaurant. With no reason to linger after work, people hit the road as soon as they can to beat the traffic.

The call center is on Shattuck Road, a modest boulevard with low-slung corporate buildings on either side. A former AT&T facility, the red brick, two-story building could be a high school or medical building with its large parking lot and sprawling green lawn with a few picnic tables scattered around. When it opened in April 1995, it brought together workers from smaller facilities in Salem, Lowell, and Malden. Officially called the Customer Sales and Service Center, it houses approximately 550 service reps, managers, and a handful of clerks and administrative assistants. Most are women between the ages of twenty and fifty.

"We're set up in what they call units," Doris, a senior rep at Andover and one of Margaret's best friends, explains. "There are twenty-four units, one manager per unit. A unit can range anywhere from twenty to twenty-five people. The building is divided into three sections: East 2, which is the red team; West 2, which is the blue team; and West 1, which is the green team" (2001a, 12).

Inside you find a fairly standard modern office setup: huge rooms filled with cubicles. Margaret describes it: "Managers have cubicles with high walls, and everyone else is just sort of back-to-back. So you've got someone with their back to you here, and then someone over here, facing this way. . . . It's just this high, four feet high. . . . The service reps' cubicles include a computer and a phone with a headset. That's pretty much it. Papers strewn everywhere" (2001a, 5).

With the breakup of the old Bell System in 1984, a worldwide telecommunications industry emerged with a host of local, national, and international companies providing a growing list of services and products. The 1996 Telecommunications Act opened the industry to a new level of competition. The next four years, as described by industry analyst Robert W. Crandall, were "exhilarating for many participants in the telecommunications sector. Investment soared as stock market valuation rose at remarkable rates" (2005, 3).

The boom, however, would not last. By 2000, scandal engulfed Worldcom, and several firms went belly up as the industry began to shake out. With the development of cable broadband and new technologies such as voice-over Internet protocol (VoIP), by which telephone calls can be made through Internet connections, a whole new set of competitors to the traditional telephone industry emerged (Fransman 2002). But on the telephone side, a small number of integrated firms dominate the industry.

AT&T was bought by SBC and then in 2006 acquired Bell South. Sprint purchased its rival Nextel. One of the giants that formed was Verizon. Several senior customer service reps at Verizon experienced the consolidation firsthand. Many began with the old New England Telephone, which then became NYNEX. NYNEX became part of Bell Atlantic, and Bell Atlantic merged with GTE in 2000 to become Verizon. Verizon continued to grow, acquiring MCI in 2006.

As one of the industry leaders, Verizon has nearly 71 million customers worldwide and operating revenues of more than $93.5 billion (Verizon 2007). Early on, rapid growth, coupled with some questionable investments, left Verizon more heavily indebted than its competitors (CWA 2003; Verizon 2004). In an effort to reduce this indebtedness, in 2007 Verizon spun off its directory services and Latin American operations and announced an agreement with Fair Point Communications to provide services to customers in rural parts of New England (Rosenbluth 2007, 2). Of Verizon's approximately 228,000 employees, almost half are members of unions, either the Communications Workers of America (CWA) or the International Brotherhood of

Electrical Workers (IBEW). The customer service reps at the Andover call center voted to join the CWA in 1994.

The CEO of Verizon, Ivan Seidenberg, describes the company philosophy this way: "There is a corollary to preserving higher than average pay and benefits. For us to maintain a competitive advantage, we have to have a labor force that is more productive than average." He continues, albeit defensively, "So this isn't a 'race to the bottom.' It is a race to create a new industry paradigm" (Seidenberg 2003). How this company philosophy actually plays out can be shown by a close look at the work and lives of the customer service representatives at Verizon's Andover call center.

"On-Line" as a Customer Service Representative

At the Andover facility the customer service reps do not make "cold calls" to sign people up for phone service with Verizon but field phone calls from customers or potential customers, advising them about what services are available, selling services, and making arrangements for those services to be provided. For example, "People call in that they want to remove services from their phone lines," Doris explains. Or " 'I want to see if DSL is available in my area, I want caller ID, three-way calling, call waiting.' A typical one is, 'What's my bill?' " (2001a, 12).

Bob, a lanky Verizon veteran who worked at Radio Shack before coming to Verizon, describes his "average" day: "I take anywhere between forty-five and seventy calls a day, depending on what the subject matter of the call is. . . . Typical, average time, we go in seconds, it's anywhere between 400 and 500 seconds, which translates to what, maybe six or seven minutes at the most." So, during the course of the day, call center reps deal with a huge number of people, problems, and personalities. He continues:

> You talk to a lot of different people in one day. Obviously, when you're talking to each different customer, each customer is in a different mood. The whole thing about this job is it's going to be stressful. That's the bottom line. It's going to be stressful. It's how you deal with it. You can't take anything personally because nobody's phone bill is personal to you. Nobody's service that doesn't work effectively or properly is personal to you. You have to take it that way. You're going to speak to a lot of people who are on edge and you have to roll with it. The stress level is high. Especially if you take seventy calls in a day. (2003, 1–2)

Doris has learned to take it in stride. There is a working-class matter-of-factness about her, and she can be tough as nails, especially when speaking about Verizon. But it doesn't stop her from caring about the customers who call, even the difficult ones. "You've got to have tough skin," she explains.

> And you got to learn, don't take it personally. The customer ain't yelling at you, the customer's yelling at the company. You just happen to be the point of contact. You get a customer who'll apologize for screaming at you. . . . Feel free. Go right ahead. I understand that it's not me you're angry [at]. . . . And then we'll go on and I'll take care of whatever it is you need me to take care of. (2001a, 8)

As Rosemary Batt and Jeffery Keefe explain, the Andover call center is typical of megacenters in the industry. They house

> between 500 and 1,000 customer service representatives (CSRs), each of whom handles 90–100 customers per day at a call cycle time of about 3–5 minutes. CSRs complete transactions with customers on-line and are discouraged from interacting with fellow employees. As soon as one call ends, an automatic call distribution (ACD) automatically sends another customer call to the "open" representative. (1999, 121)

Pat Telesco, a former call center rep and now a staff person with the CWA, remembers the work in a call center when she started more than twenty years ago. Like most customer service reps, until very recently, she worked in a small facility that serviced a specific geographical area. "The customers would get to know me as their rep. If they called in to the office they would ask for me," she recalls. "There was actually a phone store downstairs, and some of them would say, 'Rather than talking on the phone, could you come down?' Which we technically weren't supposed to do, but we would do it" (2004, 3). Work in these small centers was organized very differently from the way it is today. With little division of labor, most reps worked as generalists, solving a variety of problems that came in each day. As Telesco reports, the physical setup of the offices reflected this very different organization of work.

> We actually sat at desks. They called it a quad. There were four desks and four terminals all facing out. There was nothing between the desks. We shared one big desk area as it went around. We always joked that between the four of us we made one good rep. If I had a question, I would turn to the rep on my left or right and ask, "Has this come up before?" "What do you think of this?" (2004, 3)

Today, Verizon locates customer service and sales work in mega–call centers. The basic principle is to use economy of scale to routinize the work and create a more efficient and profitable way of both providing customer service and making sales. Traditionally, service work has been difficult to routinize, when compared with industrial work, for example. Unlike mechanical items that move inertly down an assembly line, customers and their varying demands create a different challenge. McCammon and Griffin refer to this as "a three-way workplace interaction that can occur among the employer, workers, and customers in service work" (2000, 279).

One way firms in the service sector overcome obstacles is to first segment customer service into homogeneous groupings to minimize the amount of variation in customer demand (Leidner 1993; Batt 2001). Thus, at the Andover call center as at most megacenters in the industry, Verizon has separate units that deal with large corporate clients, small business clients, and general home users. The two business units are much smaller and the work is less routinized because the customers and their problems are more complex. As Debbie Goldman of the CWA research department suggests, "The whole industry segments customers, and the higher the value of the customer, the more autonomy given to the customer service reps" (Goldman 2004, 21).

By stripping away the more complex demands associated with business customers, Verizon focuses on creating a highly routinized system for the majority of call center reps, who service the general residential user. Although some parts of telecommunications, such as operator services, have long been subject to routinization (Norwood 1990), this process is relatively new in customer service and in many ways is made possible by the mega-center and the economy of scale it creates. Like clerical work before it, service work was seen as too complex to be easily routinized. But, as Harry Braverman points out, routinizing "proved easier to [accomplish] once the volume of work grew large enough and once a search for methods of rationalization was seriously taken" (1998, 218).

Here Verizon takes a page directly from Frederick Taylor. As outlined in Taylor's classic *Principles of Scientific Management*, the fundamental principle of scientific management is to do away with individual work practice and style, which he calls "rules of thumb," and instead to "develop a science for each element of a man's work, which replaces the old rule of thumb method." It all began at Bethlehem Steel, where Taylor's job was to supervise men who picked up a ninety-two-pound bar of pig iron, walked up an inclined plane, and dropped the bar into a railroad car. After several weeks of observation Taylor recruited a worker he called Schmidt. In a dialogue recorded in the *Principles*, complete with Schmidt's German accent, Taylor persuades him to become "a high price man" who can receive higher wages if, as Taylor says, "you will do exactly as this man tells you tomorrow, from morning till night. When he tells you to pick up a pig and walk, you pick it up and walk, and when he tells you to sit down and rest, you sit down" (1911, 36, 45–46).

And so was born the basic principle of Taylorism: the separation of the conception of work and its execution. "The workman who is best suited to handling pig iron is unable to understand the real science of doing this class of work" (Taylor 1911, 59). Thus the role for management in the new Taylor system was no longer to simply "push" workers to work harder but to outline every step a worker should make. Through this scientific system the work could be done most efficiently.

This is precisely what Verizon did at its megacenters. No longer would call center reps in a community-based center be able to organize their work and the nature of their conversations with a variety of local customers. At the core of Verizon's system is a very detailed script that all center workers who deal with residential customers must use—across the Verizon system. It involves a mixture of text and prompts, and because the telephones are regulated by the Federal Communications Commission, it includes statements and procedures that must be followed. This is Taylor's scientific method at work in the service sector.

From fast food (Leidner 1993; Scharf 2003; Iadiapaolo 2007) to air travel (Shalla 2006) through medical (Amatayakul 2003) and insurance services (Leidner 1993), scripting is a fundamental building block for routinization in the service sector. Developing a script that clients and customers will accept is just the first part of the process. As Leidner suggests, firms must become adept at "persuading customers or clients to limit their demands so as not to interfere with the smooth function of routines" (1993, 31).

The narrow scripting troubles many call center reps at Verizon. Many report that it interferes with their own discretion and the approaches they have developed in their jobs, sometimes over many years. Even the Wharton Business School recognizes the down side of script writing, acknowledging that "more scripting is associated with lower job satisfaction, greater burnout and a higher intention to quit the job" (*Knowledge@Wharton* 2004, 4). Ellen, a call center rep at Verizon, vents her frustration with a script that doesn't allow her to provide basic information to the customer:

> You have the customer who is very, very unhappy because of the policies we have, and then the fact that you're not allowed to tell them anything. You are just screaming in your head in frustration that you want this person to understand that if they would just ask a question, you could answer them, but you can't give out the information. And you have the manager on the other end monitoring you constantly, and you're afraid of everything you're going to say or do on every call. It's like a tense situation. You're in the middle of these two conflicting things—this customer who thinks he has something he doesn't have and the manager who is watching you to make sure you don't tell the customer that—and by the end of the day you feel like you have been pulled at both ends. (2003, 3–4)

In addition to the scripting, Verizon has used sophisticated operations research to optimize the delivery of work to call center reps and, like many other companies, has spent considerable funding to research projected call time, call volume, and staff needs. As Batt and Keefe point out:

> Company-developed algorithms provide guidelines for the amount of time allowable in each type of activity: managers at a central control panel watch for flashing lights (green, blue, red, etc.) that indicate if any employee has gone beyond the allotted time in any one area. Supervisors then use their discretion to counsel and/or discipline employees who are at variance with the targeted time allotments or schedule known as "out of adherence."(1999, 121–122)

At Andover this central control panel is located in what is called "the force room." As one rep told me laughingly: "They sit over there and basically can see right now that I am closed [for lunch]. But they can also see when I'm not on a call and they'll call me and ask me why I'm not on a call. I tell them that I have this amount of follow-up. Then they'll say, 'We don't have time to give you. You need to get back on the phone'" (Shelly 2003, 9).

As soon as a call is completed, the ACD system routes another call to the rep, and the process is repeated throughout the day except during breaks and lunch. Reps do have a "Make Busy" button to indicate that they need a few moments to wrap up a case, but being "out of adherence" like this is recorded and strongly discouraged. "If you're on what they call 'Make Busy,' which is like a hold key," Margaret explains, "if you're on for ten or fifteen seconds, they're calling you wanting to know what you're doing. So I can't put a key in, get up and walk over and ask somebody a question about something I'm confused about. They're calling wanting to know what you're doing. There's no flexibility" (2003b, 3–4).

To ensure that reps meet expectations for the number of calls handled during the course of a day, Verizon builds no regular time into the work system for reps to finish up after the customer has hung up. Having no room for any emotional release under this system is particularly tough after a difficult call. Under the old quad system that Pat Telesco described, you can imagine a call center rep turning to the one next to her and exclaiming, "You wouldn't believe that last call . . ." and then taking a moment or two to recompose herself before moving on to the next call.

Under the current Verizon work system, workers do their best to adjust. Bob, for example, says, "Typically, I'm really adept at using the systems so I can, on most calls, wrap it up by the end of the call." But he adds, "Of course, there are ways of conversing with the customer and keeping them on the call a little bit longer to try to wrap it up" (2003, 2–3). I'd always thought the call center reps I spoke with on the phone were just being chatty at the end of their calls. As Bob explains, however, they may very well have been finishing up their work, or possibly grabbing a few seconds of peace, knowing full well that another call would be routed to them as soon as they hung up. Margaret describes it this way: "You actually have to find ways when you're really tired and just want to put your head down. A little old lady who wants to chat about nothing. I'll ask her about the grandkids. Because that's the only way you'll get that break" (2001b, 22). Since there is precious little wiggle room in the tightly controlled Verizon system, as the following discussion shows, using such tactics may be one of the few places where workers can exert control over the pace of their work.[1]

Another key component of Verizon's system is the delivery of information to the rep. Gone are the old paper service manuals. Instead, reps use computer-based programs to assist them in serving and selling to the customer. "On a typical call," Bob explains,

> you're accessing between three and four computer systems on each and every call. You have four databases that we typically do business with—a service order provisioning system, a billing system, a system showing

product availability, calling areas and that kind of thing, as well as different internet applications. All of these are open at different times. You have to access many of these to help the customer effectively. (2003, 2)

The call reps at the Andover megacenter deal with residential customers from across New England, and "each state has its own calling plans and features," reports Don, who has been at Verizon for six years. "That's part of the complexity of the job. There are so many different plans and so many differences between states that it's difficult to try to keep it all straight" (2003, 8–9). But the differences between states are still less than the differences between customers, and Verizon has been able to train its reps to deal with these differences and still adhere to a highly routinized work system.

Unlike work in the smaller, regional centers where employees had more control over the pace of their workday, perhaps working harder in the morning and maybe slowing down after lunch, or picking up the slack for a coworker who wasn't feeling well, the pace of work at Verizon is uncontrollable and unrelenting. Molly worked for GTE for five years before it became part of Verizon and has spent five years in the Andover call center. She wears the stress on her face. She describes it this way: "You can't get up and walk around. People hear, 'Oh! Well, you work in an office.' Well, yeah, I work in an office. But I'm tethered with an electronic leash to my desk. I can't leave my desk, so I can't get up and walk over to somebody else" (2003, 2).

Debbie Goldman of the CWA believes that "the technology enabled speedup." She continues:

> What I mean by that is they can figure out the maximum efficiency with which to channel the calls. You could be handling something at a certain rate for a certain amount of time. But to be doing it for 7.5 hours is what the technology enabled. They're measuring everything. They measure the length of the call, who is on when, and they're measuring whether you're on when you're supposed to be on. They're measuring if you're off when you're supposed to be off. (2004, 8)

"Managers and union representatives alike agree that residential CSR jobs are the most stressful ones in the industry," write Batt and Keefe (1999, 121). As sophisticated as it is, the ACD system does not know when a customer service rep has a headache, had a fight with his or her spouse the night before, or has a sick child. The calls just keep coming. And this organization of work has indeed created an electronic assembly line, or what Taylor and Bain refer to as "an assembly line in the head" (1999).

It is important here to contextualize this work at Verizon in relation to industrial assembly line work in, for example, the automobile industry. Although we should have no illusions about the cruelty of that assembly line, particularly before unionization imposed important controls, we should note that there was a social aspect to auto work that is not present in Verizon's call center. Workers could move up or down the assembly line to assist their fellow workers, or at least they could vent to each other about the speed of the line or the heat. No doubt it was tough, exploitive work, but there were sometimes ways to share the work, the pain, and the frustration. There were always lunch hours and break times, which in the auto industry were held at the same time for all workers. This social aspect of production was further reinforced by the geographic concentration of workers in the communities surrounding industrial facilities, at least until fairly recently. Auto workers could commiserate about the speed of the line in a local bar after work or in the grocery store on Saturday.

In the Andover call center, work is delivered individually to the reps, leaving them virtually no way to assist, support, or commiserate with other workers. Instead, the call center reps suffer alone in their cubicles, and staggered lunch hours and breaks permit few opportunities to communicate with one another. The irony of this system is that even though the reps work in very close quarters in a room with more than a hundred cubicles, they are very much alone in their struggles. And because few workers reside in the immediate area, there are few opportunities for call center reps to reflect on the week while socializing together outside work. Rather, they must deal with their frustrations individually as they speed away from the job on the interstates and return to their homes.[2]

Control of the pace of their work has been at the core of workers' struggles and demands in this country. As labor historian David Montgomery suggests in *Workers' Control in America* (1979), struggles against routinization and loss of control over work design and pace constitute a leitmotif that runs through the history of labor in the United States, from the experience of skilled craftsmen in the late nineteenth century through the Fordism of the 1930s and 1940s. This new routinization of the service sector is taking shape as the next battleground.

"Realizing All the Benefits from Communication": From Service to Sales

In addition to the ACD that automatically assigns work, the scripting of calls, and the computer-based technology that reps must use to assist customers, the work itself has changed dramatically at Andover since 2000, with a shift from customer service to sales. As Don explains, "When I first came on board there was not the sales pressure you have now. [With the deregulation of the telephone industry, companies like Verizon offer a variety of products to their customers such as caller ID, voice mail, Internet access and various long distance calling plans.] I'd say it was 70 percent service and 30 percent sales. In the past couple of years it has increased to the point that it's probably about 90 percent sales and 10 percent service" (2003, 1). His colleague Shelly describes similar frustrations: "So you could call me and complain about humming on your line. As long as I ignore you and pretend that you didn't say that and I sell you something, that's fine, that's a complete call. They basically don't want us to do customer service. They don't care that you called about humming on the line" (2003, 9). This policy places the customer service rep right in the middle of contradictory demands. The customer calls because he or she wants service, whereas the manager is pushing for sales. Trying to balance these conflicting demands in a very short amount of time, with a very tight script, is the call center rep.

It is not that the call center reps I spoke with are opposed to making sales. They are concerned, however, that sales have been elevated to such a priority that customer service reps no longer have the discretion to provide adequate service to Verizon's customers. Ellen resents this overwhelming pressure to sell and the position it puts her in.

> How do you sell something to a customer who hasn't had service in three days and is going to be told by repair that it will be seventy-two hours before he can get out there? All you want to do is to be sympathetic to this person. But while you're being sympathetic, you better get an offer in there: "When we get your phone up and running again, would you like to add this to your line?" How awkward is this? (2003, 10)

The loss of service work affects the call center reps in two ways. First, even with routinization, there is a certain challenge in providing customer service; investigation and problem-solving offer a sense of satisfaction and professionalism about the work. Second, as Arlie Hochschild points out in *The Managed Heart* (1983), there is satisfaction that comes from "emotional work," even though this emotional work is rarely recognized or compensated. The reps at Verizon value this work of "the invisible heart," as Nancy Folbre (2001) calls it, such as helping a distraught customer get phone service restored. Sales work contains very little such emotional work or agency because of the highly scripted system. With little emotional satisfaction and little need for problem-solving skills, it is no surprise that sales work provides less satisfaction, particularly for those reps who started in a service-oriented system or for those who prefer and excel at service-oriented work.

The new paradigm at Verizon, however, is all about sales, all the time. "When people hear that you work in an office" Molly explains, "they think you come in, get your coffee, sit down, and take a call here and there." She continues:

> It's not like that at all. Everything you do is timed. How long you're on a call is timed. How long you take between calls is timed. How much you sell is averaged—that's called points per call. We get something constantly from the company called "Return on Investment" that tells us, for every dollar the company spent on you, here's how many dollars you earned for the company. The goal is to earn $10 for every dollar that they spend on you. Every day you get a printout that says, "For every dollar we have spent on you, you earned us $5 today." Which you know is half of what they expect you to earn for the day. If that doesn't put stress on you, I don't know what does! (2003, 7)

Even though this push for sales is not reflected in a formal sales quota, a de facto quota system is in place. Each of the products—caller ID, DSL, and so on—is given assigned points, and customer service representatives are awarded points based on their sales.[3] For example, as Shelly explains:

> What they do is bring on a new program, like this new "Freedom Package [a bundle of telephone and Internet services]." They give it to you and everyone starts to make their sales and then they lower the points that it's worth. And then they take it away, and they say, "Oh! That's not even worth anything any more and now you have to do this!" They pick and choose and they decide what's going to be valuable to them. . . . And it can change at any time. So basically something could be worth 200 points today and the next month it could change to 50 points because you've exhausted it. (2003, 7)

Whereas the target for sales is a monthly figure, the reps I spoke with say that points are calculated constantly throughout the week and even the workday. If a rep's sales points are low as the morning or afternoon proceeds, it is not unusual for a manager to call and inquire, "What's wrong?" Customer service reps receive bonuses for exceptional sales, and those who fall below their targets are subject to discipline and discharge. As Ellen explains, "Verizon's policy or goal is for 'every customer to realize all the benefits of communication.' That's what they say." She continues:

> That's fine. But [even] if you don't need caller ID and you honestly don't need it and you've said that you don't need it and you don't want it or you've tried it once before and decided [against it], we are obligated to repeat over and over to you that you do need it. People get angry and the rep gets upset, but you're being observed by management, so the offer had better be there. When I first came here it was offer, offer, offer, but it was like, "Okay, as long as you've said it, as long as you've offered the customer the service, it's not a problem." Now, this week, it's "Close the sale. If you're not closing the sale, you're not successful and you need to learn to close the sale." So offering is off the table now. You can offer until you're blue in the face, but if you don't close the sale it does not matter. You have not met the requirements. Because the only requirement there is, is to close the sale. (2003, 8–9)

The constant push for sales, even among customers who likely don't need additional services, gets to some of the reps. "I've had reps tell me they feel that their job is driving the company's get-away car," CWA's Pat Telesco reports. "They don't mind selling, but feel like the pressure is over the top" (2004, 6). As Molly explains:

> They send us notes that let us know how many potential sales we've lost when we put a "Make Busy" on. They total the whole number of "Make Busy" minutes by a particular unit. So they'll say, "Well, this week you've had 1,000 minutes of 'Make Busy' time which translates into 10,000 easy points that you could have earned had you been online." (2003, 5–6)

Not everyone at the Verizon call center is upset about this move to sales. Chris, who comes from a background in telemarketing and never had any illusions about customer service, says:

> I do my job and nobody bothers me. It can be stressful; I can see where people would think it's stressful. But if you don't let it get to you, and

leave your work at work and your home, at home, at least for me, everything goes very smoothly. Nobody bothers me because I do so well at my job. I'm one of the top sellers of the district. I win big trips to like Puerto Rico and all kinds of cool stuff. (Chris 2001, 2)

Most reps understand that the top sellers get considerably more leeway with scheduling hours and are monitored less. "If you're a top seller, you can take all the time you need. If you're a top seller, you can pretty much write your own ticket," says Ellen (2003, 5). But even the top sellers are not immune to sales pressure. As one reports,

There's a huge push to get those points per call up around into the fifties or close to sixty points per call, hopefully by the end of the year. My manager is pushing towards that. His point is, it's a matter of survival. The company will always be willing to keep business in a place where you get a return on your investment. I can understand that from a business standpoint. I'm just a little bit concerned about how they're going to be going about it. If they start stepping [disciplining] top producers, and put them on development plans, it's going to turn this place into a sweatshop, and if it happens, my stress level will increase tenfold. (Don, 2003, 4)

Many reps, however, express little sympathy for the top sellers. They agree with Pat Telesco when she says, "They raise the bar for themselves every month. When you jump through those hoops, after you're good at it they're going to set them on fire for you." She argues that, as in most incentive programs, the high level of sales cannot sustain itself. "They make a lot of money for the time they are doing good, but the funny thing is, does the company cut you any slack when you have a bad period? They think, 'You've operated at this level before, this is how much we can get out of you, so we're going to get it out of you" (2004, 19).

Telesco wonders, "Are people's moral compasses off sometimes?" in this high pressure sales environment. She worries that

because of the company constantly telling them "Do it. Just do. Do it at all costs. Push the sale. Push the sale," you get a lot of situations where you look at it and say, "I don't know. Is it sales cheating? Did you slam the customer [push them into agreeing]? Did you cram that stuff on their account [put things on their account that they didn't order]? Did you maybe take credit from another rep for the sale that should have been theirs?" People are enticed into doing things they wouldn't normally do, in this environment.

Telesco is concerned about the questionable practices of some of the top sellers and the vulnerable positions they put themselves in. "That supervisor who is giving the high seller the wink, you know, 'Go get 'em.' When that customer calls in and complains and says they didn't order that product, that supervisor is not backing that rep up" (2004, 19, 20).

The Stick and the Carrot: Monitoring and Modern Management

It is common practice in telephone-based service and sales to monitor the calls of employees. As we are told on recorded messages, this is for "quality assurance." The telephone industry is still highly regulated, and Verizon uses monitoring to ensure that its employees comply with the state and federal regulations. Monitoring has a long history in the telephone industry. The U.S. Commission on Industrial Relations in 1915 wrote, "There is possibly no woman in any industry whose remissness is more instantly checked by the incisive action of an overseer than the telephone operator" (quoted in Norwood 1990, 38). Long the practice in operator services, this kind of monitoring is relatively new in customer service, but some 51 percent of telecommunication call centers are reported to use electronic monitoring (Batt et al. 2004, 16).

According to Verizon, the company uses monitoring as a type of formative evaluation to assist employees in developing their skills, particularly as sales reps. But the experience of many of the call center reps is that the monitoring at Verizon goes far beyond facilitating their development and is instead a form of workplace control. As Margaret points out:

> They listen in on the phone calls and they monitor us electronically. Every time they listen to a phone call, they have a checklist that's around 200 points long. And they will talk to you if you missed one. "Why didn't you do this?" And then they always want to talk about "Well, if I did it, I would have done it differently." Is the problem resolved? I don't care how you would have gotten to the resolution. I am not a Stepford. I have my own mind, I bring my different perspective to it, I resolve the issue. Did I miss something? (2001a, 4)

"The monitoring is not at specific times, nor are reps given notice," says Shelly. "They recently got the ability to record the calls too," she continues. "You can be taped at any time. Managers are recording you now all the time. I had a real problem with that. The manager plays it back to you." The taping and playback of their conversations is particularly troublesome to call center reps. Part of the reps' concern is that what they say will be taken out of context, and, Shelly worries, "The managers hold the recordings and basically pick and choose what they want" (2003, 6).

Despite Verizon's commitment to monitoring, according to Patricia Wallace, "Electronic monitoring gets mixed reviews with respect to its effectiveness as a means to improve performance." For example, one study suggests that "people who are doing tasks they find relatively easy show better performance if they are monitored, but their performance will suffer if the tasks are more complex" (2004, 231). So though the monitoring of employees may help them sell hamburgers or train tickets, it may actually hurt the performance of workers doing complex tasks like those of the call center reps at Verizon.

Many reps find this constant monitoring intolerable on top of the pressure to sell. In the Andover facility, as in most call centers, monitoring is tied directly to sales performance. If you sell above the target level, then you are pretty much assured that you will suffer very little monitoring, but if your sales are below par, you can expect to be more carefully monitored. These evaluations based on monitoring become part of the employee's record, on which promotions and pay increases are based, so the stakes are high, adding to the already high stress level. "It's very nerve-wracking," one service rep reports. "The more that I concentrate on it, it tends to bother me a lot more if I'm wondering if they're listening or not" (Mark 2001, 4).

This link between sales performance, monitoring, and discipline is recognized beyond the call center reps in Andover. Debbie Goldman reports:

> Our [CWA] members talk a lot about the pressure to sell and all of that. Even where we have language that says they can't be disciplined for failure to meet sales objectives, you still hear that . . . even though they can't get you for not meeting their sales objective, if you're not meeting it, then you might be the one they're going to monitor more. (Goldman 2004, 13)

The technology in the Andover call center provides management with the capacity to monitor employees throughout their entire workday. It would be easy to attribute overuse of monitoring to overzealous managers trying to boost sales or to those who would use monitoring to discipline and punish reps. Yet it would be a mistake to see monitoring as somehow on the fringes of Verizon's new industrial paradigm. In fact, when one looks more closely at the organization of work at Verizon, it is clear that monitoring lies at the center of Verizon's practices. Its centrality goes back to Frederick Taylor.

The starting point for the Taylor system, as discussed earlier, is replacing the individual worker's decision-making about how to perform a task with a formal scientific method. These scientific methods become practice only if managers "train, teach, and develop the workman," and "insure all of the work being done is in accordance with the principles of the science which has been developed" (Taylor 1911, 36). Taylor was acutely aware that without monitoring and direct supervision, workers would revert to their folkways of production, their "rules of thumb." Thus, the constant monitoring of workers plays a central role in Taylor's system. In *The Principles of Scientific Management* he writes:

> It is only through the *enforced* standardization of methods, *enforced* adoption of the best implements and working conditions, and *enforced* cooperation that this faster work can be assured. And the duty of enforcing the adaptation of standards and of enforcing cooperation rests with *management* alone [original emphasis]. (1911, 83)

According to the Taylor system, for Verizon to sell more, its managers need to ensure, through monitoring, that their call center reps are sticking to the program.[4]

Human Resources Practices and Stress

There is little doubt that the volume of work, how it is organized, the sales pressure, and the monitoring make the work for call center reps at Andover difficult and stressful. But the organization of work is not the only factor that defines people's jobs and how they experience them. Employers also make a series of decisions about work schedules, vacations, and sick time, and a host of other decisions regarding human resources policies and practices. We now turn to look more closely at Verizon's HR policies and practices to examine how they address issues of workplace stress.

The customer service jobs at the Andover call center pay well and have a solid benefits package—the product, in part, of collective bargaining. Although the weekly starting pay is only $308, as of 2003, the increases come quickly, and after three years weekly salaries reach $998.50. Verizon follows a historical trend, where telephone workers typically have made more than double what their counterparts in other service occupations make (Spalter-Roth and Hartman 1995). With overtime and bonuses, a Verizon telephone worker can earn considerably more than a living wage in Massachusetts. Verizon also offers an excellent health insurance program, a solid retirement package, and tuition reimbursement for college courses.

It was difficult to speak with most reps for very long, however, before they began railing about their work schedule, overtime, vacation, and sick time. There was no disagreement among them that there is little of the flexibility, particularly in scheduling, that one would expect in a job at this pay level. It starts with how the company regards arrival at work in the morning. Margaret says the company is "crazed about attendance. Three minutes late," she complains, "is a huge offense. And you have to sit there and go, 'You know what? Anywhere else in the world, three minutes late, I'm on time. My shift starts at 7:30. Granted, five, ten minutes, I can see what you're getting at. But two, three minutes just . . .'" (2001a, 2).

Beyond requiring that employees adhere to a strict attendance schedule and stay on task continually, the effort to maximize capacity and profit has led the company to seasonally impose large amounts of mandatory overtime. This is not overtime that employees can choose to take; they are required to work the extra hours or they lose their jobs. Many Americans believe that federal wage and hour laws cap the number of hours worked weekly at forty—as a result of workers' struggles over much of the twentieth century—but the regulations actually allow employers to require overtime as long as they pay time and a half for those extra hours.

Although the extra money is alluring, anything beyond occasional mandatory overtime is wearing. "I work at a pretty high level throughout the day for my sales," recounts Don. "I'm mentally exhausted, and to do another hour or hour and a half on top of that, after a while it burns you out" (2003, 6). When Ellen hears she has to work mandatory overtime, she quips,

It's pretty much hitting the "New" key, lying back in your chair, and saying, "Somebody stab me with a fork so I don't have to do another hour of this!" But you go home, close your eyes, go to sleep and all of a sudden it's the next morning and you're at your desk again! There's no down time. By the time you decompress over the weekend . . . well, Monday comes and Monday is our busiest day so you're doing ten hours. It's especially bad in the summer. (2003, 3–4)

It is particularly hard on the call center reps who have young children. If they're lucky, they have family members, neighbors, or friends who can help. Margaret says she sends her daughter to the public library after school when she has to, adding, "She's not the only one over there." It's also troublesome for parents who have their children in day care. "In the state of Massachusetts, my understanding is a child cannot be in day care more than ten hours per day. So you need to be there to pick the kid up. What are they going to do, dump him on the sidewalk?" You can see the anger rise in Margaret's face as she describes a situation she faced with her daughter.

> We had to put the cat to sleep. No big deal. Do you think I could get out of my overtime? Now it wasn't bad enough that I had to have someone else take the cat to put the cat to sleep. All I wanted to do is get out of my overtime to be home with my daughter afterwards. Couldn't get out of the overtime. I'm like, "You know what? She's a kid; it's her cat. I know it doesn't make a lot of sense but she's upset. I just don't want to do the overtime. I'm not asking to leave early. I'm not asking you to pay me for the overtime. I just want to go home and be with her." "No. Out of the question." (2001b, 10)

One of the frustrations with mandatory overtime is that, at different times of the year, reps are forced to stay but the workload ends up being very light. Sometimes in these instances the reps are sent home. Many of the call center reps are less than impressed with the predictive powers of the ACD system. "It's kind of like the farmer's almanac," Margaret says. "It's usually warm and 60 degrees on this day" (2001a, 11).

Concern over mandatory overtime was one of the major issues that precipitated a nationwide strike at Verizon in late summer 2000. The union contract that resulted capped overtime at eight hours a week maximum and required twenty-four hours' notice, which was a major victory for the reps and their union. With a day's notice, it was considerably easier to make alternative arrangements for picking up children, providing meals, and taking care of other family obligations. But according to the customer service reps at the Andover call center, Verizon has maneuvered around this language in a way that makes it even more difficult for workers. During busy times, Ellen explains:

> They just put mandatory overtime on the schedule all the time. . . . When the service level is not where they want it to be, they send an announce-

ment that you don't have to do the overtime and can go home. That's fine and at the last moment everybody rushes out of the building because they've been answering the phone all day. But come Monday, somebody's going to tell you that you have two hours of overtime on your schedule at the end of the day and still, you may get out at 3:30, but you may not get out until 5:30. You're not going to know until 3:35. (2003, 2)

While Verizon is following the letter of the agreement, it is violating the spirit—that employees should know in advance whether they will be working their regular shift or working overtime. In fact, the new policy exacerbates problems such as child care and transportation because workers must report for work every day prepared for overtime, never knowing whether or not it will be canceled at the last minute.

Verizon's obsession with timeliness and mandatory overtime is further reflected in its policy for vacation and sick days. Most employees at the Andover call center—those with less than seven years' service—receive two weeks' vacation a year; after seven years, they receive three weeks. Customer service reps also receive earned workdays (EWDs) to use as sick days or personal days. "It's based on the amount of time you're here," Ellen explains.

You get 22.5 hours per year, which you can use hourly. Then you get two full days where one of them is paid and one unpaid. But you have to take them as full days. You can't take them as half days or as hours. Usually that time is granted to you January 1. It's amazing how people use it all up before April 1 just to get out of overtime. There's no personal time or anything. That's what you have to use as your personal time. (2003, 4–5)

Customer service representatives expressed concern about the scheduling of vacation and EWDs. "As of today, June 8, the next available day you could take is September 14," Ellen explains indignantly. "Even if I have EWD time, I cannot use it." So, during the summer months, when children are off from school and families take vacations, the customer service reps at Verizon cannot use the limited time they have available unless they schedule that time far in advance. As Shelly laments, "Why give me time off if I can't use it?" (2003, 5).

Even when reps are able to schedule time off, the break is not as restorative as it might be because of Verizon's policy on sales and time off. Shelly continues: "I have to account for my sales for the five days I'm not here [on vacation]. My quota is 50,000 [points] for the month. . . . Instead of dropping me to 40,000, I'm responsible to account for 50,000 regardless. So I have to work triply hard when I come back or before I leave" (2003, 5). In the same way, sales expectations are not lowered when workers are sick or using EWDs. So, after returning from a vacation or a day off, reps need to work exceptionally hard to get their points up to required levels. Coupled with the difficulty of scheduling time off, this policy of not adjusting sales quotas just makes work harder.

As the midsummer temperatures rose on the East Coast in the summer of 2003, Verizon and its unionized workers were again embroiled in a major dispute about workplace rights and conditions. Three years earlier, failed talks had led to a strike that idled more than 75,000 workers for eighteen days as the newly formed Verizon struggled to find its niche in a rapidly changing telecommunications industry. In the 2003 negotiations, absenteeism and sick time, work hours and scheduling emerged as key issues. Verizon spokesman Eric Rabe reported in *Forbes* that absenteeism cost Verizon $600 million in 2002, which, in his words, was "too high" and "not defendable" (quoted in Weinberg 2003, 17). Things look very different from a worker's perspective.

EWDs can be used in case of illness, and they are invaluable, given the inflexibility of the work schedule. Workers at Verizon can also take up to ten sick days beyond EWDs. Unlike the practice at firms that grant sick days to be used at the worker's discretion, however, Verizon workers are actually disciplined for taking a sick day, or "stepped" as the customer service reps refer to it. To be "stepped" means to be put on the first of successive steps of progressive discipline, which can ultimately lead to discharge. Being stepped may not be a problem for a rep who needs to take only one or two sick days a year but creates difficulties for those who may need more time.

One rep speaks of "some of the horror stories" he hears as a union steward: "A person can be out because they have a doctor's appointment and they're getting stepped and walked [though subsequent disciplinary steps] and their job is in jeopardy because they got sick or they have to go to the doctor's" (Rodney 2003, 4). Because of the costs associated with "taking" sick days, CWA's Pat Telesco explains, "it's pretty much saying you don't have them" (2004, 10).[5]

So instead of being "stepped" for taking a sick day, many workers at Verizon use the Family Medical Leave Act (FMLA) to take time off without pay when they are sick. The FMLA, however, does not provide for time to be taken off in single-day increments. It is designed for more serious illnesses and family issues, and so the shortest block of time off allowed is three days. This rule creates a difficult situation for the customer service rep. As Ellen explains, "If my doctor says I only need to be off for one day, I actually need to stay off for three not to be disciplined." Thus, she says, "the company promotes the abuse of FMLA policy" (2003, 7).

Without a more routine way of dealing with minor illness, Verizon is forcing many workers to use the FMLA for something it was never designed for and, in the end, is paying the price for workers' being "off-line" for more time than they actually need to be. Frustrated, Ellen exclaims, "The union has fought this on many, many levels" and has pushed the company to revise its policy. Yet still, she says, "a lot of people come back after being out a day because they want to make their sales, they want their attendance to be okay. And they discipline them every single time." She continues:

> People wouldn't be out nearly as much if they could be out sick for one day. Who doesn't get sick? You work all this overtime and every once in a while you get up in the morning and you just can't do it. But if you just can't do it, you had better be able to go to the doctor. You have to get approved for the illness. If the illness is not approved, you will be disciplined. (2003, 7)

It is also important to recognize that the FMLA is not a real substitute for a sick policy. First, these days are not compensated. Second, workers cannot continue to use the FMLA endlessly.

Given the combination of Verizon's policies and practices (or lack thereof) around illness and their overall approach to attendance, sales, and monitoring, it is not surprising that the company faces an absenteeism problem. In fact, given the conditions in their call centers, it is surprising that the absenteeism is not much higher— which may say more about the economy than the actual working conditions at Verizon.

This "absenteeism problem," as discussed earlier, is not the result of workers' not wanting to be on the job and performing their duties but is a consequence of an extremely high pressured pace of work with few, if any, escape valves to relieve the pressure and few structural avenues for taking care of the demands of their lives outside of work. In many ways the problem with absenteeism represents the limits of how far Verizon can push their highly regimented work system. As CWA's Yvette Herrera suggests:

> If you're going to create this horrible environment with horrible stress and treat people badly, it's no wonder. They shouldn't be surprised that people don't come to work and need time off. Whether they're sick or get sick because it's a sickening place to work is hard to distinguish. . . . I think it all comes down to the fact that there is a lot of absenteeism in these places because it's grueling work. The work situation and work environment and the stress is incredibly high. You can't fix one thing without the other. (2004, 8, 11)

The only thing Verizon does on the soft side of human resources is to expend a huge amount of effort on promotional games and contests. Offering these may be Verizon's attempt to build up the morale it breaks down with its strict policies and procedures, but it is not working. The reps I spoke with for the most part felt insulted by what they commonly refer to as "trash and trinkets." Mark, for example, says, "Two weeks ago they had this Candy Land contest. Yeah, you know, "I'll sell an additional line or a whole voice mail or long distance to a customer and make the company X amount of dollars for a Tootsie Roll or a Milky Way bar." Give me a break! That's what the prizes were—candy." Besides being insulted by the idea that candy would motivate him to work harder, Mark finds that these activities distract him from getting his work done.

> I don't even do half the contests they do. If I win anything, it's usually something I don't have to track or handle myself just because I'm not going to waste my time doing that. Because it makes the job even that much more stressful. You have like six different tracking sheets to keep up with all these contests. I don't know how people do it. (2001, 9–10)

The top sellers love winning the big trips and the bonuses, but even they hate the little games. As one says, "I feel like I'm in kindergarten! They've got our atrium done up like you're walking into a kindergarten. They paid people $25 and change per hour to sit out and color" (Chris 2001, 22). The constant use of balloons to reward high performers is particularly irksome. "To think of the amount of money they spend on balloons alone," Sally exclaims:

> It's probably enough to feed a family of four for the year. It's not normal. I don't understand it. . . . Why do we have to blow up a balloon and hang it

there for every [thing we do]. . . . You come in the next morning and have twelve balloons at the side of your desk that are dead. Then they have the audacity to walk around and tell you you'd better throw them away because they look bad. But you put 'em here! Come on now! (2001, 22–23)

The Verizon reps see the irony in spending resources on these novelties. As Margaret quips caustically, "So, it's an offense that I was five minutes late because I impacted the call volume, but these people are busy blowing up balloons?" (2001a, 15–16). Shelly finds the whole process revolting:

Trips, nothing. It doesn't motivate me. What would motivate me is if we had people who cared about us. They don't care about us! When you call in sick they're like, "Oh, is there anything I can do for you?" Everyone obviously says no. I'm like, I wish someone would just say, "Well, yes, could you go pick up my prescription at Walgreen's?" and they would really do it. (2003, 12)

Bread without Roses

Not quite one hundred years ago, in 1912, 23,000 women went out on strike against the woolen companies in Lawrence, Massachusetts. In many ways it was the first modern strike in the United States, featuring massive parades and picket lines, with poems and songs written by immigrant women from diverse ethnic groups. But it was a phrase from a poem by James Oppenheim (later set to music) that captured both the essence of the strike and a fundamental notion about the dignity of labor.

> Our lives shall not be sweated
> From birth until life closes
> Hearts starve as well as bodies,
> give us bread but give us roses. (Kornbluh 1964, 196)

Without a doubt, the workers in Lawrence needed the bread—enough income to support their families. But they wanted more. They also wanted roses: dignity and self-respect on the job, time for their children and family, and the energy to do more than just work—they wanted to have a life.

Call center representatives at Verizon, who work in the shadow of Lawrence, struggle for the roses no less than did the women who worked in Lawrence a century ago. Verizon provides a very good income for its customer service reps. The problem is that the company has provided little else—little control of work, little flexibility in work schedules, and little basic dignity on the job—few of the roses that workers need to survive on the job. As Margaret puts it simply, "They pay me well to treat me bad" (2001a, 7).

Despite the money, the system is inflexible in meeting employees' basic needs as they get older, face health problems, or want to have a family. Herein lies the dilemma. Parents feel incredibly conflicted about a job that provides for their family but in fundamental ways makes that family impossible. I asked Margaret if she felt she had to choose between her child and her job. She responded:

> Absolutely. All the time. That's on a regular basis. Just trying to get her into different sports, and stuff. I don't have the flexibility in my schedule. "It's after school? Well then how are you going to get home?" She's phoned me a couple of times: "I missed the bus." "Well, walk to the library, and I'll meet you at the library in an hour." Things like that. It shouldn't be that way. I should be going, "Oh, you missed the bus? I'm on my way." (2001a, 19)

On the Verizon webpage, three happy workers provide testimonials for the company. Two of the three focus on how family-friendly the company is. One of those, Robert, reports, "Verizon has been a very family-friendly environment. I can get my work done and still make it to my daughter's soccer games and practices." Referring to benefits, the narrator announces, "We offer a generous time-off plan including vacation, personal days, and floating holidays" (Verizon 2001). The reality for call center reps at the Andover facility is quite different. Margaret, for example, says:

> I have a lot of trouble when my daughter has a doctor's appointment. Ninety per cent of the time, I'm like, "Can't you make it at 4:00 or later?" Or, okay, well, now I have to take a whole day. . . . And I'm going, "Uh-oh—we can't afford for anything to happen." Even my two weeks vacation: I can only take one because I need that other one for whatever else might happen—a dentist appointment, a doctor's appointment, Girl Scouts, trying to be the troop leader, to be involved. And that wipes out all the time that I have.

Margaret is left with very few options: "So I'm afraid to use my vacation, because what if I need it? So if I just want a day to do nothing, it can't be done. It's just not allowed for" (2001b, 7).

For young, healthy workers without children, the rigid system at Verizon is manageable. This seems to be the Verizon model—find motivated young people and pay them well enough and provide enough benefits to entice them to become permanent employees at Verizon. They come from retail, from entry-level jobs in health care and small companies, jobs where, in today's economy, there is little possibility for buying a house, having a family, or building a life. Get them excited about the balloons, the candy bars, the trips. "Yeah, I work for a corporation that tends to promote cute, young things," one service rep quips. They love you "if you're young and you're perky, and you can go in and pretend to be the company cheerleader, 'Rah, rah, rah, I love my job, I'm so happy'" (Margaret 2001a, 21).

For older workers, however, those with health problems, or reps with families, precious little time is left for anything else. The stress of having to be on time, maybe having to stay late, and worrying whether there will be enough days to take care of illness or the things that come up in life are not matters they leave at the door when their shift is done. "Some days," Margaret says, "I come home and I go, Just let me lie here for five minutes. I'll make your dinner later. Please just do your homework quietly. I'll check it when you're done. Please just don't even ask me any questions. I'll look at it when you're all done" (2001b, 10). After dinner and homework on top of a nonstop day, there's not much left for a personal life for Margaret. It doesn't start, she says, "until after 9:30 p.m."

> And I've still got to get up at 7:30, still be up early again the next morning because heaven forbid I'm two minutes late. . . . I go and I spend some time with my boyfriend. Watching a movie, doing whatever, and basically falling asleep on each other because it's so late and we're tired. Fascinating love life. A girlfriend of mine asked me to be her Lamaze coach. And I had to sit there and go, "Oh my god, what if she goes into labor while I'm at work? I can't leave." And that's going to become a nightmare. And this is nuts. (2001b, 20)

This is not the life that Margaret, Shelly, and Ellen want or dreamed of. They desperately want and need some time to make a life for themselves and their families—some of the roses.

> I heard somebody once say that Verizon is a broken dream factory, which I think pretty much sums it up. Because I don't think anybody when they're a little kid goes, "Oh, I'm going to work for the phone company when I grow up!" There's not one single person in there who said that when they were a kid. So everybody in there would really probably rather be doing something else. But to me it's the money. The

amount of money they pay me to do a job that I don't think is that difficult let's me live the lifestyle that I want to live. You know, maybe somewhere down the line if I keep socking away—maybe once I retire, which
will be at a young age—maybe then I'll be able to buy my restaurant. So
to me it's a means to an end. It pays the bills, gives me a lot of pocket
money, and hopefully someday it will let me do what I want to do. (Sally
2001, 8–9)

Sally initially came to work at Verizon to take advantage of the tuition
reimbursement. A college graduate, she was interested in pursuing a teaching career. "My mother has actually retired from the company. She said,
'Go work for the phone company. They'll pay for you to go back to school.'
That's what I really wanted to do."

But Sally, like many others who entered the factory of broken dreams at
Verizon, is staying.

> Like I said, they have you. I'm a lifer. . . . It's the money. I mean, even
> though I have a college degree in literary studies, that's an English de-
> gree, unless I want to go get my teaching certificate. . . . I don't have
> computer experience. The only computer experience I have is in that
> office. I just don't see myself being able to start over at another com-
> pany and make the amount of money that I make right now. At this
> point, I own a house, we have two cars, and we have things like a time-
> share. We have things that we pay for on a monthly basis. It would be
> very difficult to go and start somewhere else and make half of what I'm
> making now—which would probably be a typical starting salary at any
> other place—to start over. So that's what I mean when I say, "They have
> you." (2001, 12)

Like Willie Loman in Arthur Miller's *Death of a Salesman*, however, the
call center reps at Verizon may have the wrong dreams—dreams that cannot be sustained in the reality of working there—despite the high wages.
For many, Verizon's approach to scheduling, vacations, and time off just
does not provide enough roses. "You get your two weeks of vacation, and
you have your excused work days for emergencies," Margaret says. "You
can take a couple of hours here, personal time, and that's wonderful. But it's
not enough for the day-to-day, everyday stuff. I know" (2001b, 10).

The new industrial paradigm that Verizon's CEO, Ivan Seidenberg, refers to is a paradox. The wages would indicate a "high road" job, yet the
working conditions clearly suggest the "low road," despite Seidenberg's as-

sertion of the opposite. The working conditions are in many ways more like those one would expect in a sweatshop, not at a major firm. As Simon Head writes, "The call center industry and its work practices provide near-textbook examples of what I have called the new ruthless economy. . . . This is exploitation in the classic manner of the nineteenth and twentieth centuries" (2003, 109).

A work system could be designed with a variety of human resources practices to ensure that work stations are filled and the service reps are on line when the computers tell them they should be. In the auto industry, for example, there were "floaters" who had no specific job assignment but filled in for people who were sick or out of work for other reasons. In education, schools have a pool of substitute teachers they can call on when regular teachers are absent. Yet rather than maintaining a system that would provide customer service reps with some flexibility, Verizon has opted for an extremely rigid system based on (1) every employee being at work every day, with a minimum of vacation, sick, and personal days; (2) workers being "on-line" most of the day; and (3) all reps being available to work significant overtime hours as needed by the company. This "new industrial paradigm" is to have as lean a workforce as possible, to insist that employees be available for more than forty hours a week so as to avoid hiring additional workers and paying their benefits, and to expect them to sell at a high level most of the time. As Jill Andresky Fraser explains in *White-Collar Sweatshop*, "The message not so subtly being conveyed by their employers is this: We need everyone to work harder and longer, but can't trust you to do it unless we start watching more closely . . . and if we found out you're not working as we expect, we'll replace you" (2001, 88–89).

According to CWA's Herrera, management at Verizon is fully aware of the system they have created, including the costs that workers pay for company profits. She explains:

> You talk to high-level managers who know a lot about the work environment in the call centers and you have these conversations with them off the record. They know all this. It's a horrible place to work. They'll tell you that. Not in public. The turnover is horrendous. The stress is horrendous. The monitoring is horrendous. The absenteeism is high because it's such an awful place to work. It's not like you have to be a brain surgeon to figure this out.

They also, according to Herrera, understand the intimate relationship between the current work system and their ability to make a profit and hence are unwilling to change the work system.

> The fascinating thing to me is the complete resistance to change it! As far as I can tell from my conversations . . . it's too risky for them as managers. I'm talking about pretty high-up managers. You have to be pretty high up to agree to try and fix these work design problems. But it's too risky for them personally because call centers are moneymakers. It's all based on cost. It's all cost-driven. That's why we see so many jobs going to India and the Philippines and wherever else they're going. It's all cost driven. It's like a sweatshop, I mean. If you change something and try to make the work nicer . . . they see it as too risky because if it fails or if it doesn't meet the numbers exactly, they get clobbered. But it is very frustrating because you'll talk to them, and the smart ones and the ones who are real, they can't disagree, of course. They'll agree with all of this. But when you say to them, "Let's do a trial, a pilot, where we try redesigning this work so that it's better for everyone," ah no, they can't do that. (2004, 12–13)

The union representing workers at Andover is fully aware of conditions inside call centers, and, Debbie Goldman says, "would very much like to be part of projects that deal with the job design. We wish," she continues, "that the union had a larger role in that. But this is not something that management likes; . . . management has not wanted us in management" (2004, 21–22).

It is important to note how dramatic a shift this attitude represents in the telecommunications industry. In the 1980s, AT&T, responding to massive complaints by workers about working conditions, became one of the pioneers of early employee-involvement programs. "By December 31, 1983, the eve of the breakup of the Bell System," according to Morton Bahr, then president of the CWA,

> more that 100,000 CWA members were trained in the principles of QWL [quality of working life]. Much of the training took place jointly with management personnel. The key ingredient for success required the total buy-in by top management and top union. AT&T's chairman made it clear to management personnel that if they could not work in this new environment, they would be placed elsewhere. (2001, 3)

Although a number of concerns have been raised about QWL programs (Parker 1985; Wells 1987), the extent of AT&T's massive QWL efforts in the 1980s indicated that the company felt it needed to address issues of the quality of jobs and employees' work lives.

The breakup of the Bell System ended QWL but did not stop the telecommunications industry's experimentation with various labor-management programs. By the late 1980s and early 1990s, however, the whole notion of improving the quality of workers' lives began to fade. Workplace-based QWL programs transmogrified into total quality management (TQM) or continuous quality improvement (CQI), lean production and reengineering—programs designed largely to boost productivity and product quality.

In 1994, AT&T won Japan's prestigious Deming Prize for Quality Management, the first U.S.-based company to do so (AT&T 1994, 1), and was recognized as a leader in reengineering (Hammer and Stanton 1995). Like QWL, this second wave of employee-involvement programs had a variety of critics (Parker and Slaughter 1985; Babson 1995). Still, AT&T demonstrated an effort to involve workers in the production process, if only in very prescribed ways.

By the time of the meltdown and reorganization of the telecommunications industry in 2000, most of these labor-management efforts had ended.[6] For example, Batt's research demonstrated that self-managed work teams in a call center at a regional Bell company increased both service quality and sales; nevertheless, the program was discontinued. "The company," she writes, "like many others, has moved in the direction of mass production of individualized work, faster time cycles, and stricter adherence to schedules. . . . Employees are discouraged from asking questions or talking with one another because doing so reduces productive work time" (1999, 358).

Batt's characterization accurately describes the system Verizon has put in place at its call center in Andover. There were no concerns or programs about the quality of working life of its employees. There was not even a nod to TQM or the team-based production that is an integral part of lean production (Babson 1995). Instead, a system of hyper-Taylorism, pushing individual workers as hard as it possibly can. And given its comparatively high wages, it needs no QWL programs to keep workers on the job. This is Seidenberg's new paradigm—pay them well to treat them bad.

Do the Beatings Have to Continue?

With increasing competitive pressure from companies doing business off-shore, does work in call centers have to be organized as it is at Verizon for companies to remain profitable in telecommunications? Undoubtedly, the Verizon paradigm is not company-specific but reflects the way the industry is moving with regard to call centers. Simon Head points out that there is "substantial research showing that these examples of harshness of working life at call centers are not isolated incidents but form part of a work culture of the industry as a whole" (2003, 107). Yet some important experiments taking place suggest that other approaches may be more effective.

At SBC in Connecticut, for example, Pat Telesco and the CWA local have negotiated important modifications to the traditional call center work system. The first, Telesco explains, has to do with what is referred to as "call flow."

> The union always argues against tight scripting: "We're thinking people. You pay us a lot of money. I'm not going to sit and read a script to a customer." The company has the right to tell me how they want me to handle a customer, and the call flow is a list of points they want you to hit sometime in the call. . . . [But] when my supervisor is listening to see if I'm doing a good call or not, it's not, "You sold nothing on this call, you're getting scored for this." We don't have a quota for the service reps here. I'm really proud of that. It's not my fault if your product is not good, if your customers think the product is priced too high, if maybe you can't provide the product properly. All these things are out of my control. Then how can you fault me for not selling? Rather, hold me to *offering* your product. (2004, 11–12)

Additionally, Telesco explains, the union has negotiated language that restricts the practice of monitoring and the use of the information gathered in monitoring.

> When it comes down to listening to Pat, as an employee, they are limited to taping two to ten calls a month. And they can only do it on up to three days and they have to notify me ahead of time if they are doing it. . . . If they have a tape of the call, they have until the end of the month in which they took the tape to review it with me, and if they don't do it, they can't bring it up to me. (2004, 14)

These changes have had an enormous impact on the work life of the call center workers at SBC in Connecticut and have put some of the roses back into call center work. To be able to make the effort to sell and yet not be held to a sales quota makes an important difference to the call center reps, making as many calls as they do and speaking with so many customers. To be free from constant monitoring also restores a little humanity to the work system and the lives of call center workers.

Not only workers have gained from these changes in the work system: "Connecticut reps are meeting the company objectives for the products that they sell," Telesco reports. "So what does this tell you?" she quips. "The beatings don't have to continue. You can do it by developing and encouraging people." She argues, "You can control people by bullying them. It works for a short time, but after a while people get a thick skin and then they don't care anymore. And you are not effective any longer" (2004, 15).

Such results raise the question whether Verizon's new industrial paradigm has reached its limit. The nineteenth-century sociologist Max Weber suggested that bureaucracies can become so self-absorbed that, rather than fulfilling their original mission, they become an "iron cage" of contradiction (2002). At Verizon, has scientific management—the pushing and the bullying that call center reps describe—gone as far as it can go? Yvette Herrera suggests that it's time to rethink our notions about productivity and efficiency:

All those words are very loaded. I wouldn't say that [the Verizon model] is efficient and productive. But the way they look at it is cents per minute. It's a completely cost-driven operation. So that's all they look at. It's just numbers on a piece of paper. They could care less about customer service. It's numbers on paper and that's how it's driven. They don't think about the huge turnover. Well, they think about it, but not enough. They invest huge amounts of money to get these customer service reps up to speed because the training is, they keep cutting it down, but it's eight to twelve to sixteen weeks long. They're paying people while they're not being productive. Then they put them into the job and a year later half of them are gone because it's so horrible. If you were to factor all of that mess in, any reasonable person would say, "That's nonproductive and let's try to retain the employees that we're spending so much money on training. To have them walk out the door is absurd and not a good business decision." (2004, 19)

Even Frederick Taylor understood the costs of pushing workers too hard. From his purely economic perspective, human resources could easily become exhausted:

> It should be distinctly understood that in no case is the workman called upon to work at a pace which would be injurious to his health. The task is always regulated that the man who is well suited to his job will thrive while working at this rate during a long term of years and grow happier and more prosperous, instead of being overworked. (1911, 39)

This principle of Taylor's from almost a hundred years ago appears to be completely outside the framework of the new industry paradigm at Verizon. Whereas Taylor's concern was largely about physical exhaustion and physical health, the issues at the Andover call center involve stress and its impact on both mental and physical health. The organization of work at Verizon, coupled with its human resources practices, provides a textbook situation for excessive workplace stress. In a recent study Holman reports that employee well-being in call centers is "most highly associated with a high control over work methods and procedures, a low level of monitoring and a supportive team leader"—(2006, 35) all things that are largely missing at Verizon.

Globalization, Unions, and the Labor Process

The technology and the work systems in place now throughout Verizon make the shift of work offshore almost seamless. According to Debbie Goldman, the cost savings of relocating work offshore would be substantial. "We've done some costing with AT&T, and even if you add in the benefits to quality, the higher sales, the fewer errors," she points out, "there's a 30 percent unit cost gap with India. That's after you put in the overhead, the contract management, everything" (2004, 21). A study comparing call centers in the United States and India concluded that Indian employees earn about one-sixth of the salary of their American counterparts (Centre for Education and Communication 2006, 6).

These wage gaps are powerful economic constraints on what unions can do in the global telecommunications industry. At Verizon, the CWA has been fighting hard, in difficult economic circumstances, to hold the line on some of the worst low-road tactics of this new paradigm. But the union, Goldman reports, has had a "tough time" and has had to focus on trying to "block the worst of the abuse, as opposed to really reshaping the job" (2004, 21–22).

CWA's Yvette Herrera makes the connection between work redesign, profitmaking, and the threat of outsourcing:

> The dynamic is that they want to send all the jobs to India. In that context, it's tough. They put up little charts and say, "In India we can do this work for——," you know, whatever ridiculous amount it is. And here, look what we're paying your people. That's where we start. If you start there, you're just trying to save the jobs. It's tough to then talk about, "Let's not just talk about not losing the jobs, but let's make the jobs nicer." It's a tough conversation to have. We have them, but you must understand where we're starting. (2004, 17)

While this is a story of a union trying to make a difference to its members in the context of globalization, it is important to understand how the union got here. To do so, we need to step back and explore how labor relations developed in the post–World War II era and how that shaped the post–World War II American workplace.

In the context of massive union organizing by the CIO, New Deal legislation—including the Wagner Act in 1937—established for the first time the legal right of American workers to become union members. It took World War II, however, to legitimate the labor movement when labor leaders were invited to work with government and business officials to win the war, if only as junior partners. Management was constrained from the worst forms of antiunionism; the government played a much more direct role in mediating labor disputes; and the National War Labor Board codified many of labor's prewar demands, including "grievance systems, vacation pay and night-shift premiums, sick leave and paid mealtimes" (Lichtenstein 1989, 125).

In the wake of a growing shop floor activism after the war, American business fought back against labor to reestablish management rights. Nowhere was this more clear than in the automobile industry. Emboldened by wartime labor relations, in 1945 the United Automobile Workers (UAW) president Walter Reuther took his union out on strike against General Motors. He not only asked for a 30 percent increase in wages but proposed that GM not increase the cost of an automobile. GM rebuffed this demand that the union be allowed to negotiate the cost of an automobile as creeping socialism, and after 113 days the union was forced to settle a very modest contract. In many ways it marked the end of labor's ambitions to play a direct role in the industry and the economy (Lichtenstein 1989). In the end, as Howell John Harris suggests, "an aggressive union met a rather more single-minded management head-on in a struggle for authority in the workplace, and lost" (1982, 141).

The Ford Motor Company took a less adversarial approach to bargaining in 1946, focusing on securing "freedom from authorized strikes, and the freedom to maximize production as the company's return for paying the industry's highest wages and giving the UAW an unprecedented liberal contract and a large measure of security" (Harris 1982, 144). Instead of fighting the union, Ford sought to domesticate the UAW and as part of a contract put mechanisms in place that directly undermined the steward system and imposed severe penalties for job actions on the shop floor.

In many ways the 1946 Ford contract foreshadowed what labor relations would become in the United States during what has been called the "labor-management accord"—or, more accurately, an "uneasy truce" between management and labor (Gross 2003; Lichtenstein 2003). Where once disputes were settled by workers walking out and striking, there were now formal dispute-resolution processes. Gone too were many of labor's more radical elements, purged in a wave of growing anticommunism. The center of activity for the labor movement shifted from the plants and communities where it was born to union offices and management board rooms, where grievance, arbitration, and collective bargaining took place.

Although labor continued to grow throughout the 1940s and early 1950s, with union density hitting a peak of 39 percent in 1953, it stayed largely within the bounds management had set after the war. There were no major moves by labor, either in contracts with employers or in larger public policy, to challenge management's control of the organization of work on the shop floor, no efforts to shorten the workday, institutionalize worker control, or make work less alienating or less physically demanding. Early in his career, Reuther had flirted with the notion of a thirty-two-hour week, but he ended up opposing the idea, despite tremendous support for it among his members (Cutler 2004). As in Ford's 1946 contract, labor took the money but largely ceded control of the shop floor to management. According to Ruth Milkman:

> the grueling nature of production work in the auto industry changed very little over the postwar decades. Any hopes for improvement in the

daily tedium of the work or for a moderation in its intensity were relegated to the realm of fantasy. . . . [T]he UAW continued to extract improvements in the economic terms under which its members agree to submit to these conditions, and for many this was the only incentive to return to the factory gate day after day. (1997, 25)

The costs of the accord between labor and management were not obvious as long as the nation prospered and employers continued to reward workers financially. But in the late 1970s and early 1980s, with the U.S. economy stalled and international competition growing, the accord for all intents and purposes ended. Business once again waged a frontal attack on unions, and the legacy of the accord left workers without any mechanisms to constrain management as employers further intensified work.[7] And this time, in a global economy with the threat of outsourcing and offshoring jobs, there would be little money to grease the skids. Workers would have to compete just to keep their jobs.

We see the legacy of labor's disengagement from the labor process in the telecommunications industry and, in particular, at Verizon. As long as call centers were small and regionally based, the informality of the workplace, along with steady profits—often guaranteed by public regulatory agencies—protected workers from the worst impacts of workplace change. Once the industry consolidated and work was moved to megacenters, however, there was neither a framework nor a culture in place by which workers and their unions could shape workplace change, especially as the industry competed in a worldwide market. Although unions are making valiant efforts to protect their members in these new realities, this question remains: can unions in telecommunications constrain the worst management practices without being perceived as speeding up the movement of work offshore?

One hope is that there may be limits to outsourcing and offshoring. "Customers are definitely fed up with it," Pat Telesco says, because it's "not good customer service." Also, with the explosion of offshoring, she sees a backlash developing: "Politically, the climate in this country is, 'Do I want my business taken care of by someone in another country, who can't even be themselves?' They're faking who they are, making up a name and a place just to have a job" (2004, 26). Some U.S. companies are pulling back from or limiting their use of overseas workers in customer service.

As part of this backlash, Yvette Herrera sees the emergence of a two-tiered system for customer service.

What they do now is the old Taylorism applied to customer service. We see some reversals in this. I think it will be reversed eventually because I don't think it's sustainable. But what they have tried to do is Taylorize customer service so that you have what they call "Tier One" and "Tier Two." Then they put it down to the simplest kinds of things where the person only has to ask you five questions. That's Tier One. That goes to India. Tier Two, which is very difficult to get to, by the way, would be here and would be customer service by folks who actually can help you solve a problem. (2004, 13)

Herrera suggests that the future of call centers in the United States lies in the bundling or combining of services. In the cutthroat competition in telecommunications, companies such as Verizon want to provide more than one individual service to each of its customers, and they have found that bundling services works. "It retains customers for them," she points out, "and there are all kinds of studies that show that. They definitely know that bundling is the way to go and they can't compete without it." But in addition to making firms more profitable, bundling requires a different kind of service rep, one who is highly trained and more sophisticated. "We have optimism about this," Herrera explains, because "in order to continue to pursue this bundled service strategy, they're going to have to go back and expand the more sophisticated, experienced, trained customer service" (2004, 14).

The experiments at SBC in Connecticut, with work organized in a more humane way and management recognition that the bundling of products and services requires a well-trained professional service and sales staff, demonstrate that call center work need not descend to the lowest level of workplace conditions. Not only do these approaches create jobs and lives with both bread and roses, but they can make firms productive and efficient in a real, rather than next-quarter-artificial, way.

We need to recognize, however, that Verizon's paradoxical paradigm of "paying people well to treat them badly" is indeed the industry norm at this time, a juggernaut cutting a wide swath through American workplaces. The CWA and other unions in telecommunications have been fundamental in holding the line against abuses that are commonplace in an industry that is largely nonunion. There may also be a glimmer of hope for slowing down and limiting outsourcing and offshoring. But the forces creating lives of bread without roses continue.

Yet somehow, in the midst of all the monitoring, the pressure to sell, and the fear that their jobs could be offshored tomorrow, the Verizon call center reps in Andover remain committed to their union and their work. Doris is unapologetic.

I'm a service rep. I'm sorry. I'm going to do what you want me to do, not what somebody else thinks I should be doing. And until the contract language changes and my job title is renegotiated, sales is part of my job absolutely, but that's not the primary function of my job. And until someone tells me any different, whatever color my contract happens to be this time, I'm a service rep. And I'm going to remain one for the next twenty years, sitting in the same chair. (2001a, 4)

Immigrants Like Me

TOM JURAVICH

You see us in the morning, we come out of the shadows
Workers who look a lot like me
We work in the back rooms, the kitchens and the laundries
The places you don't see

We do the work nobody wants to, if they've a better place to be
You just want us hidden in the shadows
In the place you made for immigrants like me

We need to make money, to send home to our families
From our journeys, we've got debts to pay
So we work where we have to, we do what we need to
To make it, there is no other way

But we know just what you're doing, there is no mystery
No papers, no rules on how you treat us
In the place you make for immigrants like me

Up there on your high horse, you call me illegal
But I have hurt no one
With all of your venom, you say I should not be here, but then
How would all this work get done?

We do so much to make this country go, but our work you do not see
You just want us hidden in the shadows
In the place you made for immigrants like me

2

EXPLOITED

Cutting Fish in New Bedford

I started by cleaning fish, taking the bones out. Then I learned the skinning machines. Then I learned cleaning and sanitation work. I inspected the temperature in all the tanks where the fish are kept. I had to leave my job because of mistreatment. . . . I knew all the operations from the beginning. The pressure wash, all the operations in the company. I did all the cleaning for the daytime shift. I took only a half an hour for lunch. Everyone took an hour but if I didn't do it they would kick me out and say, "Oh, there is no more work for you. . . ." I was putting up with the bad treatment . . . because I didn't have any other choice. The owner of the place would always say, "You got a problem, come and see me." I tried to find somebody to speak English, to come and talk to the owner, and nobody would step forward to help me. That's how everybody works in that environment. They are too afraid to say anything or do anything because they don't have their papers and they don't want to speak up because they are too afraid. Roberto (2001b, 2–3)

AN UNDOCUMENTED worker who speaks little English, working at the bottom of a marginal industry, Roberto is vulnerable. Having emigrated from the highlands of Guatemala, he works in the fish-processing industry in New Bedford, Massachusetts. He has a broad grin and a reputation as a hard worker despite being forty-four, much older than most of the other Guatemalans he works with. But for Roberto and the other immigrants who cut fish, the struggles at work are not about sick days, health care plans, or retirement. They have none. They're not about new technology or new work systems. They don't exist. Their struggles on the job are more basic. They are about surviving abuse by their supervisors, facing on-the-job injury that would render them unemployable, cyclical layoffs in the industry, and getting cheated out of their wages. Their concern is not sophisticated, complex, or nuanced. In workplaces not all that different from the packinghouses Upton Sinclair wrote of almost one hundred years ago, it is about exploitation.

Immigrants in Odd Places

New Bedford, Massachusetts, conjures up images of a port town with fishing boats, docks, and the famous Seaman's Bethel, (the church) that looks out over the harbor, which Melville wrote about in *Moby Dick*. If you're familiar with New Bedford, you know that it is home to a large number of Portuguese immigrants and their descendants. But it's the last place one would expect to find Guatemalans. Roberto is one of between 2,500 and 3,000 Maya who since the mid-1990s have emigrated from the highlands of Guatemala to find work in New Bedford. The Maya are an indigenous people in Guatemala, sometimes called "Indians," distinct from what are referred to as Ladinos, or people of Spanish origin. They travel directly from Guatemala to work, at least initially, in New Bedford's fish-processing industry, in what are locally called the "fish houses."

Communities of recent immigrants are becoming commonplace in meatpacking and other food-processing plants across the Midwest and the South. Many such workers are undocumented, having traveled to the United States outside the formal immigration process. A large Guatemalan community works in chicken-processing in Morganton, North Carolina; Koreans make up most of the workforce in chicken-processing in Salisbury, Maryland; and Southeast Asians dominate the IBP hog-processing plant in Storm Lake, Iowa. These communities have one thing in common: they have some of the worst jobs in America—rough, repetitive, and dangerous.

Meatpacking jobs have always been tough, but a generation ago many were decent union jobs; by the 1960s, Charles Craypo points out, "the Meatcutters and Packinghouse Workers had largely organized beef packing," and "wages were 26 percent above the average for nondurable manufacturing" (1994, 63). During the 1980s and 1990s the industry went through rapid consolidation, however, and the new mega-firms orchestrated a campaign to become nonunion. Perhaps the highest-profile case was Hormel's, successfully breaking Local P-9 of the United Food and Commercial Workers in Austin, Minnesota (Green 1990). The employer campaign was so successful that by the 1990s the differential between union and nonunion packinghouse wages plummeted to 19 cents per hour (Craypo 1994, 80). In addition to the hemorrhaging of wages, as Lance Compa documents in a Human Rights Watch publication titled *Blood, Sweat, and Fear*, without strong unions, working conditions and workers' rights have returned to nineteenth-century practices in meatpacking (2004).

This deterioration of meat-packing jobs led to a dramatic shift in the demographics of the workforce. Few in the communities where this work was located were willing to work in these jobs—at least not for long, or if they could find work elsewhere—and employers began recruiting immigrant workers, many of them undocumented. The causal chain is important here. The immigrant workforce in meatpacking, Jackie Gabriel points out, is a "*result*, not a *cause* of the declining bargaining power, wages, and working conditions in the industry" (2006, 338).[1]

Until the 1980s, the fish houses in New Bedford, like meatpacking houses, were unionized, and fish cutters—drawn largely from the Portuguese community—"were very honored people on the waterfront" (Shrader 2001, 24). But by the end of July 1981, management of the fish houses forced the union out on strike, demanding massive concessions (Kogut 1981). The average hourly wage at the time the contract expired in 1981 was $7.90.

In the context of what was happening nationally—President Ronald Reagan's firing of the striking air traffic controllers, the national baseball strike, and a sluggish economy—it was not an easy time to be on strike. One fish plant closed; a small group of workers settled with another house; and by the beginning of August, seeing no real settlement in sight, the union settled for the concessionary agreement they had been offered a month earlier. The union continued at the fish houses for several years, but it never recovered. The result is clear in workers wages today, which hover around $6.75 per hour—the state minimum wage in Massachusetts. Adjusted for inflation, the average wage of $7.90 per hour before the strike almost twenty-five years ago would have been $18.64 by 2006.

Like their counterparts in meatpacking, fish processors moved to increase profits by holding down wages while simultaneously increasing productivity. They had initially turned to Portuguese and Cape Verdean workers, but as job opportunities opened up elsewhere and the labor market tightened, New Bedford based fish packers started recruiting from other immigrant communities and communities of color in New Bedford, Providence, and the surrounding areas. By the late 1990s, New Bedford had become a prime destination for the Maya fleeing Guatemala. Brothers, cousins, sons—mostly young men—began filling up the fish houses in New Bedford. They were matched perfectly with the requirements of the fish houses.

To maximize their flexibility and reduce their liability during slow times, the larger fish houses hire primarily through agencies that supply temporary workers. The temp agencies typically have Spanish-speaking staff and place large numbers of Guatemalans in the fish houses. Hiring through temp agencies is a common practice in many immigrant communities (Kwong 1997). It allows employers to isolate themselves from the liabilities of hiring undocumented workers directly and still to maintain a steady workforce, without the expenses, such as unemployment and workers' compensation, associated with having direct employees. So to the fish houses the Guatemalan workers gravitate, at least when they first arrive in New Bedford. Not many questions are asked.

The Fortunes of a One-Industry Town

From 1840 to 1860 New Bedford was the whaling capital of the world and one of the wealthiest cities in the United States. Herman Melville wrote of its splendor in *Moby Dick*. Some of the grandeur of New Bedford's golden age is still visible. A statue of a harpooner with the inscription, "A dead whale or a stove boat" stands in front of the public library, a grand stone building on Pleasant Street. Next door is the city hall, a gracious brick building, and farther down Pleasant Street is the enormous post office fronted by a dozen Corinthian columns.

The decline of whaling in New Bedford was as precipitous as its rise. Threatened by the discovery of petroleum, which was fast replacing whale oil in lights and lamps, whalers increasingly headed to Arctic waters in search of the bowhead whale and its prized whale bone. In September 1871, thirty-two ships—the majority of the New Bedford fleet—were destroyed, frozen in an unseasonably early ice pack in Arctic seas. When another dozen ships were lost in the Arctic a few years later, whaling in any real sense was finished in New Bedford (Allen 1973).

With the demise of whaling, New Bedford quickly became a major textile center. Between 1881 and the beginning of World War I, thirty-two cotton manufacturers were incorporated in the city, worth $100 million and employing 30,000 people (Georgianna 1993, 21). These mills in brick buildings on the north and south ends of New Bedford, a stone's throw from the waterfront, became central in a New England textile industry that clothed much of the country. Many textile jobs became unionized and provided steady incomes for the workers of New Bedford, who rented and later bought the double- and triple-decker homes in the neighborhoods near the mills.

A bitter strike in 1928 and then the Great Depression devastated the textile industry in New Bedford, which largely relocated to the South (Hartford 1996). Its remnants and much of the rest of New Bedford's industrial base fell on hard times during the 1980s and 1990s. In the corporate mergers and consolidations that followed, New Bedford was hit hard, losing 10,000 manufacturing jobs, nearly 20 percent of its total workforce, between 1985 and 1991. Businesses that closed during that period had been "woven into the fabric of New Bedford: Berkshire Hathaway, Morse Cutting Tools, Payne Cutlery, Chamberlain Manufacturing Co., Goodyear Tires and Rubber, Cornell-Dubilier, Dartmouth Finishing, just to name a few" (Nicodemus 2001, 1).

Like many other New England mill towns, New Bedford is doing its best to reuse some of its deserted buildings, raze others, and get funding to clean up brownfields and its superfund site. For a number of years the city saw its economic future tied to the development of a waterfront aquarium that never came to fruition; as with many other struggling cities, it has also explored casino gambling. Yet the mostly empty mills of New Bedford stand as a harrowing reminder of an economy that used to be. With no commuter-rail connections to Providence or Boston, this city of slightly less than 100,000 remains isolated from the rest of Massachusetts and from the economic development of communities along nearby Route 128.

Ironically, the same factors that contribute to the weak economy in New Bedford are exactly what attract the Guatemalan Maya. Unlike Boston or even Providence, New Bedford offers inexpensive housing that is near the fish houses. Earl Chase, founder of the American Indian Friends Coalition, a nonprofit organization created to assist Guatemalans, explains why this housing is a major draw:

> [Guatemalan immigrants] can rent a reasonably good-sized apartment with three or four bedrooms, sometimes for as low as $300 or $400 a month. You know, they pack in and share the expenses so they are able to do fairly well. That way they can send back a good chunk of change. Most of them send back at least $200 to $300 per month to their families. Even though they're making minimum wages, they send back a considerable amount. The other factor that's a good point about them living close to the factories is they can walk to work. Some of them, of course,

walk two miles or whatever a day, you know, back and forth. . . . The rest are riding bikes. (2001, 6)

The small size of the city makes it manageable and safer. Tomás, a Mayan immigrant who works in a warehouse, says, "People like it in New Bedford":

In Providence there is a lot more street crime. There is a lot more going on. There is a lot more robbery. You can't even walk out on the street after 7:00 p.m. I got kind of scared when my car broke down in Providence at 2:00 a.m. Even though there were four of us, there were a lot of groups of guys around and so it felt kind of dangerous. But over here, when I got off my job at the warehouse, even though it was at night time, I could walk home. A lot of people take their bikes to the fish house and they can ride from the south end to the north end. (2001, 3)

Jeffrey Passel from the PEW Hispanic Center estimated in 2005 that there were 11 million undocumented workers in the United States. In 2006 that number was adjusted upward to between 11.5 and 12 million (Guskin and Wilson 2007, 17). It is estimated that there are between 200,000 and 250,000 undocumented workers in Massachusetts as a whole (Passel 2005, 6), which places it in the second tier of states with the most undocumented workers, behind the first tier of eight states, including California, Texas, and Florida, that have the largest concentration of undocumented workers.

The number of Guatemalans in the United States doubled from 221,943 in 1990 to 463,502 in 2000, according to the U.S. census (1990, 2000), and many immigration activists believe the actual figure is considerably higher: in March 2006 the PEW Hispanic Center estimated that there were 320,000 *undocumented* immigrants from Guatemala in the United States (*Migration Information Source* 2006). Census figures from 2000 report 12,020 Guatemalans living in Massachusetts (Uriate, Granberry, and Halloran 2006, 59)—On the basis of national figures, the majority of them likely undocumented—and again, immigration activists believe the actual number to be much higher. Guatemalans are among the most poorly educated immigrants in Massachusetts: less than 15 percent have a high school diploma, and occupationally, they have the highest concentration in blue-collar jobs of any immigrant group in Massachusetts (Marcelli and Granberry 2006, 39, 42).

The Tragedy of Guatemala

To understand the exodus of the Mayan people from Guatemala, we need to turn briefly to their history. In Guatemala the arable land along the coasts made up the plantations, which, as in much of the rest of Central America, were owned and controlled by colonial powers; peasants cultivated small plots of land in the highlands. In 1950, under the guise of fighting a growing communist tide in Central America, the United States (foreshadowing what it would try in Cuba and succeed with in Chile) began clandestine operations against Jacobo Arbenz Guzmán, the democratically elected president of Guatemala. For thirty years after Arbenz's fall, Guatemala was ruled by a series of military-dominated regimes that used terror to maintain their positions (Popora 1990, 85).

After Gen. Efraín Ríos Montt took over the government in March 1982, "the terrorism reached genocidal proportions. Entire villages were wiped out where the people, mostly Indians, were suspected of sympathizing with the growing guerrilla movement" (Popora 1990, 85). "Between early 1982 and the end of 1983, the Guatemalan army destroyed hundreds of towns and villages, driving two hundred thousand rural people out of their homes and killing between fifty thousand and seventy-five thousand mostly unarmed indigenous farmers and their families, and violently displaced over a million people from their homes" (Schlesinger and Kinzer 1999, x).

By the mid-1980s the country began moving toward peace, but not until 1996 was a formal peace treaty signed by the guerrillas and the Guatemalan government. The economic impact of thirty years of fighting in Guatemala was devastating, especially in El Quiche (Carmack 1988), home of most of the Maya who have immigrated to New Bedford.

One recent immigrant, Juan, comes from a family of tenant farmers. He was nineteen when I first met him in New Bedford, newly arrived from Guatemala. Lanky, with just a hint of the slouch that teenagers have, Juan has an easy smile. But age descends quickly on his face as he begins to tell his family's story. "We didn't even have a meter of land. . . . My parents and before them my grandparents" farmed the same land. The person who "owned the land was cultivating coffee. There were two farms. One where we lived and one where they had the coffee plantation. To pay for the land we had to work three months on the coffee farm, and they didn't pay us a dime." But as the war intensified, he continues, they had to leave the land entirely.

> I was born in 1981. My parents told me the story. . . . I was a baby and my other brothers were very young too. We would hear about how the soldiers would just kill people. . . . We were nine brothers and three sisters and they would hide us in the mountains. We were without food sometimes. As it was, we didn't have enough food at home, but when we had to go to the mountains we had nothing. . . . The only thing to eat sometimes was bananas. We would find some green bananas and cut them up and toast them on the fire. That's what we had to eat. My parents would give food to us and they would suffer the hunger. . . . They were very tired because they carried us on their backs or carried us through the cold. They brought nine babies up to the mountains. That's what happened during the war. (2001c, 2)

Older than Juan, Diego, who now also works in New Bedford, saw first hand how the war affected his family: "We were living pretty well before that. My father always had enough to cultivate. He had cows and it was enough to maintain the family." But that ended with the resumption of fighting, he continues, barely able to fight back the tears:

> In 1982 I was about eight years old and it was when the war was going on. That impacted our family a lot. I remember I was eight years old because at that point you remember things that you don't forget. We all had to go to the coast when the war started. That's when I started working. . . . We left everything in our house, abandoned. The soldiers started burning down the houses and took the roofs off. They stole all our cattle and just grabbed everything. It was in about 1983. From there I became a man. I just continued to work on the coast. . . . We were on the coast for about twelve years. We never went back until everything calmed down, which was in 1996. . . . It calmed down a little . . . that's when we went back home. We struggled really hard until we were able to build our house over again. During that time we suffered very much from poverty. (2001b, 5)

For the Guatemalan Maya, whose peasant community was economically marginal to begin with, thirty years of civil war—the *violencia*, as it is known in Guatemala—left them incredibly vulnerable.

With their indebtedness growing, many Latin American countries moved rapidly to increase their agricultural products for export—to generate cash as part of their structural adjustment programs (Kay 1997). In Guatemala and throughout the region, plantations were modernized and capitalized, shifting to cash-generating export crops. The shift in production created a demand for seasonal labor that coincided with the increasing difficulty of peasants to maintain their traditional subsistence farming, in part because of the fighting. This "semi-proletarianization," as it has been called, forced many—having few other choices—to join the ranks of seasonal farm workers (De Janvry et al. 1989). Roberto describes the work:

> I worked in Guatemala on sugar harvest, on coffee harvest. We used to go to the coast for three to four months, about the distance from here to Washington, D.C. For months you leave your wife behind and go to the coast to work and then you come back. When you come back you have to farm our beans and our corn and vegetables and we work together with our family to do that. But all summer we'd be working on the coast. On the coast it is really tropical and hot. We used to cut fifteen tons of sugarcane a day. After we burned the fields [to remove leafy material they do not process], we would cut it down. All the sugar gets all over you and you're all covered with the ashes. It's all piecework. You cut more, you earn more. (2001b, 8)

The workers on the coast are housed in large group quarters, with little or no personal space or personal property. Food is rationed, and the work hours are unrelenting. In many ways, working the harvest on the coast is the last resort for peasants who can no longer make it on their farms. "What bothers me and hurts the most," Juan explains, "is to never have lived a childhood. . . . The first thing you learn in Guatemala is how to work in the fields. Never to learn about how to become a professional—or anything. We don't have any hope that a child will become something." Juan loved school, however: "Fortunately I was always good at school. I was always one of the best students. But my father never had enough money to send me to school, I convinced him, so that I could continue studying." Juan would help with the harvest and go to school from January to October (2001c, 9).

After sixth grade Juan's father told him, "Sorry, you can't do that any more" (his older brothers had gone only through second or third grade). After leaving school, wanting to do more to help his family, Juan at the age of fifteen joined his cousin working in a garment factory in Guatemala City. "I worked in a clothes factory. I didn't even speak Spanish at the time. I would speak in my own language [K'ichee]. I didn't understand anything.

I didn't understand any Spanish. . . . They used to make fun of me when I didn't speak it properly" (2001c, 5). Always a student, Juan enrolled in night school to learn Spanish along with one of his coworkers. He was also able to cover his expenses in the city and send money home to his family.

The Journey

There is not much to keep young men in Guatemala—little hope, little future. So, as in other diasporas, the young and strong are sent away, to Mexico, from which many cross the border to the United States. Because there are virtually no visas available for young men without education or means, almost all cross illegally. Juan tells his story:

> A lot want to come here from Guatemala. . . . If you are working down there, the more you work, the less you get paid, it seems. There is more discrimination. . . . We don't have our own land and we want to help out our family, my little brother. My parents are old. I think about the future a lot. It's this fear that if the landowner says "get out," then you get out. But where are we going to go, because we don't have any land. So I decided to come. (2004, 4)

To make it possible, "my dad borrowed some money. To come here it is 35,000 *quetzales* [approximately $5,000 American] to get here. To pay the interest on the loan, it is 10 percent or 8 percent. It depends. When you leave from your home, it is not very easy" (2001a, 5).

Yet for Juan and thousands like him, the lure of the North is strong. "For decades," says Rubén Martínez, "the message has been: We have a job for you" (2001, 9). Juan Hernández, an adviser to the former Mexican president Vicente Fox, called these immigrants from Central America and Mexico "the new American pioneers." He argued, "I work for Mexico, and we must create the opportunities in Mexico so they don't have to leave. But the United States is the wealthiest country in the world. And they will try to get there however they can" (2001).

A few try to make it on their own, but most spend between $3,000 and $7,000 for a *coyote* (as smugglers of illegal immigrants are called) to guide them to the United States. As U.S. Immigration has intensified border control since September 11, 2001—erecting miles of fences and walls and stepping up patrols—more immigrants are forced into the desert and mountainous areas, where they move north often at great peril. Each year we hear more horror stories as the desperation to leave intensifies (Ellingwood 2004; Martinez 2001).

Stories of the journeys taken by the Maya coming from Guatemala are chilling. Juan tried three times before he was able to cross into the United States. The first time, he says, he never got past Mexico: "I met someone who said he could bring me into the country legally. I trusted him. . . . All he really wanted to do was rob me. . . . I spent 10,000 *quetzales* [about $1,500 U.S.] on that and never got anywhere with it and nothing out of it. Then I just forgot about everything. I had a debt to pay back of 10,000 *quetzales*." On his second attempt he was caught in Mexico and returned to Guatemala. On his third try he discovered just how hard the passage is for many.

> Once I got over the border to go to Arizona, that's where it started—the terrible life. They gathered about fifteen people together and brought us all together. We had to cross the desert so immigration wouldn't get us. The guides knew what we needed to have on the road. We really couldn't bring that much food because we were walking for five days. Night and day, night and day, we were walking. There were helicopters passing us overhead. We had to hide. It was a life that nobody should have to go through. We got to Arizona and there were people who only wanted money. They were pressuring us about money. They treated us like a thing, not even human. They brought us to a house where there was no light and no water. It was just an abandoned house. We were there for twelve days and didn't have any food. We were afraid to go outside. Then they got us out of there and put us into an old car. The car broke down in Atlanta. The drivers took off from us and just abandoned the car. We were stuck in the parking lot of a store. By that time there were only ten of us. A guy I met in the parking lot was Guatemalan, and we talked to him and he brought us to his house. We had been two days without eating or drinking, and he gave us something to eat. He said we needed to get in touch with our families to send us money. (2001c, 8)

Juan was fortunate that his cousin David, who was already living and working in New Bedford, was able to send him money to get to New Bedford. But Juan has not forgotten about those who made the journey with him.

> The others—I never knew what happened to them. There are days I think of them and what we suffered together. Towards the end we had to support each other because people would fall down. We gave each

other a hand and we helped keep one another's hopes up until we would finally arrive. . . . Sometimes I like to remember, especially when I'm alone, that I'm proud of the pain I've suffered. That's how my life began here. (2001c, 8)

A guide brought Diego and the people he was traveling with part way, then gave them a hand-drawn map to use to navigate through the desert. Diego points out that

you're not really sure with the hand-drawn maps if the map is accurate. We went into the Alta Sonora desert. We walked for a week in the desert. And all the nights too. We were with a group of about eighteen people. It was a desert without anything. All you would see is big mountains without end. You went walking, walking, walking and you'd never make it to the mountains.

At the end of the week they stumbled onto a ranch "in the middle of the desert." Diego continues:

This man had tractors. He had his land. . . . He saw us and he started shooting at us. We were hiding. There was a little wall that we had to hide under. The bullets flew over the wall that we were ducking under. He didn't want to kill us, but he was trying to scare us by shooting the rifle up in the air. He really didn't speak too much Spanish. He yelled at us, "What are you doing over here?" We said, "Please, can you give us some water and some tortillas?" I couldn't even stand up because I was so hungry and thirsty. The man brought us out a big container of rice and he gave us some cooked potatoes and green chili. That was on his land where he had a bunch of chilis. We were so hungry that we didn't care, even though they were really hot chilis. We just ate them anyway. (2001b, 8, 9)

Somehow, miraculously, they made it across the border into the United States. Diego continues his story, telling how he ended up in a truck heading to Denver: "There was a truck that held about twenty-three people. Not in a seat or anything like that. You're all crunched in there. He went from Phoenix to Denver, Colorado, for about twelve hours in the truck with twenty-three people. No air. In Denver it was cold. We were freezing inside that truck. It was almost like a freezer, and there were all these drops from the condensation. Just as we were entering Denver on the highway, the police stopped us. . . . It took him about twenty minutes, and then immigration ended up coming. They put handcuffs on the driver. Immigration opened up the door and there were the twenty-three people. . . . They had peed on themselves. No place to go to the bathroom. They said, "Everybody put your hands up! Don't move." (2001b, 11) After all this—the hand-drawn map, the week walking through the desert, and the hours crammed into the van—Diego was sent back. On the next attempt he made it, spending much of the trip "in a wooden crate underneath a car."

Cutting Fish

Working in the fish houses is tough work. The Guatemalans are used to hard work, but few have had any experience outside of agriculture and virtually none in fish processing. It takes some time, as Hector explains, to get used to the work.

> I didn't like it at first. I despaired because you have to put your apron on, your boots on, and I had not done anything like that before. The cutters, they work for piecework, so they don't care if they are working really fast. But the packers work per hour, so there is that difference. The supervisor is always pushing them to work faster. Sometimes twelve-hour days every day. . . . It's seasonal work and you have all this work at once, then it just stops" (2001, 2).

Fish processing varies by the kind of fish and the size of the fish house. Processing scallops is fairly simple. They are typically shucked at sea and in the fish houses are washed, sorted by size and grade, and packed in various-sized containers for different markets. Clams are usually steamed open; the meat is extracted from the shells and then cooked or packed raw.

The processing of groundfish—both fresh and frozen fish—is the most complex. Most of the larger fish houses have machinery that performs some of the basic operations. Rosa, one of the few women who have emigrated from Guatemala, describes the process: The fish "goes through the deboning machine—it separates the bones from the meat—then it goes through a skinning machine and then it goes back to the table where people start to clean it off." The fish are moved in and out of the machines and to the fish cutters in large plastics tubs, weighing about thirty-five pounds each. "You pull those tubs down and those are the ones that need to be cleaned off. And then, after they are cleaned off, then you stick it on the belt. . . . You put it in another tub and from there it goes into the water tank. You have gloves, you have a smock, and a nylon apron" (2001b, 2). All the workers wear boots to keep their feet dry, although they hardly keep their feet warm during New England winters.

Doing the hand work is where the Guatemalans come in. "You can do a whole tub of cod in between ten and twelve minutes," Rosa says, "if your knife is sharp enough and if you know what you are doing and you are accustomed to doing it. Supervisors keep a keen eye on the workers." She continues, "If you are cleaning the fish all right, then you don't get scolded, but if you leave some fish bones or some worms on the fish, then they will come and call you on it, what you're doing" (2001b, 1). Roberto elaborates:

> They would compare the amount of bone and waste. They weighed the waste product. People who had too heavy of the waste of the fish and bones, they got in trouble. Those were the people that were sent home. People who were masters would leave three to four pounds of waste. Some who didn't have experience would leave twenty-eight pounds to thirty pounds of waste fish. You had to be really careful when you are boning fish that you don't take off a lot of the meat. (2001a, 9)

Many of the larger fish houses have excellent reputations for delivering high-quality fish products to their customers. Kyler Seafood, however, had a reputation of treating workers poorly, and compromising the product, as Roberto saw:

> They are selling bad fish. If there is some stuff that doesn't pass inspection they bring it back and they treat it with this special liquid that makes the bad smell go away. They mix it up with the fresh fish, so they slip it in. They like having the workers that don't say anything. Sometimes all the fish will fall on a dirty floor and they just pick it up again and go on. . . . You're mixing up fish from the floor and putting it in with the good fish. At Kyler they have cameras, but that doesn't matter, they do all this stuff that's not up to the inspection. I worked a little at [another fish house] and saw the difference. (2001a, 4)

Like meatpacking, cutting and packing fish is hard and dangerous. Sharp knives move in repetitive motions at lightning speed on wet surfaces; there is constant reaching, moving of bins, working very close to dangerous machinery—some better maintained than others—in constant wet and slippery footing. Linda Barros Ruiz, who works with the YWCA in New Bedford and does outreach work as a health advocate among the Mayan women, says, "I'm seeing a lot of injuries. I have a client right now, she doesn't have any feeling in her hands" (2001, 3). Cuts, strains, back and neck problems, and numbness and loss of full range of motion from repetitive work are common-place. Not all injuries are minor.

Tragedy struck the Guatemalan community in New Bedford on July 30, 1998, when Antonio Ajuqui, forty years old, was killed "when the fish-meal grinder he was cleaning was accidentally switched on" in the Atlantic Coast Fisheries Corp. The New Bedford paper reported that the victim's nineteen-year-old son, Francisco, also worked at the fish-processing plant and was nearby when the accident occurred (Rising 1999, 1). The company was fined $115,500 by OSHA (Occupational Safety and Health Administration) for this "willful and serious violation." Other major fish processors, including Eastern Fisheries, Frionor, Kyler, Marleys, North Coast, and others, have been fined by OSHA, though for less serious violations (Lorkin n.d., 7). Al-though the death of a fish-processing worker in New Bedford is not an every-day occurrence, it is a reminder that meatpacking and related occupations continue to be incredibly hazardous. The Human Rights Watch report on conditions in U.S. meat and poultry plants found that "employers put work-ers at predictable risk of serious physical injury even though the means to avoid such injury are known and feasible" (Compa 2004, 1).

Added to the physical hazards the Guatemalans face in the fish houses in New Bedford is the attitude of the managers, who have no incentive to take care of injured—especially undocumented—workers and show little interest in doing so. Linda Barros Ruiz describes a situation in one of the fish houses:

One lady who was pregnant, who was almost eight months pregnant and needed to work. . . . I guess she was working the day shift. Then suddenly a big order of fish was coming out and she needed to stay until 11:00 o'clock. She left early. She couldn't take it any more. She was on her feet all day. They threatened her, they were going to fire her. I think this is wrong. No matter who they are or where they come from, everybody should have the same rights. That's a lot of abuse going on there. When it comes to work and when it comes to, you know, if they're feeling any pain in their neck, or on their hands, they need some time off, a leave of ab-sence, whatever. They can't get it because you're hired to work certain hours and you have to be there during those hours. . . . They feel like they have to work. If not, they'll lose their job. They feel that they can't afford to be out of their job. They are here and they have to support a family back home. So no matter what's going on, they have to work. (2001, 4)

Despite the danger, the hard work, the dampness, and the constant monitoring by supervisors, the Maya working in fish processing in New Bedford complain very little. One young man, eighteen years old, told of leaving home at age ten to avoid being a burden to his mother after his father was killed. He then worked for six years in the *maquiladora*[2] plants in Mexico before taking four months to cross the border into the United States. After another four months he was working in a bottom-of-the-line job in a fish-processing plant, cleaning fish as they arrived and picking maggots off them. When I asked him what he liked about New Bedford, he replied, "What's not to like!" After his experiences in Guatemala and later in Mexico, he felt fortunate even picking maggots off fish.

This attitude, which arises from the deprivations and hardship of living and working in Guatemala, makes for highly productive workers. The Mayan immigrants are known as hard workers, in part because so much is at stake: they must repay loans used to come to the United States, send money to families back home, and make ends meet in New Bedford—from wages that are at or below the minimum wage—and all under the specter of being caught by the Immigration Control and Enforcement (ICE) and returned to Guatemala. "In my case and our cases—all the Guatemalans'—we go after the money," Juan explains. "It's not because we love the money, you know? It's because we need it. Everybody sends money to Guatemala. They send money to their kids, their wife, their parents, or to their little brothers. Everybody's taking care of their family down in Guatemala" (2004, 13).

The Guatemalans are also known for working a tremendous number of hours—whenever they can get work. Tomás's story is typical.

> My brother is working two shifts, eighty hours a week. . . . I used to work up to 106 hours a week. I used to work from 7:00 a.m. to 8:00 p.m. at [one fish house], go home, eat, rest a little bit, then at 10:00 p.m. go to [another fish house]. I am doing the same thing. I am working at a scallop place 7:00 a.m. to 2:00 p.m., then 3:00 p.m. to 11:00 p.m. at [a garment shop]. (2001, 7)

When I asked Tomás how he made it through these long weeks, he replied, "We take a risk on our life for work, for necessity. Not because we want to, but for necessity" (2001, 7). There is no word or phrase equivalent to the word stress in their vocabulary, according to Corinn Williams, director of the Community Development Center in New Bedford. She has worked a great deal with the Mayan community and says the Maya sometimes speak of people who have problems with their nerves, but hard work is what they learn, and there is little complaining about it (2001a, 12).

When asked, "What makes a good day?" most workers typically respond that a good day is one during which the workload is light or the supervision is minimal or there are no problems with production. Among the Guatemalans I interviewed, however, it was always the same: "When there's work, that's a good day. . . . It makes us happiest to have like ten or eleven hours' work. That's what makes us happy" (Rosa 2001b, 4). No questions about work flow, supervision, or dignity on the job. A good day is when there is work—and plenty of it.

They keep their heads down and continue to work hard to pay back their loans for coming to the United States, to send money home for their families to survive, and to save enough money to buy land and build a house back in Guatemala. For the first year and a half that he was in the United States, Juan worked two full-time minimum-wage jobs, saved $10,000 in cash, and bought a piece of land near his parents' home in Guatemala. It is the first land his family has owned in three generations, since the Ladinos took the land the Maya had traditionally farmed. "If some day the immigration is going to catch me here and they send me back to Guatemala, at least I got a piece of land. . . . Or I give it to my parents to live there if some day their landlord is going to kick us out" (2004, 17). Over the next three years, Juan brought five of his brothers, along with several cousins and his brother-in-law, to New Bedford. Each brother has also bought land back home.

This situation, with workers who want and desperately need to work, coupled with the inability of most of them to speak or understand English, is ripe for exploitation. As Earl Chase, a New Bedford immigrant advocate, tells it, "Exploitation is the name of the game in these fish houses, pretty much. . . . [T]here are a couple [of fish houses] that treat them really good," he explains. "But the problem that we see here is, with such a large part of the workforce in the fish houses, if they were to be shut down, these people would have absolutely nothing to live on" (2001, 14).

The lack of a labor agreement and the workers' lack of status as regular employees make their treatment even worse. As Williams has observed in her work over the past several years with the Maya, "Someone will say, 'Unload this fish. We need you to unload it.' But then they don't end up paying them. So there are a lot of abuses that happen here" (2001b, 14). One Guatemalan reports of his employer, "I understand this is a small operation. I know he doesn't have the money in the bank to create a payroll. I know there are different laws that affect different owners. Sometimes he says, 'I'll pay you every fifteen days.' And then he says, 'I'll pay you, I'll pay you.' But sometimes he doesn't pay us" (Diego 2001a, 4–5).

In September 2000, conditions in the Kyler Seafood plant in New Bedford boiled over. The workers sought assistance from outside, and a coalition formed, comprising the American Indian Friends Coalition, the Community Economic Development Center, Massachusetts Jobs with Justice, Organizaccion Maya K'iche, a Latino coalition, and several unions interested in organizing in the fish-processing industry. Before meeting with management, coalition members gathered testimony from workers at Kyler. "Eddie assaulted me and then I was thrown out of the plant." "I was on a filleting machine. Eddie came over and jabbed me in the side of the ribs hard, telling me to hurry up." "Eddie swears at the women and says bad things to them" (Kyler Workers 2000).

Management agreed to investigate, but several days later exonerated the supervisor, arguing that the whole issue was just a matter of miscommunication. The coalition brought public attention to the plight of the Maya in the fish houses and provided a support network for the Guatemalan workers. It was time for the Guatemalan workers to come together to stand up against the abuses of management, especially now that they had the support of the community organizations and leaders. Yet to the frustration of their supporters, no one came forward. The level of fear was still too high, and the workers still seemed to be focused more on what was happening in Guatemala and how their wages, even if acquired under oppressive conditions, were providing something good for their families and their future.

Union Organizing and Immigrant Workers

The indignities the Guatemalan workers suffer daily in the fish-processing industry make the question of union organizing important. These jobs were once unionized, and recent years have seen a number of exciting union victories in other industries among immigrant workers, including asbestos removers (Kieffer and Ness 1999), dry-wall hangers (Milkman and Wong 2000), garment workers (Juravich and Hilgert 1999), and janitors in the highly celebrated Los Angeles Justice for Janitors campaign (Waldinger and Der-Martirosian 2000). The numbers confirm that nonwhite workers are more interested in and more likely to join unions than their white counterparts

(Bronfenbrenner 2004). Yet as Ness reminds us, "Evidence from immigrant and native-born organizing efforts reveals that low wages and poor conditions alone are not enough to rouse workers to action" (2005, 5).

In *Birds of Passage: Migrant Labor and Industrial Societies* (1979), Michael Piore has suggested that in the early stages of immigrant settlement, workers are still connected most closely with their extended families and countries of origin. "The logic maintains," Hondagneu-Sotelo points out, "that the longer immigrants stay, the less likely they are to deliberately live in extreme frugality and to work as many hours as possible, and hence the more likely they are to permanently settle" (1994, 16).

Undoubtedly many of the Maya in New Bedford are still very much in the first phase of this transition. In general, the men stay in close touch with their families in Guatemala. They send money home religiously and talk on the phone regularly. For many of the men these long-distance family skills are an extension of the skills honed over many years of spending part of each year away from home within Guatemala, working sugar and coffee crops. Given this orientation, many of the Maya in New Bedford tend to shoulder abuse rather than fight back. As Roger Waldinger and Claudia Der-Martirosian suggest in their research on immigrant workers, "Continuing homecountry ties generate a dual frame of reference, which in turn blunts the impact of frustrations encountered in the United States." Describing the situation of many of the Guatemalans in New Bedford, they go on to suggest that "workers emanating from groups with a history of circular or temporary migration will be more likely to retain a dual frame of reference, which in turn reduces the impetus to seek out union jobs" (2000, 59).

This is not to suggest that the workers in New Bedford do not feel the abuse or understand how wrong and destructive it is. Yet organizing to change these circumstances is another matter. A frustrated union organizer told of his failure to get a group of workers from the fish houses to admit that anything was wrong. He had heard the stories; he knew there was severe exploitation and abuse taking place; but the workers refused to talk about it. As union organizer and longtime New Bedford resident Peter Knowlton suggests, "The workforce is so new here, and they used to live under such oppressive conditions and horrible economic conditions, that I think to them it's like, 'Wow, why should I risk this?'" (2001, 3). Jennifer Gordon in *Suburban Sweatshops: The Fight for Immigrant Rights* reports a similar story of an immigrant worker on Long Island, New York, who says,

"Why should I put myself at risk? I'm earning money, I work 40 hours a week . . . and I'm only going to be in this country for two years" (2005, 37).

Closely connected to their strong ties to Guatemala, and another significant drag on union organizing, is the lack of a public Guatemalan community in New Bedford. In the same way that the Maya became invisible in the mountains during the fighting in Guatemala, they have remained hidden in New Bedford. Until fairly recently, few in the town knew of their presence. The only place you would see them was "on their bicycles in the early morning, traveling to work in the fish houses and other places of employment. Quiet. Law-abiding. Hard working" (Seaman 2004, 1).

As their English improves, the Guatemalans venture out of their communities more often, to go to the mall or eat at a restaurant. Yet their lives are still largely centered on their home and the homes of other Guatemalans. Juan, for example, says: "I got some friends who I work with. . . . Sometimes they invite me to go to their house and have some dinner. That's real nice but I stay with my people. I stay with my people, you know, because I feel better with my people, because we talk in our language" (2004, 7). They live with friends from their villages back home or new friends made in the fish houses. They share the cost of rent and the cooking of meals, and they help each other out as they struggle to make a new life here. They gather in their homes, or in the homes of friends, to drink, talk, and watch the single channel of Spanish-language television.

Leon Fink describes a very similar situation in his examination of the Mayan community in Morganton, North Carolina: "Given their language, the places of work, their physical presence on the outskirts or in the shadows of the town's daily life, the Guatemalan workers—though less so their children—lived a world apart. It took nearly a decade, for example, before any Mayan/Hispanic presence showed up at the annual Historic Morganton Festival." Fink goes on to suggest that one of the frustrations of the Maya is the lack of public space in the United States. "In Guatemala, as in other Latin American countries, one is used to a central plaza, with space to walk and talk, and time to sit and 'hang out'" (2003, 26, 153). Without this kind of space available, they are left in isolation in their apartments.

The one thing that draws the Guatemalans out of their houses is soccer. Every weekend, except during the coldest months, Juan reports, "Everybody goes on the field and plays soccer or watches all these guys playing. That's all we do every weekend. We get all the Guatemalans together and we have fun" (2004, 7). Beyond soccer, there are few public gatherings and no festivals or celebrations. One of the only groups organizing within the Guatemalan community is the Maya K'ichee organization, a local chapter of a national organization that promotes Mayan culture, dress, and spirituality. Local Maya K'ichee leader Aníbal Lucas has been a supporter in a variety of issues, including the situation at Kyler Seafood, but the organization's central mission is focused on cultural and spiritual matters.

The Maya in New Bedford miss the rich community lives of their villages in Guatemala. Juan describes what holidays were like back home:

> Everybody's worried about making their breads. And to eat turkey. Everybody is happy. It is a time when all the families get together. All the kids get together. I have eleven brothers and sisters and they all get together, even the ones that are off married. It's great. It's a time for everybody to get together. You can bring prepared food or a chicken or some of the breads and then you sit down and everybody is there and you spend the whole day at a table talking and passing the day. All the families do that. Those are the happiest days of the year. (2001c, 6)

Even when Juan worked in Guatemala City, he was given fifteen days off to celebrate Christmas. He found his first Easter in New Bedford very different. "I was anticipating a lot would happen and Easter Sunday kind of came and went like any other day. It wasn't very celebrated. . . . Maybe you eat something and watch a little TV and that's it" (2001d, 7). Now that his brothers have joined him, they have a family celebration, although nothing that rivals what they experienced in Guatemala. During an interview, Diego wistfully showed us a videotape of his hometown festival to the Holy Spirit, the patron saint of Zacualpa. This is as close as he gets to having a community life in Massachusetts.

The existence of a *public* immigrant community is important to unionization because it can provide resources and support during union struggles. This support may include monetary and in-kind contributions from more established and well-off members of the community, as well as the kind of emotional and moral support that is dramatized in films such as the early *Salt of the Earth* (1953) and the more recent *Bread and Roses* (2001). A public community also provides avenues for leadership development from which a union campaign can draw directly and indirectly. Finally, union drives can be part of larger community efforts at self-improvement and hence are likely to draw on resources and support beyond the immigrant community. Although many of the workers in the Los Angeles Justice for Janitors campaign, for example, were immigrants newly arrived from Central America, "there was also a sizable component of seasoned activists with a background in left-wing or union activity back home" (Waldinger and Der-Martirosian 2000, 116). It is important to note, however, that no such support exists for those who work in the fish houses in New Bedford, given that the workers come almost exclusively from the rural Guatemalan highlands, with very little organizing experience.

In addition to having little public community of their own, the Guatemalan Maya as a group participate only modestly in outside organizations. For many other Latin American immigrant groups, the Catholic Church becomes a surrogate community from which they draw support and comfort. Support from Catholics and other communities of faith has been key in the struggles of a number of immigrant groups, elevating their struggles beyond the concerns of a few immigrant workers. For example, in another Massachusetts community, the Catholic Church played a major role in the strike and recognition of the largely El Salvadoran workforce when Richmark organized with the Union of Needletrades, Industrial and Textile Employees (UNITE) in 1999 (Juravich and Hilgert 1999). As a primarily indigenous population, however, the Maya do not exhibit the same level of enthusiasm about the Catholic Church that many Latino cultures do—although some are members of the Catholic Church, and Catholic Social Services has assisted the Guatemalans in New Bedford.

Others, however, belong to a growing number of Pentecostal communities in New Bedford, reflecting the growth of Pentecostalism in Guatemala. Sheldon Annis (1987) identifies two major roots of Pentecostalism in Guatemala. The first relates to the changing economy and the urbanization of the peasant population, and the second to the civil war in Guatemala. "As the Catholic Church became increasingly identified as the chief (and thus most dangerous) institutional voice of opposition to the army's spreading repression in the countryside the evangelical Protestant churches beckoned as seemingly safe havens for those wishing to steer clear of the contest for worldly authority" (Fink 2003, 48).

Lack of participation in public life has allowed New Bedford's Mayan community to remain politically marginalized. Organizer Peter Knowlton laments, "The part that really distresses me, though, is that the city itself has not recognized and developed any structure to help out that community" (2001, 21). A Latino group based in the Puerto Rican community in New Bedford has reached out to the Mayans politically, but their response has been lukewarm. This effort to "Hispanicize" the Maya and other Indian communities in the United States is not uncommon (Fink 2003, 135).

Union organizing among the Guatemalan Maya is also hampered by the irregular demand for workers in the fish-processing industry. That demand changes dramatically from season to season and from day to day in response to the irregular supply of fish, which depends on the actual catch and the price fluctuation at the fish auction. Given that uncertainty, coupled with the continued presence of small mom-and-pop fish processors, the industry at times appears more like part of the informal economy than a manufacturing economy. "Informality itself," Jennifer Gordon points out, "makes unionizing difficult—in the words of one union representative, 'It's hard to organize someone who for all formal appearances doesn't exist' " (2005, 48). Further, a significant number of workers in fish processing in New Bedford are employed by temporary agencies. Although the use of temps is common in all sectors of the U.S. economy, it is especially prevalent in low-wage industries with a concentration of immigrant workers.

Undocumented in a Documented World

In her best-selling *Nickled and Dimed: On (Not) Getting By in America* (2001), Barbara Ehrenreich chronicles the difficulties she encountered creating a life around minimum wage jobs while she struggled to find a decent place to live and to afford food and clothing. As difficult as it was for Ehrenreich and her coworkers, they were for the most part white, citizens, and at least conversant in English. For the Guatemalans in New Bedford, the indignities of being low-wage workers are just the beginning of their struggles. While they look like other low-wage workers, it is amazing how much even low-wage American workers take for granted that undocumented workers are denied.

Many of the Guatemalans are regular employees who receive paychecks at the end of the week and, like everyone else, have federal and state taxes and Social Security deducted. Here, however, the similarity ends. Despite paying taxes, they are unable to take advantage of many of the programs their tax contributions fund. For example, as one Guatemalan in New Bedford reports: "Now I'm on this landscaping job and it seems to be working out really good with the company. It's a small company and the guy says, 'You work from like March to Christmas-time and then January, February and March you collect.' But I can't collect. Unemployment, workers' compensation, disability—they just don't apply" (Roberto 2001b, 6).

· Nor do they have access to Social Security payments if they become disabled or when they grow old, despite their contributions to the system. It has been estimated that undocumented workers in the United States contribute as much as $7 billion a year (Porter 2005)—money they will never receive. Aviva Chomsky notes that this $7 billion has allowed Social Security "to break even, because that's about the same amount as the difference between what is paid in benefits and what is received in payroll taxes" (2007, 38). So while undocumented workers bail out our Social Security system, "there is no safety net for them" (C. Williams 2001a, 16).

In addition to the contributions the Guatemalan workers make to New Bedford and to the local, state, and federal government, they are part of a network of immigrants who send billions of dollars to their home countries. Representative Eliot Engel, chairing a congressional hearing, sketched out the scope of remittances to Latin America and the Caribbean:

> In fact, $63.2 billion in remittances reached Latin America and the Caribbean in 2006. For the fourth year in a row, this exceeded the combination of all foreign debt, investment and development assistance to the region. Seventy-five percent of these remittances, or $45 billion, were sent from the United States. Our foreign aid to the Western Hemisphere pales in comparison to the figure. (U.S. House of Representatives 2007, 1)

Remittances sent from the United States to Guatemala alone in 2006 totaled $3.6 billion, an increase of more than 23 percent from 2005. Remittances continued growing in 2007, but growth stalled in 2008, as did remittances sent to Mexico and the rest of Central America with the slowing of construction in the United States (Garr 2008, 1). Remittances tumbled even more dramatically with the U.S. financial crisis, those to Guatemala falling 2.9 percent in October 2008 alone (*Economic and Financial Reporter* 2008).

Even with the recent drop, Corinn Williams refers to these figures as "a very significant flow of dollars for poor people from Central America who are still poor people in the United States," pointing out that it has been "a very effective means of developing communities that foreign aid can't even touch. In Guatemala, for example, it exceeds what the coffee exports are"

(2004b, 6). Donald F. Terry, manager of the Multilateral Investment Fund of the International Development Bank, suggests, "We want to bring this out of the shadows so people understand the critical contributions these hard working people are making" (quoted in Becker 2004, C4).

Activism has been growing around what is a largely unregulated industry that often overcharges unsuspecting people on both ends of the transaction. There has been a call to boycott Western Union, which charges up to $25 per $100 sent to Latin America (Pina 2007). The PEW Charitable Trust reported in *Billions in Motion: Latino Immigrants and Banking*, "Remittance senders are often unaware of the full costs they are paying to send money home. Reducing the cost to 5 percent of the remittances would free up more than $1 billion next year for some of the poorest households" (Suro et al. 2003, 3).

As was discussed at the 2007 congressional hearing, one of the foundational issues with remittances is that many undocumented workers do not have access to bank accounts either in the United States or in their country of origin, forcing them into the informal world of money transfers, which is largely unregulated. When the Guatemalans first arrived in New Bedford, no banks would provide them with accounts because of their lack of Social Security numbers. Even though most banks have provisions that allow non–U.S. citizens to have accounts, banks in the New Bedford area were very slow in providing services to the low-wage workers in the Mayan community.

Still, many Guatemalans live almost entirely in a cash-based world and, like Rosa, "cash their check at a bar." They send money back to Guatemala by money orders they get at the local courier service, Kings Express. "I usually try to scrape together $500 or $600," Rosa explains, "and send a money order down" (2001a, 13). Having this much cash on their persons or in their homes makes them vulnerable to crime. Although New Bedford is safer than Providence or Boston, robberies and physical abuse in the form of beatings are not uncommon in its north end neighborhoods (Seaman 2004, 1). Fink describes a similar situation among the Maya in Morganton, North Carolina [2003, 23]. Corinn Williams relates a case involving "these three punks [who] went after the Mayans":

> Where the fish processing places are is very isolated and these guys would come up and would just prey upon these Mayans. Either knock them off a

bicycle and mug them or attack them or steal money or what have you, and they never went so far as to call it a hate crime, but it certainly was very close to [one]. The perpetrators would say things like "Well, let's go down to Guatville and pick off some of these guys." (2004b, 30)

It is difficult to assess the amount of crime experienced by the Maya in New Bedford because, as with workplace abuse, they are reluctant to come forward or report crimes to the police. This behavior is based on more than simply the fear that comes from their undocumented status. It comes from their experience with the police, among whom, Corinn Williams admits, "there have been real jerks as individuals" (2004b, 24). In a number of incidents the Maya have been victimized by the police, and they have been the subject of racial profiling, mostly involving traffic violations.

Without Social Security numbers, Maya cannot get driver's licenses in Massachusetts. Before 9/11, the state of Rhode Island did not require a Social Security number, and some of the Maya maintained Rhode Island addresses and got Rhode Island licenses and plates for their cars. But local police, they report, used the Rhode Island plates as a way to identify and harass Guatemalans. As Hector says, for example, "We don't get equal treatment if we go to the bank or if we get stopped by the police. They notice we are Hispanic and we notice we don't get the same level of treatment that you might get. We get treated like garbage" (2001, 5).

Because of the difficulty of getting licenses and registrations, many Guatemalans simply drive without licenses. Diego tells of being stopped by the police:

Sometimes it's snowing out and you have to go to the store. So, I took my key and drive again. But you always worry. The officer asked if I had a license. I said, "Sorry, I don't have one." "Well, how come you're driving?" "Out of necessity." Then they searched the car and I got sent to the police station in handcuffs. They put me in a van and sent me up to the jail. There was a Puerto Rican police officer there, the policeman said, "Oh, you're going to Guatemala." I said, "Why? If you're going to be sending me back to Guatemala, I'm not the only illegal person here you know." I said, "I don't have any papers. I would go to the registry to get my license and take the exam and that's what I'd do. I'm not taking any drugs. I don't create any scandal here." (2001a, 7)

Several years later, Diego and his wife had driven to a yard sale, and while they were parked, their young son slipped out of their hands and was struck by a passing truck. The boy was seriously injured and had to be air-lifted to a Boston hospital. Even though Diego's car was parked at the time, when the investigating police officer discovered that Diego did not have a valid driver's license, his car was towed, and he was detained and unable to accompany his son to the hospital. The person who struck the child drove away.

Out of their desperation to get driver's licenses and bank accounts, the Maya in New Bedford often fall victim to schemes for obtaining phony Social Security numbers or immigration papers. After his brush with the law, Diego bought an "International Driver's License" by mail for $750. It turned out to be nothing but a scam. Roberto reports buying an ID in Boston for $40. It had a Social Security number on it, but when he showed it at a health clinic, it was checked and he was told, "No, that belongs to a different name" (2001a, 6).

Access to health care has been problematic for the Guatemalans in New Bedford. Without citizenship and a Social Security number, they are barred from many state and federal programs that serve low-income families. There is a health center in New Bedford where they can get basic care, but there are real concerns about the quality of that care. Linda Barros Ruiz reports:

> Sometimes it's a language barrier. Sometimes it's that the doctor is in such a rush that they don't have time to listen to them. The doctor does a quick diagnosis. A quick version of whatever the short story they give them. They don't even care or go into details with these patients. I sometimes wonder if this has to do with the doctors. Like they feel, "They are immigrants" or whatever. I had an incident with a client of mine that was complaining about some difficulty she was having, and they had called me in the room to interpret for her and I did go. But the doctor was in such a rush. I stood at the doorway so the doctor was forced to hear the whole thing. (2001, 9)

The Ground Shifts

By 2004 things were changing for the Maya in New Bedford. Some had been in the United States for five years or more. Many had a working knowledge of English, or at least enough to get around. Some, like Juan, were able to have a life they never could have imagined in Guatemala—to save enough money to buy land and, on an even more basic level, to have enough food to eat. "I go to the buffet where you can eat whatever you want," Juan says, "and I think about my family all the time in that way. Because I wish I can help them here and share all this food" (2004, 9). More women have joined the men in New Bedford. New families are being formed and babies born; Juan's girlfriend from Guatemala, who vowed never to cross the border, did come to New Bedford, and in 2004 they were expecting their first baby. Most of the men still worked long hours for the same minimum wage they started with, years ago, but life was beginning to settle down for many, as they knew more about what to expect in the United States and the likelihood of their returning to Guatemala dimmed.

For several years there was almost no activity by the immigration service. The Maya in New Bedford were fortunate that Tom Reilly was attorney general in Massachusetts because, unlike some state attorneys general, he championed the cause of undocumented workers. "Human dignity," he said, "is a very important value. Allowing people to be exploited and then punishing them if they report it—that doesn't sound right to me" (quoted in Ranalli 2001). But changes far above the Massachusetts attorney general's office would soon render his intentions powerless.

In March 2003 the Immigration and Naturalization Services (INS) was disbanded, along with the customs service. In their place a new investigative branch of the newly minted Department of Homeland Security (DHS) was established—U.S. Immigration and Customs Enforcement (ICE). Its mission is "to more effectively enforce our immigration and customs laws and to protect the United States against terrorist attacks." Explicit in its mission statement is the linkage of undocumented workers with terrorism: "ICE does this [protects Americans] by targeting illegal immigrants: the people, money and materials that support terrorism and other criminal activities" (ICE 2007a, 1).

For undocumented workers in New Bedford, however, little changed until December 6, 2005, when ICE agents staged an early morning raid at the waterfront. They arrested thirteen people, including eight at one of the fish houses, AML International. Many of the undocumented workers at AML had been placed there by S&D Staffing, a Rhode Island–based temporary agency. The AML plant manager, Frank Ferreira, told the press, "All these people want to do is work" (Nicodemus 2006, 1).

This was the beginning of a new era in New Bedford, one that would affect not just about the thirteen workers who were detained but the entire community of undocumented workers. The impact of the morning raid was felt far beyond the waterfront, as undocumented workers around the city stayed at home instead of reporting to work on the second shift. The headline in the city's paper, the *Standard Times*, read "Fear Grips City's Immigrants after Feds Raid Fish Factories" (Nicodemus 2006, 1). "It didn't take long with the cellphones, the whole city emptied out, all the plants. People were just leaving because they didn't want to get in trouble. Even the legal ones left. Nobody knew what was going on. It looked like an invasion" (Abraham 2005, B1). Diego recounts what happened to him that day:

> Somebody called me while I was at work and I heard that immigration was coming in at the waterfront. All the family members got the phone calls and all the people around the city. The rumor and confusion was that immigration was going to come to all the companies across the city. But thankfully it wasn't like that. But everybody abandoned their work; abandoned their job. Everybody who worked on the first shift left their job. On the one side the boss was thinking—well everybody's working and it's fine—then everybody just took off from the workplace. So the next day he told everybody they were fired and that there was no more work. Eighty people were laid off. (2007, 3)

It was different at Michael Bianco, Inc. (MBI), a local company that provides backpacks and other equipment to the U.S. military and is a major employer of undocumented workers in New Bedford. The plant manager "announced over the loud speaker that Insolia [the owner] has stated that all MBI employees were free to leave the building. After the announcement, approximately 75 employees ran and hid—some in their vehicles and others in boxes on the third floor at MBI" (ICE 2007b, 2). Unlike the management where Diego worked, the owner of MBI reportedly told his workers after the raids, "I'll take care of you guys. Nothing's going to happen to you" (C. Williams 2007, 3).

The raid in New Bedford took place less than a week after a major tour of the U.S.-Mexican border by top officials in the George W. Bush administration and a new initiative to get tough on "illegal immigration." In early 2006, Congress proposed HR 4437, which, among other provisions, would classify undocumented workers and those who assisted them as felons. Millions of immigrant workers and their supporters rallied in opposition to the bill in mid-April and, on May 1, staged the largest protest of immigrant workers in U.S. history. In New Bedford, more than 500 immigrant workers and allies attended a rally at City Hall. Corinn Williams spoke: "Our friends and neighbors deserve to come out of the shadows. Our city is a city built by immigrants. Immigrants are hard at work in the factories, in the fields and in the fish houses" (Nicodemus 2006, A7).

Given widespread opposition, HR 4437 failed to make it through Congress. In the aftermath of the defeat of the bill the Bush administration and the anti-immigration wing of the Republican Party continued a fierce anti-immigrant rhetoric. It had a tremendous impact on communities such as New Bedford. Corinn Williams describes the difference:

> I think a lot of the change had to do with the failure of comprehensive immigration reform in 2006. . . . That kind of threw all the issues out onto the table. In the years leading up to that I think both employers and the community and the immigrants had sort of tacit agreements about how things worked. People were getting jobs, employers weren't very skittish to hire people. . . . [They were] navigating between those boundaries of state government and local government, with federal policy that wasn't working. (2007, 1)

Now, she says, "the press picked up on the language of illegal aliens and illegals, the fiery rhetoric of lawbreakers. AM radio stations across the country seized on the issue to turn the immigrants into the problem instead of the immigration system into the problem, or the employers." Williams suggests that they adopted the language of the Department of Homeland Security "and started to equate immigrants with criminals" (2007, 4–5).

Raids continued across the United States in 2006 and picked up sharply after the Republican defeat in November (Plunkett and Mulkern 2007). On December 18, 2006, 1,300 workers were detained at six facilities of Swift & Company meatpackers—"in what the government said was the largest but not the last assault on the underground immigrant economy" (*New York Times* 2007). Homeland Security Secretary Michael Chertoff unabashedly connected the raid to the Bush administration's political agenda, saying, "I've made no secret about the fact that we need a comprehensive program. Vigorous enforcement clarifies the choice we have" (quoted in Plunkett and Mulkern 2007, A1). The *Boston Globe* reported that "arrests of undocumented immigrants have grown 750 percent between 2002 and 2006" (Abraham 2007b).

As Congress began work on immigration reform early in 2007, with the introduction of a reform bill cosponsored by John McCain and Edward

Kennedy, ICE raids continued. More than fifty workers were arrested at the Swift meatpacking plant in Amarillo, Texas (ICE 2007a); sixty-nine workers at Jones Industrial Network—a temp agency in Baltimore (Jones 2007); forty-eight employees at Republic Services in Houston (Kilday 2007), and many more.

As the debate on the McCain-Kennedy bill continued in earnest in Congress, on March 6, 2007, ICE returned to New Bedford—to Senator Kennedy's home state of Massachusetts. This was not just another low-key raid but a major operation referred to by ICE as "Operation United Front." Under police escort, 600 ICE agents traveled the sixty miles from Boston for an early morning raid at MBI in the south end of New Bedford.

The company, founded in 1985 by Francesco Insolia, originally made handbags and other leather goods, but between 2001 and 2003 it received $10 million in contracts from the U.S. military for vests and backpacks. It moved to a larger facility and grew to 86 employees. By 2004 these military contracts had ballooned to $82 million, and by 2005 MBI had 520 employees (ICE 2007b, 2); however, its 2007 Dunn and Bradstreet filing—a filing that virtually all U.S. firms use to borrow and lend money—lists only 62 employees.

In what was reportedly an eleven-month investigation, ICE documented incredible violations of employment law and workers' rights: "docking of pay by 15 minutes for every minute an employee is late; fining employees $20 for spending more than 2 minutes in the restroom and firing for a subsequent infraction; providing one roll of toilet paper per restroom stall per day" (ICE 2007b). Juan explains that his brother-in-law worked at MBI and said everybody knew about the conditions.

> All the people knew how they got treated. You can't spend more than three or five minutes in the bathroom. You can't use a lot of toilet paper. You have to work fast. Everybody knew about it. We talked about it all the time. But we always said, what are we going to do about it? We have no voice. You can complain and cry about it but where are you going to go? If you go to somebody who can do something about it, who's going to lose their jobs? All the people. So the people decide to deal with it. They say, you know what, let's just deal with it. That's what my brother–in-law used to say and a couple of friends. Just deal with it. (2007, 10)

The workers also all knew about the overtime scam at MBI. After eight hours, wage workers in the United States are entitled to overtime pay at one and a half times their hourly rate. Not wanting to pay this extra amount, managers at MBI came up with an ingenious plan. Corinn Williams became suspicious of MBI's operations while helping Guatemalans file their taxes. She noticed that some had two W-2s, one for MBI and another for a company she had never heard of before, Frontline Defense. Workers' testimony helped her piece together the explanation: "Essentially what would happen is that people would work an eight-hour day. They'd go to the time clock to punch out and then they'd punch in at Frontline" (2007, 10). This way the employer would not have to pay overtime.

Guatemalans in the community knew about these practices and that MBI exploited workers who were hungry for extra hours, even at standard pay. As Juan explains:

> My people, we're here to work. If there's a company that can give us extra hours we'll take it. That's what we want. We don't care how many hours we work a day. We'll do it. My brother-in-law—he used to work somewhere else—but [at MBI] he was making like $6.75. If you go there and work six days a week you can make $325 a week. That's some money. So we talked about it with him and he said, you know, I'm going to go there. So he left the place he was working and went there for more money. (2007, 10)

Corinn Williams describes the morning of the raid. "I'm home. It's just down the street from the plant. I live by the water over there." About 8:15 she got a call from the wife Earl Chase (the founder of the first organization to work with the Guatemalan immigrants in New Bedford). "She said, 'I'm on my way to work and there's something really crazy happening down your way.' So I jumped in my car, and it was a bitter, bitter cold morning. It was just freezing." Williams met a worker for whom she had just done taxes. "He had started this wonderful little family and I just looked at him and he looked at me and it was deer in the headlights. He said, 'Oh my God, Maria is in there, my wife. My sister-in-law is in there.' We just kind of looked at each other in shock. We didn't know what to do" (2007, 13).

Inside, ICE had arrested the owner, the plant manager, the payroll manager, and the office manager. In town, they had also arrested Louis Torres, who had reportedly supplied fraudulent documents for many of the workers at MBI (ICE 2007). In a massive show of force, hundreds of agents entered the factory. When they announced their presence over the public address system in the plant, some employees started to run, but all exits had already been blocked. ICE detained every worker and began methodically checking their immigration status.

Outside a crowd began to gather as the news spread, despite the bitter cold. Corinn Williams received a call on her cell phone from the police chief to meet him at the command station set up by the New Bedford police. He introduced her to the public information officer from ICE, who told her, "Don't worry ma'am, we do this kind of thing all the time. Everything is under control. Not to worry!" (C. Williams 2007, 14). Inside, however, it was a very different story. Anna was one of the detainees. She reports:

> I heard someone scream. When I moved back to see, I saw a whole bunch of people enter. I saw they were grabbing people. They mistreated the men especially, because they tried to get loose, and get away. So they grab them and throw them to the floor, even hitting their faces. The word I kept hearing them use was 'fuck you.' " (2007).

The raid was especially hard on the women at MBI. Unlike men who had worked there for many years, many of the women were new in New Bedford and at the company. Many had been in the United States for only a short time, and few spoke English. Anna continues:

> The truth is they did treat us badly. Because some of the women who had young children, who breastfed. I saw, because I was near them. They even made them take the milk from their breasts to see if it was true that they had young children. They had almost all of them take milk from their breasts. They even made fun of them. They [the male agents] said— one of them told another to pass an oreo cookie to eat with milk, that they were milking the cows. We were in the next room listening and the women were crying. It was so ugly. (2007)

As in the earlier raid, news traveled quickly around the Guatemalan community. Juan says he was at work when his wife called him at 1:00 p.m. "She called me crying. I got scared. . . . She told me. She said, 'My brother got caught. All the people working in the factory got caught.' In that moment I felt terrible. I didn't know what to say because if I thought about—someone knows my kid? What's going to happen now? Are they going to come up to us?" Juan and his wife agonized over whether she should go to work that evening. Juan came home early to be with her. "I said to myself, if they come, I'd rather be with my family. If they take us, they will take us. I

shared a moment with my family. We watched the news—about what happened to all those people and how they treated them" (2007, 5, 6).

Slowly, workers who had documents emerged from the plant, while
those detained in handcuffs sat in the plant for hours. By nightfall 361 detainees were left. They were shackled and herded out to board corrections
buses, as their family members wept and cried out to them. The buses, es-
corted by police cars with sirens blaring, took the detainees to nearby Fort
Devins for processing. The shackles, the corrections buses with reinforced
metal doors, the police escort with sirens blaring were incredibly frighten-
ing to the detainees—most of whom were very young women—and their
families. Such treatment also reinforced the link the Bush administration
and ICE were trying to make between undocumented workers and criminals or terrorists, the idea that these were dangerous people.

A Humanitarian Crisis

Meanwhile, people started to gather at St. James Church, which became an
impromptu center for families of the detained and their supporters. "We
began organizing around the information flow and trying to reconstruct the
list of who was taken in," Corinn Williams remembers. But activists were
not prepared for what they would see. Many of the women were mothers,
and because they had been in New Bedford only a short time, most of their
children were very young. As darkness approached, babysitters, family
members, and husbands of the detained women descended on St. James with
the children. "There were men with their infant babies who had never taken
care of them before," Williams reports. "They were just devastated" (2007,
17–18). The scene was chaotic as volunteers tried to cope with the many children of the estimated 200 detainees whose small children had been left behind. By the end of the evening it was clear that New Bedford was facing
what Corinn Williams called "a humanitarian crisis"—a phrase that would
be quoted hundreds of times in the news media over the next several days.

Back at Fort Devins, Williams reports, the detainees, most of whom had
been in custody since early morning, suffered further indignities: "Once they
got into detention they were strip-searched. They were treated like criminals. One woman told me it was as if we were the Medellín drug cartel or
something. This was treated like a major criminal investigation" (2007, 17).
As Juan tells it, "Like my brother-in-law was saying, the way they were

treated like animals . . . they were laughing at them, you know? They were asking them why they were here. They should be happy to go back because they don't belong here" (2007, 6).

A tug of war started almost immediately between ICE and state officials over access to the detainees. The newly elected governor, Deval Patrick, and the commissioner of the state's Department of Social Services, Harry Spence, got involved. Despite ICE's assurance to Corinn Williams that everything was under control, she says, it was not. ICE had done a huge amount of planning to bring 600 agents to New Bedford but had made no plans for what to do with mothers—or their small children, almost all of whom were American citizens. The agents had no social workers on staff, and it wasn't until 10:00 p.m. that they finally relented and allowed a few state social workers to visit some of the detainees at Fort Devins. To their horror, state social workers discovered that ninety detainees had already been sent to a facility in Harlingen, Texas. Governor Patrick told the *Boston Herald*, "What we never understood about this process is why it turned into a race to the airport. By the time we got access, a number of them had already been flown to Texas" (Ross 2007, 4). The following morning 116 were flown to a detention center in Albuquerque, New Mexico.

Early the next day, on March 10, a federal judge barred ICE from moving any other detainees out of state, but the damage had already been done (Szanisalo 2007, 4). At the end of the day, under pressure from the Massachusetts Department of Social Services, ICE released fifty-nine detainees for humanitarian reasons. But there was no mechanism to review the cases of those who had already been shipped out of Massachusetts.

Anna, one of the detainees sent to El Paso, was desperate to speak with her six-year-old daughter, who had chronic stomach problems. She had been refused access to lawyers before leaving for El Paso and was allowed only five minutes at Fort Devins to use the telephone. She heard that her daughter was "doing poorly" and "said she wanted to kill herself because her mom wasn't with her." The abuse continued on the plane. Anna tells about the flight to El Paso.

When we were in the plane they put chains here on our waists, our hands and feet were also tied. When they brought the food, which they brought in bags, they threw the bags like we were dogs. Some people, since their hands were tied, dropped them. Within five minutes they came by picking up the bags—some people were still eating. They would grab the bags and throw them away. (2007)

Senator Kennedy, in the midst of desperately trying to save his compromise legislation to provide basic rights to immigrant workers, was incensed by the reports:

> They have said that they had planned this raid for months, but had made no provision to house the workers they had arrested. Instead, the workers were rounded up and immediately transported by DHS to Texas and other states, far from their families, without even an opportunity to say goodbye. The DHS knew that many of these workers had children at home, but they did not do nearly enough to protect them. As a result, children came back to empty homes; at least one nursing baby went to the hospital with dehydration; and hundreds cried themselves to sleep, wondering where their loved ones were and why they had disappeared. (Kennedy 2007, 1)

Kevin Burke, the state's public safety secretary, lamented: "It left kids and families in a position of potential danger. The moral rudder was somehow lost in this. There was more concern getting these folks out of the state than there was concern at making sure mothers and children had a chance to connect with each other" (quoted in Abraham 2007b). "We go all over the world to protect families," Scott Lang, the mayor of New Bedford, said. This raid only "wreaks havoc in New Bedford and doesn't do anything to move the debate forward. These kids are U.S. citizens. Taking parents away from them makes no sense to prove a point" (quoted in Alexandra and Lupsa 2007). Speaking after a meeting with families of the detainees within days of the raid, Kennedy announced, "I don't want to go back to the Senate and hear from Administration officials about family values when what we have seen here is the tearing apart of families. . . . [T]he Immigration Services performed disgracefully" (quoted in Mullenneaux 2007, 1). Juan put it more directly:

> My question all the time is if they have a family and if they have kids, they must know how much a father loves his kids. How can you do this? How can you not think about all these families who are only looking for a better life and now they have families? You have the heart to separate them from their kids, and leave their kids with who knows who? How are they going to live? You know those kids are going to suffer. They're

going to ask for their parents. But yet, it's still happening. They still do it. It's something I will never get, that they do that. What kind of people are these? (2007, 4)

The scene at St. James that night demonstrated the practical difficulties of the policy of the Bush administration and ICE to detain and deport large numbers of immigrant workers in a community. The anti-immigration wing of the Republican Party advocates the removal of the estimated 12 million undocumented workers in the United States, as if this could be accomplished with some kind of surgical precision, without causing any harm to others. But as the events in New Bedford reveal, immigrant communities are not entirely isolated. People intermarry and, perhaps even more important, have children who are U.S. citizens. Do these children have fewer rights as citizens because they were born to immigrant parents? And can government policy subject them to cruelties that we would never accept if they were suffered by the white children of U.S. citizens—cruelties that would undoubtedly in any other context be termed child abuse? The events that day in New Bedford clearly demonstrate the difficulty of implementing a policy of repatriation of undocumented workers and how much that implementation would compromise American values.

Hardly a Guatemalan family in New Bedford was untouched by the raid. Juan's brother-in-law was seized, as was one of Diego's brothers and a nephew. His brother, Diego says, "has a daughter and two little boys who were asking, 'Where's my daddy? When is my daddy coming home?' The little girl was asking the same thing" (2007, 17). A photographer from the *New Bedford Standard Times* took a picture of Diego's three-year-old niece, scared and sobbing, the night of the raid. The photograph became emblematic of the raid and was reprinted in newspapers and featured on picket signs at rallies and demonstrations around the country. Visiting Guatemala on March 12, President Bush came under fire for the raid by the Guatemalan president, Oscar Berger.

Still in El Paso, Anna was still trying desperately to reach her daughter: "Some officers came asking who wanted work—that they were going to pay. Since I didn't have money . . . I raised my hand and they signed up seven people first to clean all the rooms we were in." They spent more than two hours cleaning bathrooms, washing windows, sweeping and mopping. When they were finished, Anna said, "They then called us one by one and gave us a dollar each, no more" (2007).

For the next several weeks, many of the Guatemalans in New Bedford clung to their cell phones, waiting to hear from their loved ones. A local church took donations so phone cards could be sent to those in detention. Senators Kennedy and Kerry, along with Congressman Barney Frank, heard testimony of dozens of traumatized families at St. James Church on March 11. Families and friends tried to work out child-care arrangements. Massachusetts social workers were finally allowed to travel to Texas, where they recommended that ten detainees in the city of Harlingen and twenty in El Paso be released (Daley 2007, 1). As the courts began to process the detainees, everyone focused on the pending immigration reform legislation, desperately hoping a bill would be passed quickly that would allow the Guatemalans to stay in New Bedford and stop all this suffering.

On the Edge of a Cliff

As the immediate shock of the raids passed, however, the cold, hard reality began to set in among the Guatemalans in New Bedford. In some very fundamental way, things would never be the same. The specter of being detained and deported, so fresh in their minds, haunts them still. Juan, now six years in New Bedford, is in some ways a poster child for the immigrant worker who made good. He saved money, bought land back home, got married, had a daughter, and moved out of the fish houses to a fairly skilled position in a small business. But the raid, he says, changed everything. "I feel like I'm building a future right on the edge of a cliff. Every day you get better, but you never know when the future is going to slide down and disappear. We know that can happen any time." He continues:

> This is my dream, I'm here for my dream, but now that dream can disappear any time and I will suffer a lot. It's not just me but also my daughter and my wife. I can't imagine how all the parents feel now that they're in jail in Texas. They left their wife and their kids behind. Because I know how much I love my daughter and I wouldn't be able to live without them. But like I said, it's the risk that we take every day because we don't know if they're going to come back and who's going to be next. (2007, 2, 3)

Juan moved his family to another apartment after the raid, fearing that authorities had his address because his daughter attends public school.

Diego describes the effect of the raids as a kind of hypersensitivity now about being in public. "You're always paying attention to what you're going to do and looking around. It's like you're being pursued and persecuted. You're afraid at work and on the street" (2007, 6–7).

This high level of fear has had a strong impact on the behavior of the Guatemalans in New Bedford. Before the raid, with their English improving, many were more easily navigating the city and its surroundings. And though they were a long way from having a vibrant and thriving public Guatemalan community, individuals were moving more easily between communities. This all stopped after the raid. As Juan explains:

> In my case with my family, we changed a lot. I'm not going out unless I have to. . . . You never know what's going to happen. . . . Every time we hear something about Immigration, everybody gets scared. Our reaction isn't the same any more. I get nervous. That's what I'm saying. I'm not the same person any more. I'm not free any more. I am, but I'm not, you know. I stay closer to home and my family. I share time with my family because, as I said, we don't know how long we're going to be together. Things have changed a lot. It's not just with me but it's with a lot of my friends. (2007, 8)

Like Juan and his family, a great many other Guatemalan Maya returned to something they had known very well in their home country, a fear honed during a decade of hiding in the shadows during the fighting in the highlands.

The Guatemalans have also been forced to make contingency plans in case of seizure by ICE. "We're ready for that and now everybody knows what they're going to do if something happens," says Juan, who has worked out plans with his brothers and friends. "Now they know and will do what I've told them to do with my stuff, or whatever, left behind." But he chokes up when he starts talking about plans for his daughter. "If we both get caught what's going to happen with her? Who's going to take care of her? That's what I don't want to think about all the time" (2007, 7–8).

The raid had as strong an impact on the Mayan work life and the kind of work they do as it did on their community life. Many of the Guatemalans in New Bedford found themselves without a job in the days after the 2007 raid. As Diego explains, "When the tragedy happened, all the companies who knew that they had illegal people, they sent them home. Then those people who lost their jobs went looking for work. They didn't pick up new workers because they weren't hiring. So there's no work. . . . So many people. So many people affected by the raid" (2007, 8).

The overall effect of the raid has been to drive the Guatemalans deeper into the underground economy in their search for work. Part of ICE's rhetoric about the raid in New Bedford concerned the workplace abuses they had documented at MBI over many months. "That was what the U.S. Attorney's first press release was about. This horrible plant, this sweatshop with all these bad conditions and we're doing everybody a favor by having this raid, because this is a bad employer" (C. Williams 2007, 11). Yet in its wake, the raid has driven Guatemalan workers into small, informal workplaces where in many instances even the protections they had at MBI are not in place. With employers fully aware of how desperate they are to find work—any kind of work—there are virtually no restraints on employer behavior. It is a situation ripe for abuse. As Corinn Williams explains, "What we found in the aftermath of the raid is that employers have become that much more emboldened and that conditions are that much more abusive. And you know, if you don't like it, there's the door" (2007, 28).

In many ways the Guatemalan workers have been pushed right back to the same circumstances as those when they first arrived: take the first job you can get, any job; don't ask too many questions; keep your head down and, in Juan's words, "make do." The hope of moving into more stable jobs, which had been growing over the previous several years, has been dashed. There will be no talk of unionization, no hope of jobs with bread and roses. It's back to survival.

In all its inhumanity, maybe this is what ICE has in mind: by limiting employment options, you create conditions so bad that immigrant workers will return to their home countries. Yet there are fatal flaws in this argument, both economic and logistical. First, the economic conditions that led to mass emigration from countries like Guatemala have not changed. Relative to the situation in the Guatemalan highlands, jobs at minimum wage in the United States are still highly desirable. Even if the working conditions are barely tolerable, there is no financial incentive to return home. Second, many of the newly arrived have huge debts to repay for their journeys to the United States. It would be impossible to repay them on Guatemalan wages, and failure to do so would put the workers and their families in harm's way. Third, Guatemala continues to be a very dangerous place. A United Nations Development Programme report documents that 5,337 people had their lives cut short by violence in 2005 alone (Munaiz and Mendoza 2007, 1). Further, because so many of the Guatemalans send a significant portion of their wages home to support their extended families, returning home themselves would not just affect them individually but damage their families as well. Finally, for the Guatemalans with children who are U.S. citizens, returning home is incredibly complicated. The children have grown up in a world very different from the peasant communities in which their parents were raised. Juan explains:

> I'm stuck but I have no choice. Like I said, any time I can be sent back, but I want to be here. I have a daughter here now, and I don't want to take my daughter back there to a country that's not her country. So now I have like a family from two countries. Because I'm from Guatemala and my daughter is from here. She doesn't know my country. If we get sent back, if I can take my daughter with me, so she's going to pay the price too. (2007, 13–14)

The Failure of Immigration Reform

As the spring of 2007 passed in New Bedford, the detainees' cases were slowly processed. When Diego's brother was released, the family was overjoyed, and a *New Bedford Standard Times* photographer once again shot an award-winning photograph of his brother's daughter, this time with a grin from ear to ear. But as Diego noted, "Now he can't work. How's he going to support his family? Help from his friends? He has gas bills, food—so many things. He can't work. He has to respect the law" (2007, 13). On May 16 the Greater Boston Legal Services filed a class action lawsuit to recover the wages lost to the overtime scam at MBI. OSHA began an investigation of the MBI plant.

But all eyes were on developments in Washington, where the Comprehensive Immigration Reform bill was being debated in Congress. The passage of an immigration bill was the only way out for those still in detention and those already facing deportation. The bill was a grand compromise that offered the Republicans increases in border security and Democrats a form of amnesty for immigrant workers already in the United States— although they judiciously avoided the word amnesty. The president, bruised and battered by how poorly the war in Iraq was going, and with his popularity at an all-time low, made immigration reform the centerpiece of his priorities. For a moment it seemed as though there were enough forces aligned to overcome the gridlock that had paralyzed Washington.

By May, debate had risen to a fever pitch as amendments were proposed from both sides of the aisle. As a bipartisan bill, there is something in it for everybody to dislike. The left, including many immigrant-rights activists and unions, opposed it because, in the words of the AFL-CIO president, John Sweeney, "The bill abandoned long-standing U.S. policy favoring the reunification of families and failed to protect workers' most basic rights" (quoted in Bacon 2007, 1). It proposed instead a points-based system.

The revolt of the anti-immigration wing of the president's own party, however, ultimately torpedoed the immigration reform bill. "Senate conservatives fought the legislation from the start, saying it rewarded those who broke the law by entering illegally." Several right-wing organizations, including Numbers USA, whipped up support in the conservative base, and moderates like John McCain and even Mitch McConnell, the Republican leader of the Senate, never stood a chance. On June 7 the Senate rejected a Democratic call for a vote, and, despite pleas from Edward Kennedy, majority leader Harry Reid pulled the plug on the legislation, saying, "We're finished with this for the time being" (Hulse and Pear 2007, 1).

Reid left the door open for further developments, however, and the wrangling continued through much of June. On June 28, with no clear compromise in sight, Congress called it quits. As Senator Richard Durbin told a new conference, "Tomorrow, when this is reported, there will be millions of people across America who will be disappointed, who will continue to live in fear and uncertainty. There will be people who wonder what America will mean to them and their children" (U.S. Senate 2007, 1). Senator Diane Feinstein added, "Well, this is not a proud day for the likes of Emma Lazarus," whom she paraphrased: "Give me your poor, your huddled masses yearning to be free; send these, the homeless, to this great country" (U.S. Senate 2007, 3).

Friday, June 29, 2007, was just another workday for the Guatemalans in New Bedford. For them and the estimated 12 million undocumented workers in the United States, it was another day on a long journey as they showed up at some of the worst jobs in America in order to feed their children and send money back home to their families. In some ways nothing changed with the failure of the reform bill; nothing was lost except their dreams—their dreams to move out of the shadows into the light of becoming American citizens, their American dream. I spoke with Juan the following day about how he felt in the wake of the failure of immigration reform. He responded:

> We get so disappointed. How much more will it take for them to see and realize how important we are to this country? How long? It's already

been a long time. I don't know why. There are so many questions that we ask all the time that we can't get answers to. We can't understand what's going on and why they're doing what they do. All the people ask, "What have I done wrong?" I know I crossed the country, I crossed the border without papers, it's like, I tell my friends sometimes, Americans . . . I bet if you were in my shoes you would do the same thing. (2007, 16)

In other fundamental ways, things would never be the same for undocumented workers in the United States. The anti-immigrant frenzy that was whipped up to defeat immigration reform could not be put back in a box. Stymied by their inability to restrict undocumented workers, federally, anti-immigrant activists went to work on the state and local levels, passing hundreds of antiimmigrant ordinances in states and municipalities. Hazelton, Pennsylvania, a city that grew from the work of immigrant miners in the adjacent anthracite coalfields more than a century ago, was the first to pass ordinances that, in the words of Mayor Louis J. Barletta, would make the city "one of the toughest places in the United States" for undocumented workers (Preston 2007a, 1).

Although a federal judge struck down the Hazelton ordinances, the action did very little to stop the flood of anti-immigrant activity in other cities and towns. The National Conference of State Legislatures reported that "state legislatures, grappling with the failure of the federal government to overhaul the immigration laws, considered 404 immigration measures this year and enacted 170 of them, an unprecedented surge in state-level lawmaking on the issue" (Preston 2007b, 1). Many new state laws restricted the hiring of undocumented workers, outlawed contracts with them, and prohibited them from obtaining driver's licenses and receiving other social services. These issues were mirrored on the local level. Provisions were made so that state and local law enforcement could assist ICE in the arrest and detention of undocumented workers.

The Bush administration was not silent on immigration. Despite the president's legislative defeat, he swiftly moved administratively. Early in August 2007 the Department of Homeland Security instituted new rules that would require employers to comply with Social Security "no match letters."—letters from the Social Security Office indicating that the Social Security Number does not match the name of the individual submitted it. Currently these letters have long been ignored with little consequence. Now employers would have to fire employees who did not have correct Social

Security numbers or face a stiff fine. "We are tough and going to be even tougher," the DHS announced. "There are not going to be any more excuses for employers, and there will be serious consequences for those that choose to blatantly disregard the law" (Preston 2007c, 1).

At the same time that the Bush administration was moving against undocumented workers, ICE increased its activity with raids across the country like the one in New Bedford—against meatpackers in Postville, Iowa; poultry processors in Greensville, South Carolina; and another defense contract in Asheville, North Carolina, among many others across all sectors of the economy. The only silver lining was that the work of Massachusetts senators Kennedy and Kerry in the wake of the New Bedford raid forced ICE to institute humanitarian guidelines to release mothers and other caregivers of children.

In an extremely troubling development, ICE agents began arresting workers in their homes. In early October 2007, ICE conducted a raid in Nassau County, Long Island, purportedly looking for gang members among undocumented workers. The *New York Times* described

> armed squads bursting into homes in the dead of night with shotguns and automatic weapons, terrorizing families and taking away anyone who lacks identity papers, even if they have raided the wrong house. It may sound like Baghdad, but it is the suburbs of New York City, the latest of hundreds of communities around the country where federal agents have been invading homes and workplaces in search of immigrants to deport. (2007, 1)

As *Newsday*, the Long Island newspaper put it, "Leave it to the feds to use a sledgehammer when the job calls for a scalpel" (2007, A44). In Nassau, Police Commissioner Lawrence Mulvey described it as "a seriously botched cowboy" operation by dozens of ICE agents—some in cowboy hats—who had not trained together, used inappropriate weapons, and mistakenly drew them on Nassau officers (*New York Times* 2007, 1). Using these paramilitary tactics, ICE was bringing the war on terrorism to the homeland in a way few Americans could have imagined.

It is the link ICE is making between terrorism and the immigration of undocumented workers, and how it is being used to justify injustices against hard-working immigrants, that the Guatemalans in New Bedford find so troubling. "They're saying all these terrorists are planning to attack from the border," Juan argues. "So now all these cops and immigration officials, they are there on the border to make sure all these terrorists don't come from

Mexico. That's what they're thinking. I don't think so. Are all these terrorists going to cross the desert? You don't attack the United States that way. That's a dumb thing to do! The only dumb guys who cross the desert are us!" he says laughing. "They got all their papers in order. What do they need to cross the desert for?" (2004, 21–22). Diego picks up the argument:

> In my point of view they are throwing it on us that we're terrorists now. We're not terrorists. It wasn't us who were the terrorists! We didn't knock down any buildings like what happened on 9/11. It's the point of view that's doing the damage. These are experts and sometimes they are legal. I can't fly a plane! I don't carry arms to do damage like that. The U.S. government knows what's happening. Now they're coming to clean up the country. I'm not against that. Now they're picking up the bad guys and that's OK. But if I'm not doing anything bad and I'm not harming anybody—I'm just maintaining my family and my life and working. I'm helping increase the economy of the United States. That's why we came. We came to work! (2007, 4)

Yet in the absence of comprehensive immigration reform, the raids continue. In many ways it is becoming similar to the so-called War on Drugs. Even though many question what they really do to eradicate drug use, law enforcement agencies focus a great deal of energy and resources on high-profile raids and arrests— demonstrating U.S. government resolve on the drug issue. Yet these raids often have little more than symbolic value. Similarly, although raids like the one in New Bedford may appease the anti-immigration wing of the Republican Party, they do nothing substantively to solve the current crisis of undocumented workers in the United States, besides showing that we are "getting tough" with undocumented immigrants the same way that we "get tough" with drug dealers.

Despite its political appeal to some, ramping up the prosecution of immigration crimes, which nearly doubled from 2007 to 2008, does not have widespread support in the law enforcement community. "The emphasis, many federal judges and prosecutors say, has siphoned resources from other crimes, eroded morale among federal lawyers and overloaded the federal court system." They report that this focus on immigration has hampered their effect on "gun trafficking, organized crime and the increasing violent drug trade" (S. Moore 2009).

As Senator Kennedy points out, "There are 12 million undocumented workers in the United States. Arresting 300 of them may generate some headlines for [the Department of Homeland Security], but such raids do not begin to solve the immigration issues" (2007, 2). In the wake of the New Bedford raid the *Houston Chronicle* reported, "In the bigger picture, it showed again that symbolic sweeps are pointless substitutes for workplace immigration laws that function" (Kilday, 2007, 8).

The Bush administration's decision to increase raids against undocumented workers, a policy change that resulted from its inability to get its own party to support real immigration reform, is not without victims—in particular, as in New Bedford, children who are American citizens. After the ICE raid on the homes of Smithfield workers in Tar Heel, North Carolina, Greg Tarpinian, the executive director of the labor federation Change to Win wrote:

> It becomes clearer every day that the Bush Administration has decided that pleasing its base with acts of political theater is more important than finding a real solution to immigration. And the human cost of that decision becomes clearer every day as well. We see the cost in families torn apart by armed agents at gunpoint. . . . We see the cost in communities coming to fear the knock on the door in the dead of night. (*PRNewswire* 2007, 1)

As was also clear in New Bedford, ICE did not force Guatemalan workers out of the United States but instead drove them deeper into the informal and underground economy. This action only further encourages the exploitation and abuse of immigrant workers rather than eradicating it. It is impossible to see how encouraging such exploitation is a good thing either for immigrant workers or for the country. Are we going to "fix" the immigrant problem by driving immigrants into servitude? Are we going to "fix" our economy by the hyper-exploitation of our most vulnerable workers?

Of those taken in the ICE raid, 168 were deported, including Víctor García. Back in Guatemala he "wonders how we will feed his four young children. "When he worked for Michael Bianco, García was able to send home $500 a month. Now he is lucky to earn 40 *quetzales* ($6.00) a day working in the fields. "I wasn't stealing anything," he says. "I just wanted to work" (quoted in Carl 2008, 2). In New Bedford, in November 2008, former Bianco owner Francesco Insolia pleaded guilty to the charges stemming from the ICE raid. He was ordered to pay a $30,000 fine and will be sentenced to at least one year in prison (Kibbe 2008, 1). Later that month Bianco settled the overtime suit and paid out $613,000 to workers who were not paid for overtime

(Evans 2008, 1). OSHA fined Bianco $45,000 (later reduced to $37,000) for safety and health violations.

In this season of fear it has been difficult for the Guatemalans in New Bedford to hold onto their dreams. But they do, somehow, to get themselves through the long days of tough work that, now in the aftermath of the raid, is even harder. Juan says:

> I always compare myself to a river. I would always go walk by the river to console myself. I would look at the river to see it flowing, without knowing where it came from or where it was going. I'm just like the river because I have had to go through the mountains and through big rocks. . . . It seems like this is what's happening to me too. I have obstacles that I come up against every day. That's why we have that saying about every day is a new day and what happens, happens. . . . That's what gives me some consolation as every day goes by. Every day is a new day. To remember all of what you've lived through, you could close yourself up in the pain and loneliness and sadness. Sometimes I try to console and energize myself because I have a life to live and I have to struggle and do something. Whatever God lets me do. That's the way I think. (2001b, 12)

Juan says if he gets his papers, he is going to take a trip with his daughter: "Someday I'm going to take her back to Guatemala and we're going to cross the desert together. That way she can understand what I did for her! To get citizen papers. To be a citizen in the United States." He knows it may be a long time.

After Eight

TOM JURAVICH

Friday night, it's getting late, I've already done my eight
I've been on my feet since half past three
Outside the clinic, the evening went, time, money, passion spent
Me, I'm so tired, I can hardly see
I'm dreaming of my cool, crisp sheets, stretched out from my head to feet
Just got two hours left, I could stand a little rest

It's two a.m., I'm finally home, it's quiet and I'm so alone
I can finally get some sleep
I read the paper, sort the bills, I forgot to eat, I'm hungry still
Make myself a bite to eat
I flip the channels on TV, I'm still awake; it's a quarter to three
Ah, this night is such a mess, I could stand a little rest

I can't believe it's one o'clock, did my old alarm clock stop?
I've gotta be at work at three
I told mom we'd go to the mall, I guess I'd better make that call
What the hell is wrong with me
I need my coffee, I need my fix, I'm hungry but I'm feeling sick
A shower might be best, I could stand a little rest

Back at work, it's three p.m., out here on the floor again
Did I ever really leave this place?
The patients they're an endless stream, did I end up in some bad dream?
I'm not sure I can stand the pace
I'm dreaming of my cool, crisp sheets, stretched out from my head to feet
Just got two hours left, I could stand a little rest

3

EXHAUSTED

Nursing at Boston Medical

It starts around four a.m., so you've been there a good nine hours and all you think about is your bed. That's all you want to know is your bed, your pillow. It's true, it's fantasizing about sleeping. . . . It was exhausting and it was worse because you'd go home, you'd sleep, maybe at noon you'd wake up. You'd have a headache because you haven't had caffeine, because you stopped drinking coffee in the middle of the night, but your body needed the caffeine. So, now you wake up, you have a headache, you're disoriented, you don't know what you need to eat. So, I think it's really very unhealthy. But, it was quite an experience, the bond that you form with your coworkers in the middle of the night. Because we are all there pretty much in the same boat, trying to keep each other awake. Some nights were worse than others, but the whole entire process is wicked. Janet Killarney (2002, 2)

JANET KILLARNEY works as a nurse in the operating rooms at Boston Medical Center. She originally trained and worked as an obstetrical nurse in the delivery room. "It was really my passion," she recalls, but there was only one hitch: "You had to do the twelve-hour shifts. After I did that full time for almost four years, I just had no interest in it. I had a husband. I'd just been married. I wanted to be home. I wanted to feel human when I was home" (2002, 2). But Janet's move into the operating room ended up being no less demanding.

Janet started at Boston City Hospital, a public hospital with more than a century of commitment to care for Boston's poor and working class. Then Boston City was merged in 1996 with Boston University Hospital, and things changed dramatically, especially for nurses in the operating room. The new hospital took an aggressive business approach to surgery, filling surgical suites to capacity far into the evening, without adding additional nursing staff. This intensification of the nurses' work compromised their professionalism and left them scrambling to work overtime and to cover for one another's shifts. Feeling their commitment to patient care undermined, and facing unmanageable working conditions, many have decided to leave the profession, further exacerbating the nursing staffing situation. Those left, like Janet, struggling to maintain some of their original commitment to patient care, are exhausted.

Boston City Hospital

Built in the south end of Boston in the 1860s, Boston City was one of a number of public hospitals constructed in major U.S. cities in the latter half of the nineteenth century to serve the poor and indigent. "The actual impetus for the hospital's establishment came from the insufficiency of Massachusetts General, with its hundred forty beds. Boston had grown, and the segment of its population potentially in need of hospitalization had been greatly enlarged by Irish immigration" (Vogel 1980, 33).

City Hospital's Training School for Nurses was founded in 1878, proclaiming itself "the first in America to adopt the method of having its training school for nurses as an integral part of the hospital organization" (Boston City Hospital 1891, 5). A publication from the school in 1900 announces that "all nurses are required to be sober, honest, truthful, trustworthy, punctual, quiet, orderly, clean, neat, patient, kind and cheerful." It continues with detailed instruction in eight areas, including "the applying of leeches, and subsequent treatment" (Boston City Hospital 1900, 1–2).

Later, several private hospitals would be built in Boston, and some would go on to become among the finest medical facilities in the country—Beth Israel, Brigham and Women's, and the expanded Massachusetts General. But throughout most of the twentieth century, Boston City remained the hospital for Boston's working class and poor. It was where their babies were born, their parents died, and, if they were lucky, their children were treated for no more than the normal childhood injuries and illnesses.

Sharon, a nurse at Boston City, describes patients who were not your typical suburban clientele:

> There's a very special type of patient that you take care of at City Hospital. They are by no means the wealthiest. They're people who need health care. We can always give it. Nobody told me, "That patient is supposed to leave at 8:00 so they're gone. We need that bed!" This was, of course, before managed care. But even after managed care they might have stayed an extra day or two. Natasha, a famous bag lady from the

Boston Common, was a resident of ours in the medical building on one of the medical floors from October until March. Then we'd discharge her to her address at Boston Common. We were here for the people that live in this area and in a lot of the city neighborhoods—to come and get their health care. I never knew whether they had insurance and didn't care whether they did or not. It wasn't my job to ask. (2002, 2)

These patients were incredibly appreciative of their nurses. As Esther tells it, "The people love us. They love their Boston City nurses. If you go to downtown Boston, on any corner, during the daytime, they'll go, 'Hey, Boston!' One of the homeless people you had last night or the night before, they know all of us" (2002, 4).

Starting in the late 1960s, however, Boston City was on the front line of a new wave of drug abuse, handgun violence, and homelessness. Esther, a nurse with sixteen years' experience, describes what working at City Hospital felt like then:

I [had] worked in the suburbs, and it was very quiet and very suburban. I came to Boston, and it was a knife and gun club—it was the height of the violence. The gangs were ramped. . . . We did at least two gunshots a night, several stabbings a night. Every night of the week, seven nights a week, it was trauma central. (2002, 4)

Celia Wcislo, who started at Boston City and went on to become president of the union that represents the nurses and other health care workers at the hospital, describes the scene when she arrived in 1973:

It was like a war zone. It was sort of urban. Everyone had a funny accent. It was very street tough. But everyone was very friendly. You didn't have paper. You didn't have pencils. You had to bring your own stuff in. The girls told you how to dress. If you're going to wear blue jeans, iron them. If docs put their hands on you, here's what you do. And you do it in front of [everyone], when they're on rounds. "Dr. So-and-So, if you ever put your hands on me again, I'm going to have to report you to somebody." And so I sort of felt like they took me under their wings because I was like, wow this place is huge. It was anything goes. There would be druggies running through the clinic shooting at people. I loved the place. (2002, 2)

Boston City Hospital was the model for the television series *St. Elsewhere*, which ran from 1982 to 1988. The first of a series of gritty, reality-based programs (like Hill Street Blues and others), it fictionalized what was all too familiar to Boston City's nurses.

Wcislo captures the two sides of Boston City. The nurses and staff were overwhelmed, yet they were extremely dedicated to their patients, and they pitched in and did their best to make it work. "So, we're like the wrong side of the tracks. We took all the indigents and the crazies and gunshot wounds," Janet Killarney explains. But she goes on to say, "I don't think you could find a better group of trauma staff than you can find here—everyone from the EMTs [emergency medical technicians] to the emergency room, to the operating room, to the intensive care units" (2001, 16).

Mary Katides relates how unlike Boston City was from the private hospitals in the Boston area.

> I worked at Mass General before, and a lot of those nurses are from Wellesley and Newton and they have nice fingernails, go to the hairdresser, and things like that. I do see that Boston City has a different personality altogether. One doctor from New England Medical Center came to our place and he says, "What's the difference between a Boston City emergency room nurse and a junkyard dog?" and he says, "Lipstick." That pretty much sums it up. We're good to our patients but the doctors do feel the rough edge there, you know. (2001, 35)

Boston City worked, in part, because many of the nursing staff came from the same working-class and poor communities as their patients. Janet Killarney, for example, like her friend and coworker in the operating room Jean Griffin, came from a family of modest means. Jean, who just turned fifty, has twenty-nine year's experience as a nurse. Her husband has worked many years for Boston Edison. "We come from South Boston, both from blue-collar backgrounds, and we had that little dream of a house in the suburbs with a nice school system. We were married at twenty-two," Jean explains. "And we knew it took hard work and we were willing to make all the sacrifices for our dream" (2001, 3).

Mary Katides is forty-one and has worked as a nurse for nineteen years. She grew up in the housing projects in South Boston. Mary's brother Michael Patrick MacDonald has written about the Irish in South Boston in *All Souls: A Family Story from Southie* (1999). His recounting of his family's life in the Lower End of South Boston is harrowing. "I was thinking about this," Mary says. "A lot of us do come from poverty, or close to it, from big families. We come into nursing because taking care of the families, it just comes so natural" (2001, 34). Mary started early taking care of herself and her brothers and sisters.

At twelve years old, actually, I was always the sick one in the family. So I had to be good at taking care of myself. I had tonsillitis all the time. In fact, I took myself, I jumped on the trolley when I was in Jamaica Plain, went over to Children's Hospital, and I had abscessed tonsils. But they were saying, "Is anybody with you?" And I'm saying, "No, I'm by myself." You know, I just knew I was really sick and I needed to go into the hospital. My mother she'd give us a hot toddy and we'd be drunk for the day from the whisky and everything. I just had to do that at a real young age, take care of myself. My mother had eleven of us, and usually you had to wait a few hours in the emergency room. When you are one of the oldest, you know that your mother is too busy with the younger kids. (2001, 30)

As she got older, Mary had to handle more than just tonsillitis. Right after she had passed her EMT test, she got a call from her mother. "She called me up and she says, 'Mary, Jackie's here with Frannie [her downstairs neighbors] and I think they're dying. Sonny [their father] stabbed them and,' she says, 'they're on the floor here bleeding to death.' She was afraid to call 911 because the boys didn't want anyone to know that their father stabbed them. My mother wanted me to fix them up. I called 911" (2001, 32). It wasn't the only time such a thing happened. Mary explains:

My brother Kevin came to my house after being shot in the leg. His partner in crime had just shot a jewelry store owner [who in turn shot Kevin]. Kevin was furious about what his friend had just done. His leg was bleeding profusely, and he didn't care. He just called Whitey Bulger [a notorious South Boston gangster] to see if he could help him get out of town. I had my two sons in the house at the time so wasn't happy about this. I turned on the TV, and it was all over the news. It talked about the jewelry store owner was in critical condition and is paralyzed. Kevin was shaking and crying, saying "He's paralyzed!" He then called his wife to talk with her, and within fifteen minutes the state police were at my house with their guns drawn. Kevin went peacefully, but they trashed my house looking for a gun that wasn't there. Kevin didn't have a gun, and they saw that later on video. But throughout my life I've always been exposed to traumas, guns, suicide. A lot of my patients in the operation room were my neighbors from South Boston. (2001, 31–32)

Mary's connection with Boston City Hospital is deep. "My brother Davy," she says, "went to Boston City. I think I kind of got that in the back of my head, these emergencies and traumas in my life. He died in the operating

room. My sister Kathy fell from a roof and was rushed into Boston City. . . .
I just felt like I had a real connection with Boston City. And I felt like I could
maybe save people" (2001, 27).

The Creation of Boston Medical Center

In 1994 Boston City moved out of its nineteenth-century building into a new
facility adjacent to Boston University Hospital. But the health care system
was in deep trouble in Boston and throughout the United States. Demand
for new procedures and testing was rapidly increasing the cost of medical
care. These increased costs, coupled with decisions to rein in government
spending on Medicare, made it increasingly difficult for hospitals to balance
their books. Public hospitals bore the brunt of these changes head on. They
also had to absorb the skyrocketing numbers of uninsured patients.

By the 1990s the industry had decided that the only way out of this fiscal
crisis was for hospitals to merge. As Dana Beth Weinberg writes in *Code
Green: Money-Driven Hospitals and the Dismantling of Nursing*, "Not only did
these mergers neutralize a rival hospital, but they promised hospitals cost
savings from the realization of economies of scale" (2003, 26). Taking its cue
from the corporate world, the new paradigm for hospitals became "bigger
is better." By virtue of their size alone, they would squeeze inefficiencies
out of the system to compete in the new economic reality. Between 1990
and 1996, 176 hospitals were involved in mergers, more than in the entire
previous decade (Spang, Bazzoli, and Arnould 2001).[1]

Merger mania struck Boston hospitals with a vengeance. Massachusetts
General merged with Brigham and Women's in 1993, and Beth Israel with
Deaconess Hospital in 1996 (Knox 1996b). With health care costs escalating, city officials began to worry about the long-term viability of City Hospital, and merger talks with Boston University Hospital started in earnest.

The possibility of merging Boston City raised many concerns, however,
especially about its mission. John Rich, a staff specialist in adult medicine,
spoke of "differences between BCH's culture and every other hospital in
town," explaining, "there is a sense of caring for people for whom it doesn't
matter if they can pay, and fighting through impossible systems to do it.
That's why most of us are here, despite the hassles" (quoted in Knox 1996c).
Staff members were also worried about their jobs. One reason for mergers
is to create efficiencies, but these are frequently accomplished by major
downsizing, and Boston City officials suggested that "up to 1,500 jobs would
be lost," 400 by direct layoff (Knox 1996a).

Still, concerns among the staff and the public about City Hospital and its more than one-hundred-year tradition of serving Boston's poor could not stave off the avalanche of escalating costs, or the desire of city fathers to limit their liability. With support from the mayor, the governor, and the state legislature, the merger of Boston City and Boston University Hospitals was completed in 1996, creating the Boston Medical Center. City Councilor Albert L. O'Neil was quoted in the *Globe*: "I will be 76 years old tomorrow, and I never dreamt I would see this day in this hospital. If James Michael Curley were alive today, he'd be turning over in his grave" (Knox 1996a). Curley, the populist if somewhat scandalous mayor of Boston in the 1930s, had been an ardent supporter of public services, including City Hospital.

As Sharon, a City Hospital nurse, put it, "Maybe we weren't so cost conscious and, at some point, around [the mayor] Mr. Menino's neck, we became the albatross. And he sold us into bondage to the group that has us now, Boston Medical Center" (2002). Menino continued to be a thorn in the side of nurses from Boston City. After the merger, a portion of the building was named after him. When the Menino Pavilion was dedicated, an order for hospital staff, including the nurses, to use the back door made nurses furious. "I'm thinking, twenty-two years I've worked here . . . and I had to go out the back door" (Meagan 2002, 16). "Until him, we had mayors that actually were treated in the City Hospital. Menino chooses to go to Beth Israel or Brigham and Women's when he gets sick" (John 2002, 2).

Boston Medical Center has 582 beds and an operating budget of $929 million, and it employs approximately 1,600 nurses. Now a not-for-profit organization, its stated mission is to "provide consistently excellent and accessible health services to all in need of care regardless of status and ability to pay" (Boston Medical Center 2007, 3). Despite Boston City's merger with the upscale Boston University Hospital, the majority of Boston Medical patients are still working class, poor, and at risk. According to Boston Medical brochure:

More than half of all Boston Medical Center patients have an annual income of $17,000 or less

Approximately 50% of Boston Medical Center patients are uninsured or have Medicaid.

Nearly 40% of patients seeking care in Boston Medical Center's Emergency Department have no primary care provider.

Last year more than 40% of the patients treated in the Emergency Department were identified as having a substance abuse problem. (Boston Medical Center, 2002)

As in many other corporate mergers, Boston Medical continues to maintain two separate facilities, under different administrations. Few connections exist between the nurses at the two campuses. Nurses at both are unionized: those at the former University Hospital are members of the Massachusetts Nurses Association; those at the old Boston City site belong to the Service Employees International Union (SEIU). Thus, despite the merger, nurses from Boston City felt the separateness. As one of them tells it:

> The police, fire, ambulances all still think of us as City Hospital. They bring us all the City Hospital patients. So in that respect nothing's changed. In other respects, we are the redheaded stepchild of Boston Medical Center. It's hard to explain that one. We feel we're treated as less than the East Newton Campus nurses and . . . we've been told that the doctors over there don't want their patients at our hospital. Like it's someplace inferior. (Esther 2002, 3)

"And you can feel it. I can't pinpoint it, but you can feel it. They treat our patients differently," Jean Griffin declares. "I remember the first few times some of these anesthesiologists from New England Medical came and said 'Oh, I didn't know we had to wear gloves to touch them.' I said, 'Excuse me?'" (2001, 13).

Celia Wcislo remembers "a punitive period where the culture of City Hospital was seen as the enemy. . . . If you were a City person, you're still City. It's almost like a brand on your forehead. You can't help it, you are like the new kids who don't understand what they're talking about" (2002, 6). "There was a lot of uncertainty from the standpoint of people losing the BCH and not knowing what they'd face. I think it was a day-by-day thing. There was a lot of fear of management and the takeover," Janet Killarney recalls. "For many people, we just basically got the hand-me-downs. If there were two positions [to be merged], say, even in midlevel management, say in accounting, if there were two comparable positions, the guy or gal from the City side was given the severance pay and the other person was taken" (2001, 16).

City nurses worried especially about the encroachment of the new corporate model into patient care. As Sharon sees it, "We are allowing nonmedical, nonprofessional people to answer medical questions, to dictate whether I get care or not." She continues:

> Was I going to send that homeless person to the street? Because that's what the address was. Discharge to street in a snowstorm? Am I going to do that? Or am I going to wait until tomorrow morning when they can get over the snow bank and get to where they want to go? . . . It's not humane. These are human beings that we're dealing with every day. They're not numbers. The bean counters can count the admissions and the discharges and make themselves look good, but it's not what I went into nursing for. (2002, 11–13)

And one of her colleagues points out, "The bottom line is financial. It's the health care industry. . . . Years ago it was a hospital, Boston City Hospital, University Hospital. Now it's a center, Boston Medical Center. You're in an institution. I feel like I'm in a prison sometimes" (Meagan 2002, 13).

Mary Katides reports that at Boston City, "everyone mixed much better, management and workers. . . . BU seems to be very business-like." This change is reflected in how people dress: "Our manager was in a scrub, scrub attire just like we wear. And the new ones have suits on and they don't get their hands dirty. It gives you a different attitude about them" (2001, 7).

As we have seen in the corporate world, with the mergers of firms such as Daimler and Chrysler, and Hewlett Packard and Compaq, the actual process of bringing together disparate operations with different traditions and cultures is not always easy. In one of the only detailed case studies of a hospital merger, Dana Beth Weinberg points out the difficulties of the merger of Beth Israel and Deaconess Hospitals. Of the promised cost savings she writes, "Three years after the merger, the gamble had not paid off. Despite the original optimism, the Beth Israel Deaconess merger did not deliver on its financial promise and even weakened the hospital's situation" (2003, 28). The president of the newly merged unit resigned after "the hospital's bonds were reduced to 'junk' status" (Kowalczyk 2001, 1).

The merger's impact on nursing and patient care was devastating. Weinberg documents a shift away from the "primary nursing" that had made Beth Israel a national leader, and an overall erosion of nursing skills and control. "The hospital, in adopting the standard set of changes in vogue in hospital cost-cutting across the country, also adopted an implicit philosophy of patient care that was foreign to the primary nursing practice in place at Beth Israel" (2003, 177).

Because my exploration of the impact of hospital restructuring on the practice of nursing in what was Boston City Hospital began five years after the merger, I focus less on the details of the merger than on how the merger has affected the practice of nursing at the former Boston City. With almost 1,600 nurses in the facility it is not possible to examine all aspects of nursing, so I look primarily at the work of nurses in the operating room.

The Soul of the Operating Room

With 29,000 admissions and more than 24,000 ambulatory surgical procedures each year at Boston Medical Center, the operating rooms (ORs) are in great demand (Boston Medical Center 2007). Jean Griffin describes the basic staffing of the OR, where hundreds of different procedures are performed:

> In an operating room situation where there is a procedure going on, you would have the nurse, who is circulating, and the scrub person or the scrub tech. You would have an anesthesiologist—again, it's a teaching hospital, so it would be a resident learning. You would have the attending surgeon and you would have either one or two residents at various educational levels, and possibly a med student. (2001, 17)

Although the personnel lineup is fairly standard, nurses in the OR must be flexible enough to assist in a myriad of procedures at a breakneck pace. Janet Killarney describes it:

> It's non-stop. It's absolutely non-stop. . . . You need to make sure that the orders are what they should be. You do know after years and years pretty much what doctors have for standard orders, for pre-op orders, and things like that. [But] it's non-stop; it changes by the minute. You have to be pretty much proficient in everything because from one day to the next you might go from pediatrics to general surgery to plastic surgery to ears, nose, and throat. (2001, 11)

Even more than the physician, who is focused on one specific task, the nurse in the OR has a sense of the whole patient and is responsible for the patient's overall care. The role carries a great deal of responsibility, especially when things start going bad. Mary Katides describes one such situation she faced:

> One day they were waking a patient up who had just had his tonsils out. Now, he's a twenty-one year old kid, really big. He's waking up. He's really not breathing well. So I look up at his oxygen level, it's going down

and down and down. He's obviously got an obstruction and, you know, I can see that. And I just had to tell the tech, "Keep everything right there, available, just in case." Sometimes you have to do a tracheotomy. . . . Now this kid's kind of waking up, thrashing, so they're kind of holding him and I'm running for the trach kit, opening things up. A lot of times, you will even be the one pointing stuff out to the anesthesiologist. Like I said, "I think he's got an obstruction." You hear a certain noise and you just know it. But you feel sometimes like you're alerting the whole room and a lot of them really don't see the whole picture. We see the whole picture. It's what makes us different. (2001, 8–9)

Jean Griffin asserts, "I always describe the OR circulating nurse as the soul of the OR. If there is nonsense going on, she would be the one to say, 'Enough already.' If there was a trauma going on, she would be orchestrating everything in the back so that the blood would be there and the extra instruments would be there. But also she sets the tone" (2001, 14–15).

Until recently there were often two nurses in the OR, one who would circulate and the other who would scrub, or hand instruments to the physicians. But today at Boston Medical, as in many other major hospitals, they use "scrub techs" or "surgical techs," as they are sometimes called, not registered nurses (RNs). Griffin describes the techs' role:

> They cannot do anything else. They are not licensed. They are basically technicians and they pass the instruments to the surgeon. It's an important role, but it's not the most important role. The most important role is circulating. [The circulating nurse] make[s] sure there is safety for the patient, that the patient is positioned correctly, safety strap on, patient's warm, patient's clean. Assist anesthesia if they need anything. (2001, 15)

Janet Killarney adds that scrub techs are "limited to a technical role. They aren't responsible for sponge and instrument counts. They aren't responsible for medications. You give them the medications they need to administer, and you need to make sure they know what it is. But they're not really responsible in that sense" (2001, 14).

The use of scrub techs is the latest development in the deskilling taking place in hospitals and health care facilities. Beginning in the 1940s and 1950s, hospitals in the United States introduced "team nursing" in an effort to cut costs. In these new teams, "the most skilled tasks were to be performed by RNs, semi-skilled tasks by LPNs [licensed practical nurses], and unskilled work by nurses' aides" (Brannon 1994, 99). According to Suzanne Gordon,

"Hospitals believed that they could 'extend' the better-educated and more expensive registered nurses by hiring only a few RNs on any particular ward and deploying cheaper labor—LPNs and aides—to work under them" (1997, 44).

Far beyond what developed in the 1940s and 1950s, from the 1990s the deskilling of nursing continued rapidly as the economics of health care changed. As Baer and Gordon point out, "With saving money as their first priority, financial consultants deconstruct the bundle [of tasks nurses perform] into parts and delegate the pieces to someone they can hire for less money" (1996, 228). While it may have indeed helped balance the books, the question that remains is what impact this deskilling has on patient care. Even though nurses may be happy to be relieved of some of the mundane tasks of patient care, these tasks often provide ways for them to check on and monitor their patients. Money managers who argue that "by liberating nursing from what they call menial tasks they are elevating nursing practice to a higher level" reveal "how little consultants knows about or value the direct patient contact that is the hallmark of bedside nursing and the key to quality care" (Baer and Gordon 1996, 99). As one nurse explained to a health care researcher:

> "Well I just take temperature and blood pressures and I write them down on this thing and ask them how old they are." . . . So the person who was running this thing, the PhD lady said, "Why would we have a registered nurse?" And I said, "Because if I put that child on a weigh scale and weigh them, I check out the child's spine, I check out that child for bruises, I check that child's muscular development, I check the child's hair, I check that child's ears. I check a lot more on that child and I can scan that; in 15 seconds I can know more about that child by looking than this person who can just take a temperature and stuff like that and write it down." (Quoted in Armstrong et al. 2000, 103)

Another big change in the OR resulting from the new entrepreneurialism in the Boston Medical Center has been in the pace of work. In the City Hospital, elective surgery was scheduled only between 7:00 a.m. and 3:00 p.m., " perfect timing," according to Jean Griffin (2001, 20). The day shift would finish up and a smaller night shift would come in to deal mostly with trauma. "In the old days, years ago, when it was Boston City Hospital," Janet Killarney remembers, "at three o'clock in the afternoon you went down to four people in the OR." She laments, "The surgery doesn't run that way any more. I'm sorry to tell you when [a doctor] schedules two gastric bypasses, they are an average of about five hours each. Guess what? That's ten hours. We're only here eight" (2001, 27). Jean Griffin adds. "We're running more cases and we're running cases much later, until 7:00, 8:00, 9:00, and 10:00 at night" (2001, 20–21).

The most frustrating thing to the nurses in the OR at Boston Medical is that even with these changes in the length of the surgical day, management has made few adjustments to the daily staff schedule. As Janet tells it, the OR runs all day, "but they don't have the staff to run it." Venting her frustration, she says, "It's not my fault. These aren't secret documents. This is how the OR runs every day. It's up on the board" (Killarney 2001, 28). The changing use of the OR forces a large number of nurses into what is essentially mandatory overtime. Unlike in other workplaces, where a coworker might come in to complete the task for someone who needs to go home, the culture and the practice in the OR make this sort of shift highly unlikely. The nurses, who have tried to explain their problems with the new system, are frustrated and angry about the lack of responsiveness by Boston Medical Center management.

Janet Killarney describes how this intensification in the use of the OR affects the way patients are prepared for surgery:

> It used to be, before a patient could go into the operating room, . . . I would want to make sure my doctor was here, to at least see the doctor before [the patient] went under anesthesia. . . . But now, we rush the patient into the room if the surgeon is somewhere in the vicinity, if he's just getting out of his car and coming to the campus, if he's in the elevator, somewhere, we page and he says, "This is where I am. I'm coming now." As long as he is somewhere near the building, then we can proceed. (2001, 18)

Janet, like her colleagues, is also concerned about both the requirements of informed consent and the impact on the patient of being rushed through what they describe as "an assembly line."

> You can't ask somebody to sign consent when they've been given a narcotic or some anesthetic. The doctor's in the change room putting on his pants. Your patient is out. Before, it used to be that if you saw the face of

the surgeon, you could bring the patient into the room. . . . This [new system] doesn't fare well to me. It's just that the bar is getting lower so you can get the patient in the room on time. What have you actually gained? . . . You're trying to make a business out of something that really has to be an art form. You have a patient who's scared. I can't imagine you're twenty-eight years old and you've got cancer in your breast. All you're concerned about is getting the patient in the room because that is going to make us $500 at the end of the day. (2001, 18–19)

As Janet explains further, many nurses in the OR at Boston Medical feel squeezed between their professionalism and concern for patient care and the demands of a corporate hospital:

The more operations you can do in one day, the more money you can make. It's a rush. They want you to be thorough, and they want you to be committed to the patient, and be culturally sensitive, and aware of all the ramifications of what it means to give anesthesia, what it means to do tonsils on a four-year-old baby, but hurry as fast as you possibly can to do it. (2001, 13)

While filling the ORs with elective surgery, the economics of managed care can have the opposite effect on emergency surgery. Physicians sometimes refuse to perform surgery, and it makes Jean Griffin furious. She explains:

I have been many a night in the OR calling a plastic hand surgeon or an orthopedic hand surgeon to come take care of this firefighter's crushed hand injury. And they'll say, "I'm not getting paid for it. I'm not coming in." And that's a big difference that I've seen over the last ten years . . . And I questioned a few, "Didn't you take the Hippocratic Oath? How could you do this?" (2001, 18)

A Culture of Caring in a Corporate Environment

What we see among these nurses is the clash of two cultures: the nurses' culture of caring, and the corporate culture of Boston Medical. Back to its earliest roots, nursing is about caretaking. Thomas Rotch made this point clear in his address to the graduating class of the Boston City Hospital Training School for Nurses in 1890:

By a glance we indicate to you, who are behind us at the helm, what must be done, quickly, firmly, unhesitatingly, without question, . . . [you]

whom alone in the hour of danger we can trust, are at your post, cool, trained, unswerving in your absolute obedience to us. . . . One great secret in nursing is to have tact. Do not talk too much. Do not consider it necessary to instruct your patient in anatomy or physiology, nor in the symptoms of the different diseases. In nursing a child, be gentle and sympathetic to its mother as well as to the child. (Boston City Hospital 1891, 26)

Though much has changed in the skills required of nurses since 1890— they no longer need to know how to apply leeches—in many ways what is expected of nurses has changed very little. SEIU Local 2020 president Celia Wcislo points out that the expectations for nurses are inextricably linked with expectations for women in general.

I sort of see nursing as the epitome within the institution of the role of women in the narrowest sense. You're to take care of everyone, pick up the slack for everyone else, keep the floor clean, get the food there, get the kid's temperature taken, get them their medicine, go to work, do everything, make sure the house is clean so that your husband, the doctor, is happy when he shows up. If you're taught that is your role in life and you have a job that reinforces it institutionally all the time, it is very hard to separate your work life, what you've always thought you were going to be as a woman, and what your role was. (2002, 7–8)

These values are strong among the working-class women who became nurses at the City Hospital and now work for Boston Medical. Many, like Mary Katides, were the caretaker in their families as they were growing up. This made them incredibly dedicated to their patients and the doctors they served. Jean and Mary, like many women, were attracted to nursing because it was one of the few professions—when they were coming of age— that allowed women to be the primary caretakers of their own children and still hold a job. Many nurses accomplished this by working nights, weekends, and other alternative shifts to avoid day care. In her early days in nursing, Jean worked as a visiting nurse and made arrangements to bring her infants along with her. Later, she explains, when she came to Boston City Hospital,

I got this job in the operating room, with full-time nights. And, I might add, I've done full-time nights for about twenty years. Again, to prevent day care. And it took its toll on me, basically going sleep deprived for so many years. But I don't have any regrets, you know, because my children always knew that their mother was going to be there for their school plays and to pick them up. (Griffin 2001, 6)

Mary had a similar experience:

I worked mostly at a nursing home right close to home because I had two young kids at that time. So I worked eleven to seven shifts usually, whenever I could, because of the whole child-care issue and everything. At that time I was married, so my husband was home [at night]. It always was me who did the sacrificing. I mean, I don't like working eleven to seven, but it was always me who was ultimately responsible. (Katides 2001, 1)

Sharon, who also worked nights, says, "My kids used to think I made doughnuts. I'd come home with doughnuts in the morning, and so they thought that's what I did at night—when they were very little" (2002, 3–4). Jean describes the toll working the night shift and alternative hours can have on nurses, particularly as they get older:

I didn't know how abnormal my life was, or how tired I was, till I went on days. Because I call it "being on a merry-go-round." Laundry, food shopping, my house was getting done, the family was happy. Everyone was happy; I was miserable. But again I was willing to make those sacrifices as long as this one was happy and this one had his ironed shirt and there was food in the pantry. (Griffin 2001, 8)[2]

Even working these alternative hours, it is not always possible to arrange complete coverage for children, especially for single parents. As Mary remembers, "All my money was just going to day care. The girl across the street, I had to pay her eighty to a hundred dollars just to fill in the spaces, and then I'd have another day care for after school. It was just unbelievable the money that you go through." But even finding day care was not easy. "For nurses it's always been a problem, even for regular day care. They don't open at six in the morning" (Katides 2001, 5, 22).

Mary has found a way to resolve some of her child-care issues. Her older sons, twenty-four and twenty-one years old, live downstairs in a duplex; she and her nine-year-old daughter live upstairs. While she still needs to use other people for child care, having her sons available takes the edge off and cuts down on expenses. "They come upstairs at night, they help out a lot" (2001, 4). But work still intrudes on the life she is building for herself and her daughter.

Even though many nurses, like Jean and Mary, worked nights and weekends so they could raise a family, it is difficult to find a nurse who enjoys the erratic schedule and working nights. Janet Killarney describes the impact on her of working nights:

> I don't think my sleeping patterns will ever be the same. I'm disrupted. I'm damaged goods, I tell you. I have a panic, even if I'm not tired, if it's getting to be ten-thirty, eleven o'clock at night and I'm not near where I should be. It's like, panic is kind of a dramatic word, but it's some anxiety of being in bed, because of being sleep-deprived. (2001, 23)

Esther confesses that "some people actually vomit every time they work nights, and it's tough because your whole biorhythm is really—you're trying to train something or re-train something that shouldn't be re-trained." Like Jean's, her sleep patterns have been permanently altered.

> Four hours is the most I can sleep in a row, and that's unusual. I usually sleep three hours and I wake up and have to do something, take a walk, because since the kids were in school I could sleep three hours in the morning while they were in kindergarten, while the youngest one was in kindergarten. So I just over the years, I sleep a three-hour nap, when I go home I'll sleep for two or three-hours, get up, go back and sleep two or three hours before I come to work. Even through my nights off I have a tough time staying asleep. (2002, 8–9)

Shift work has been associated with many health risks. The Nurses Health Study found for example, that "women who worked rotating night shifts for more then 20 years had an 80% higher risk of breast cancer than women who did not work such shifts" (2006a, 4).

Besides what it does to your body, nurses point out, working nights also puts you out of step with the rest of the world. Janet says, "The worst part is that no one who works the day shift, who has never worked a night shift, really quite understands it." She continues:

> My mother would call me like at noon, when I had just gotten to bed, and say, "Hi, what are you doing?" knowing that I had to work. She just didn't understand. It would be like calling someone at 2:00 a.m. and waking them up to have a conversation. No matter how you explain it, you just have to take your phone off the hook, and you miss messages. (2001, 4)

Another nurse, Jessica, explains how her work schedule affects her marriage:

> My husband and I are not even on the same schedule and I go, "You know what, I can't hang with you. It's my work schedule day. I just can't do this. You know? I have to be in bed with lights out by ten." Then I go, shit! I can't sleep! What is my problem? Am I thinking about this job that I'm hating to go in for because I know you can't go to work without a brain. You can't go to work half-assed, in plain English. Because people's lives depend on you being able to jump, your neurons have to pop like crazy. You can't go in there emotionally a mess. (2002, 12–13)

In addition to their working irregular schedules, the culture of caring means that, if there is an emergency or if someone calls in sick or if the hospital is short-staffed, nurses stay past their regular shift as a matter of principle. The patients come first, no matter what. In some hospitals this principle was a formal part of the employer's rules—nurses who left patients unattended at the end of their shift could lose their licenses—but it hardly needs to be mandated, given that it is an integral part of the nursing profession.

Even in the best of circumstances, in small, community-based hospitals and before the ravages of managed care, nurses had challenging working conditions: irregular hours, no regular lunch and break times, and dual loyalty to patients and doctors which often left them exhausted. But the intensification of work resulting from the corporatization of health care has, for many nurses, pushed an already a tough set of circumstances over the top. Some nurses at Boston Medical work ten-hour days. Others work twelve. A few, like Janet, work the day shift from 7:00 a.m. to 3:00 p.m., but unlike senior employees at most other workplaces, all nurses at Boston Medical are required to work an evening shift and a weekend shift once a month, according to explicit language in their union contract (SEIU 2001, 10). At the old Boston City Hospital, nurses with ten years' seniority were exempt from this requirement, but that exemption "went by the wayside" when the hospitals merged (Killarney 2001, 10).

In addition to the already grueling regular schedule, nurses in the OR at Boston Medical are regularly required to work mandatory overtime. Sometimes, as Jean explains, eight hours can be stretched to sixteen:

> I was upset that I was handed this mandatory overtime Saturday night, 11:00 p.m. to 7:00 a.m., because I am working Sunday 7:00 a.m. to 3:00

p.m. And I don't mind doing a double, 7:00 in the morning till 11:00 at night. I choose to do that now and then, to have that extra day off. But I can't be here all night and then work all day at age fifty. I can't. (Griffin 2001, 22–23)

It is hard to think of another profession where a senior worker, with more than twenty-five years' experience, making close to $100,000, is expected to work double shifts, evenings, and weekends. At Verizon, management asserted its control by the Taylorization of the labor process of customer service representatives. While portions of nursing work at Boston medical have been stripped off and given to less skilled workers, nursing remains a highly skilled profession and not subject to the same kind of management control that obtained in the call center. Yet as at Verizon, management exerts its control at Boston Medical through the scheduling of hours.

In the OR, overtime results when surgery that extends beyond one's normal shift—which happens frequently because of how tightly the ORs are booked as Boston Medical Center continually works to increase revenue. "It's quarter of four," Jean explains.

> I'm going to assume, I guess I have to stay and finish the case. The case could end at 4:30 or the case could end at 5:30. Now, what if I was a mother who has to pick my child up from day care? And if I was up front, I can't break scrub to go on the phone. I could ask my circulator to call. If she's too busy, she can't call. So these are the things that are happening, and this is why we are losing OR staff. Because people need to have control of their lives. (Griffin 2001, 21)

Nurses at Boston Medical cope with the tough schedules, the off-shift work, and the overtime by swapping shifts and covering for each other. Doing this feels less like helping out the hospital than helping out one of their colleagues, and, by their reports, they do a lot of it. Like soldiers on the battlefield, it is the commitment to their colleagues that drives nurses at Boston Medical to work more than they should. As Mary explains, "There's a woman who's in her sixties, who doesn't have a car, and she has to do night rotations every so often, or be on call. Now I'll take hers. You know what I mean? There's some people that you will step in [for]. Another woman has kids and I'll take the second half of the three to eleven, seven to eleven. I'll take the seven to eleven, find somebody for three to seven" (Katides 2001, 24–25). No matter how tough it gets, Sharon says, "Somewhere in that group of nurses will be somebody who's going to say, 'I'll do the floor tonight.' Nobody's going to walk off a case. Nobody's going to walk out" (2002, 13–14). Mary adds, "At this point, you don't even care about the money. A lot of times it's really just kind of helping each other" (2001, 25).

Helping each other out and being called on by management to fill in for irregular hours, however, often affects nurses' health and well-being. One of the first things to go is mealtime. "Sometimes," Jessica says, "you'd like a good meal and you go sit down and you'll be eating and you'll get, 'Sorry to interrupt your lunch. I need you. . . .' They have no problem about interrupting us. The patients don't have any problem about it. Visitors don't have any problem" (2002, 17). In her research on nursing and break times, Ann Rogers found that "nurses reported having a break or meal period free of patient care responsibilities less than half (46.6%) of the shifts they worked" (Rogers et al. 2004, 512).

Food in general is a problem. "Eating Chinese food at three a.m.? Even though you're working and you're active," Janet says, "it's just not a healthy way to live" (Killarney 2001, 4). And, Suzanne Gordon suggests, "obesity, which is associated with stress, is a significant problem among nurses, particularly in North America" (2005, 307). As Jean Griffin tells it, "It was taking its toll on me. I was miserable, being I'm older. I was 35 when I had my youngest. I had started to gain weight. I called it silent weight gain. You know, a few pounds every month when you are working nights, and you just try to attack that and you can't. When you are tired you just gain" (2001, 6). Given the culture of caring, nurses tend to sacrifice their own health to take care of their patients. Jean Griffin talks about running "from 2:30 to 11:30 nonstop, no bathroom privileges, no water privileges, no supper. I would go home and I would be so crippled, the next day I don't know if this is worth it" (2001, 26).

Jean, Mary, and Janet agree that much of the overtime and the need to call nurses in on their days off is just poor management. Despite surgeries routinely taking more time, management has failed to adjust staffing in the OR. Unlike scheduling at Verizon, which is overly formal and mechanical, scheduling at Boston Medical, according to the nurses I spoke with, seems underplanned and poorly executed. Janet asserts:

I'm of average intelligence. So if I can figure it out, the people who are getting paid to figure it out, what are they doing? That's what I don't understand. You are unwilling to let people balance their schedules, so then this poor person has to stay, and I have to make three phone calls for her from the [operating] theater. How effective do you think she is being? How much do you think she wants to come here tomorrow, because the same thing might happen. She had her eight-year-old son get off the bus and there is no one there to pick him up. How dare you! What are you doing in all these meetings that you can't figure this stuff out? (Killarney 2001, 28)

The SEIU Local 2020 president, Celia Wcislo, tells how the union conducted research on the problems with scheduling at Boston Medical. "[We] just sent one person to every floor over the last four hours and we got a calculator and added up" the holes in the nursing schedule for the week. Doing this very simple experiment, they discovered 1,100 regularly scheduled shifts for the current week that were unfilled. Even management, she reports, was surprised with the number: "I mean they turned white . . . you could see them think, 'No wonder this sucks'" (2002, 10).

In the 1980s I conducted research in a small New England electronics assembly plant (Juravich 1985) where, I found, industrial workers were plagued by "chaos on the shop floor": materials that weren't right, machines that didn't work, and bosses who gave contradictory instructions. The workers found these conditions extremely frustrating. Boston Medical personnel feel very similar. Despite the large and growing number of managers, management just hasn't been able to figure out how to make staffing work. Maybe it works on paper or on financial spreadsheets, but it is clearly not working in the operating rooms or on the floor at Boston Medical. Or maybe the administration there lets the inadequate staffing happen as long as the revenue keeps coming in. Celia Wcislo suggests that this is not only the case at Boston Medical but a problem nationwide: "The whole health care industry is in such economic turmoil that they're reacting and not planning" (2002, 4).

As it is for the women at Verizon, the impact of mandatory overtime is especially tough on nurses with children, particularly single parents. Not knowing what your schedule may be from day to day makes planning extremely hard. Mary tells how something as simple as a birthday party becomes impossible, with all the demands on her time:

The last morning I worked was Thursday morning, and my daughter had a birthday party Saturday. So I was supposed to work Friday night and then I was going to do my daughter's birthday party Saturday. Well, they threw it at me Thursday morning that I'm going to have to be on call Saturday night. . . . As it was, I'm going to be tired Saturday for her party. And, you know, I'm not getting any sleep that day, not too much, then I've got to worry about a call Saturday night. So, I was pretty upset with that, although I ended up not getting called in on anything. But it's always, "You need to be waiting." (Katides 2001, 4–5)

The rotation off shift continues to be difficult for Mary Katides and, she explains, interferes with the things she wants to do with her daughter, things that many other parents take for granted:

When I worked days and was thrown onto one or two nights, I knew it was going to take me a week to recover, whether I was twenty-five or thirty-five or forty. It just does a bad job. It is a tough balancing job. I work four nights a week. I can't do the five. That would just throw me for a loop. Because I'm a Girl Scout leader right now. I mean, I do want to do that stuff on the side. I'm very involved with kids. I'm a Girl Scout leader and then I work at the Y doing strength training for kids. . . . My boyfriend always says, "Can't you get a nine-to-five job?" (2001, 12, 11)

Jean Griffin recounts the story of a nurse she worked with and later had to represent in a grievance meeting:

She got a phone call from her son at school, he's seven years old and has delayed speech. He bumped his head and he wanted her to come get him because they cannot take the chance of sending him on the school bus. She doesn't get any support from the nurse supervisor, so I tried to comfort her. . . . Three months before she'd put in a request, "Please drop me down to 24 hours." And she was told no there was no position, she has to stay working full-time. . . . She said, "I'm going back to being secretarial." (2001, 28–29)

Staffing, Overtime, and the Nursing Shortage

Over the past several years the popular media have been abuzz with stories about the shortage of nurses across the United States. The Health Resources and Services Administration, a division of the U.S. Department of Health and Human Services, reports that "by 2020 the national shortage is projected to increase to more than 1 million FTE [Full Time Equivalent] RNs"

(HRSA 2007, 1), which means that nurses will be able to fill only 65 percent of the projected demand. "States with the projections for the most acute shortages, such as Alaska (70 percent) and Connecticut (57 percent), are scrambling" (Holtz 2007, 2).

The most common explanation for the nursing shortage is that too few young people are entering nursing. Typical is *RX for the Nursing Shortage*, published by the American College of Healthcare Executives. Authors Julie Schaffner and Patti Ludwig-Beymer argue that the shortage is "driven by a fundamental shift in the labor market . . . characterized by fewer nurses entering the workforce." Further evidence for this argument is that those working in nursing are significantly older as a group than those in many other occupations. RNs in their forties "dominate the workforce," outnumbering those in their twenties "by 4 to 1"[3] (2003, 3, 6). As part of this argument about why too few nurses are entering the profession, recent attention has turned to the limited capacity of nurses' training programs. In 2005, for example, "147,000 qualified applicants were turned away from U.S. nursing schools" (National Public Radio 2007, 2). Part of the problem is the shortage of nursing faculty and the difficulty of attracting nurses to teaching. As Jeff Holtz points out, registered nurses with master's degrees "can make about twice as much working for a hospital as they can serving on a faculty" (2007, 2). In an effort to remedy this problem, HRSA and a number of states have put together grants and programs for potential nursing students and more recently for the expansion of nursing programs.

The problem with this explanation—which has been unquestioned by government and business leaders alike—is that it ignores the large number of nurses who *leave* the profession each year. Gordon Lafer writes:

> Despite the dire projections, there is not an actual shortage of nurses at this point in time. Instead, there is a shortage of nurses willing to work under the conditions currently offered by the hospital industry. In the year 2000, there were nearly 500,000 registered nurses in the United States that were choosing not to work in the profession for which they trained. (2005, 31)

In short, the issue is not that we have not trained enough nurses but that those we have trained are not willing to work under the conditions they face in today's corporate health care environment. Suzanne Gordon points to a "shortage of people willing to put up with the conditions under which they are asked to deliver hands-on care to the sickest, most vulnerable people in our societies" (2005, 9). And Fay Satterly, in *Where Have All the Nurses Gone?* writes: "It is not difficult to understand why nurses are unhappy. The major change that occurred in the work environment in the 1990s—including a big increase in workload—were all instituted without their input. They feel undervalued, unheard, and worry that they cannot provide safe, adequate care for the patients they serve" (2004, 13).

Reinforcing what I have seen at Boston Medical, Lafer reports that almost half (47.5 percent) of nurses surveyed, when asked why they had left the profession, cited "more convenient hours in their new jobs" more than any other factor (2005, 31). The issue of work hours is real, as the stories of the nurses at Boston Medical attest, and the current situation is forcing nurses from their field. Lafer cites research conducted by the American Nurses Association:

> When one recent survey asked nurses to describe how they felt at the end of the day, nearly 50% report feeling "exhausted and discouraged," 40% felt "powerless to effect change necessary for safe, quality patient care. . . ." Perhaps most disturbingly, 55% of nurses report that they would not recommend a nursing career to a friend or child. (Lafer 2005, 32)

An abundance of survey research demonstrates how dissatisfied nurses are with their work conditions (e.g., Aiken et al. 2002; Sochalski 2002). And the problem is not just in the United States. According to Public Services International, a global union federation that represents 7 million health care workers worldwide, "The working conditions are driving many nurses from their profession early. They are the victims of shrinking budgets, mismanaged privatization and the urge for market-driven policies, leading to unreasonable nurse-patient ratios, excessive workloads, growing incidence of workplace violence, low wages, under-valuing of work, and inadequate protections for occupational hazards" (2007, 1).

With the rapid changes in health care, the work they face is now fundamentally different from what it was when they entered nursing. "I think that's why there are so many RNs in Massachusetts," Wcislo says, "I bet a third to forty percent or more aren't practicing because they are sick of the profession. Wouldn't go back if you paid them. They might pick up a shift here and there but they're not permanently going to tie up their lives" (2002, 11).

In some ways nurses have reached the tipping point in terms of what they can withstand in the corporate-run hospital. As part of the culture of caring, Sharon suggests, "Nurses have always been expected to say, 'How much harder can you grind that wheel?' Our nurses need to know that they can stand up and say, 'Look, I'm exhausted. I cannot. I have kids. I cannot. I need to be out of here'" (2002, 13–14). And, because of the portability of their training and the high demand for nurses, they do get out. Unlike the Verizon customer service representatives in Andover, who feel trapped in a job they cannot afford to leave, nurses are showing how they feel about their jobs by leaving.

In an important development for the nursing profession, research conducted over the past several years has demonstrated a clear link between staffing levels, nurses' hours, and patient care. A series of studies by Linda Aiken, for example, has shown a clear link between staffing level and patient morbidity (Aiken et al. 2002). According to the Department of Professional Employees, "Patients in hospitals with the lowest nurse-to-patient ratio (eight patients per nurse) have a 31% greater risk of dying than those in hospitals with four patients per nurse" (2004, 2).

A major study by the National Academy of Sciences found "overwhelming evidence that, as levels of nurse staffing rose, the quality of care improved, because nurses had more time to monitor patients and [could] more readily detect changes in their conditions." These researchers also examined the impact of long nurses' hours on patient care. They report, "Long hours pose one of the most serious threats to patient safety, because fatigue slows reaction time, decreases energy, diminishes attention to detail, and otherwise contributes to errors" (Pear 2003, A20). Similarly, Ann Rogers found that when nurses work over twelve and a half consecutive hours, "they triple the risk of making an error" (2005, 1).

Fatigue is a major issue among nurses, but controls on nurses' hours are largely nonexistent in the health care industry. A member of the National Academy of Sciences panel points out, "Virtually every other industry in the country pays more attention to fatigue than we do" (Pear 2003, A20). As Boston Medical nurse Sharon argues:

If the eighteen-wheeler driver can't drive more than 16 hours, why not me? If I'm a nurse and I've worked a sixteen-hour shift or a twelve-hour shift in a place where acuity is [important] . . . even when acuity is not high, at the end of 12 hours, I'm looking at meds that all start with the same letter and end with the same letter, and I have to take ten extra minutes to figure out that it's really what I'm supposed to be giving. I'm tired! And if my age is forty-five and above, I'm more tired! (2002, 8)

Another Boston Medical nurse describes how she feels after working a twelve-hour shift: "I go home . . . and I'll tell you, I don't want any sensory stimuli. I don't think my husband understands. I don't want lights on. I don't want noise" (Jessica 2002, 4).

The National Academy of Sciences report goes on to suggest that "state officials should prohibit nurses working more than 12 hours in any 24 hour period or more than 60 hours a week" (Pear 2003, A20). Of course this is an important policy initiative—but *what has happened to the American workplace when a major scientific body has to argue the need to reduce the work week to sixty hours and to limit mandatory overtime to twenty hours a week?* And even at those levels, what kind of patient care and quality of life for nurses is possible?

Historically, hospitals have always been twenty-four-hour operations and have always had language in employee handbooks or union contracts specifying nurses' obligations to adequately staff their facilities. Given its commitment to patient care, the nursing profession hardly needed this to be codified in an agreement with the employer. Regardless of what a contract says or doesn't say, the culture of caring has always kept nurses on the job long past what might be healthy for them.

In smaller hospitals and more informal work organizations such as the original Boston City, it was considerably easier to balance out hours and shifts, in part because there was an adequate supply of nurses. With the current shortage of nurses, however, employers like Boston Medical are loath to create more flexibility, even though more flexibility would lead to higher retention of nurses. Nurses, like workers at Verizon, have extremely difficult and stressful but well-paying jobs. And while workers at Verizon stay in their jobs because they can earn much more there than anywhere else, nurses at Boston Medical stay in positions with massive numbers of regular work hours and overtime not because of the money but because of their commitment to patient care. Even though contractually limiting hours in this new corporate environment might be a very good thing for nurses, in some ways it is anathema to the nursing profession.

Rather than focusing on contractually restricting hours of work, nursing unions, along with patient groups, have advocated guidelines ensuring minimum staffing levels, largely on the state level. In 1999, California was the first state to pass a "safe-staffing bill" (Gordon et. al. 2008). The evidence is overwhelming that a lower nurse-to-patient ratio saves lives. "If all hospitals increased RN staffing to match the top 25% best staffed hospitals, more than 6,700 in-hospital patient deaths, and overall 60,000 adverse outcomes could be avoided" (California Nurses Association 2005a, 1). The California legislation resulted in adding more than 80,000 nurses to the workforce from 1999 to 2007, and many were "nurses returning to the profession" (Hall 2008, 2).

Although other states have been slow to follow California's lead, in 2008 efforts were under way in Massachusetts, where Boston Medical is located, to enact safe-staffing legislation. Despite stiff opposition from employers, a report by the Massachusetts Department of Health Care Finance and Policy shows that with "record profits in 2007 approaching $500 million in the second quarter," a 35 percent increase over 2006, the industry could indeed afford to introduce safe-staffing measures. John McCormack, co-chair of the Coalition to Protect Massachusetts Patients, calls these profits "shocking" especially because they coincide with the publication of a Department of Public Health report that "an estimated 2,000 Massachusetts patients a year die needlessly from preventable hospital-acquired infections, infections that recent scientific studies link to poor RN staffing in hospitals" (Massachusetts Nurses Association 2007, 1)

A Finger in the Dike: Techs, Travelers, and Subcontractors

Despite overwhelming evidence of the beneficial effect of safe staffing on both patient care and the work lives of nurses, the health care industry in the United States, as at Boston Medical, has largely moved in the opposite direction. Although desperate to attract and hold on to RNs, hospitals and health care providers, rather than creating manageable jobs to stop the flight from nursing, have for the most part responded by offering more money—the bread but not the roses. Some hospitals, adopting a practice from professional sports, provide signing bonuses. In Columbus, Ohio, nurses receive up to $6,000 for signing on to hospital work (Hoholik 2005, 1). St. Peter's Hospital in Albany, New York, has gone so far as to use a model right out of eBay and Priceline: it has nurses bid on the hours they want and the pay rate at which they are willing to work (Grow 2003, 14).

The problem with this approach is that for many nurses it's not about the money. As Mary Katides tell it: "At this point, you don't even care about the money. A lot of times it's really just kind of helping each other out or something. The money does look nice, but you do want a life, number one, outside of work" (2001, 25). For Janet Killarney, too, it is about much more than just money:

> I think as you get older your values, or what's important to you, changes. I don't want to be tied down to my job. I have a profession, I don't have a career. It's something I want to incorporate into my life, not have it be my life. I don't feel that, in any place I've ever worked as a nurse, you get back what you put into it anyway. (2001, 21)

When financial incentives have not worked, U.S. hospitals and health care facilities have recruited nurses from overseas, largely from countries such as China, India, and the Philippines. The proportion of internationally trained nurses is growing rapidly. According to the *American Journal of Public Health*, "foreign-trained nurses made up 8.8 percent of all new registered nurses in the United States in 1990 and 15.2 percent in 2000." The same study reports that more and more of the nurses from outside the United States come from low-income countries: "In 2002, 21 percent of foreign-trained RNs originated from low-income countries, a doubling of the rate since 1990" (2007, 2).

Internationally trained nurses from less developed countries face economic and social pressures very different from those of their U.S.-trained counterparts. This difference often makes them more willing to accept overtime and erratic work schedules. Many are economically vulnerable because of debts for training and travel, and many, like the Guatemalans, send money back home to support their families. For example, it has been estimated that Filipino nurses, one of the largest groups of internationally trained nurses, sent $8 billion in remittances to the Philippines in 2004 (Brush, Sochalski, and Berger 2004).[4]

While the use of internationally trained nurses may provide a temporary solution for hospitals in the United States, it accelerates the shortage of nurses in the global South (Bieski 2007, 23). The availability of internationally trained nurses, especially from poorer countries, also allows hospitals

Jean Griffin, Boston

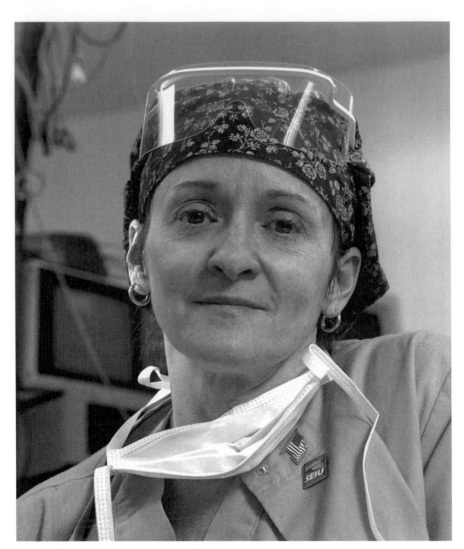

Janet Killarney, Boston

Mike Blair, Dalton

Glen Boden, Dalton

Pete Peras, Dalton

Glen Boden, Dalton

Bob and Gaye Sargent, Dalton

"Rosa," New Bedford

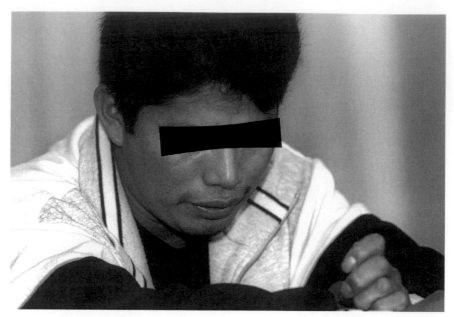

"Diego," New Bedford

Fish House Worker, New Bedford, MA

Call Center Representative, Andover

Call Center Representatives, Andover

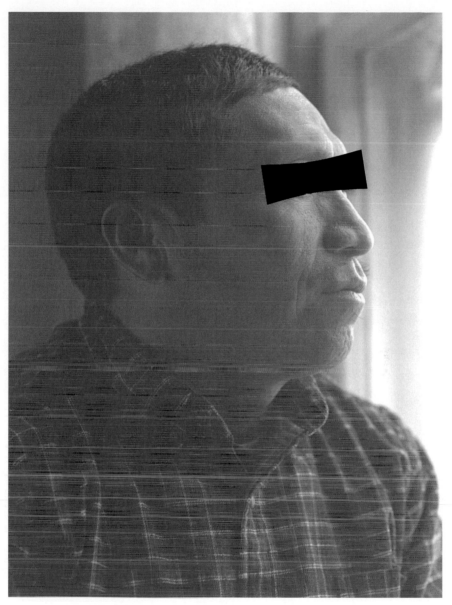

"Roberto," New Bedford

"Juan," New Bedford

to ignore the very conditions that led to the massive nursing shortage in the first place. "As long as hospitals feel they have access to an unlimited pool of foreign nurses," Cheryl Peterson, senior policy fellow of the American Nurses Association, argues, "there is much less pressure to address problems in the working environment" (Calbreath 2007, F-1).

Another Band-Aid that is growing in popularity is the use of part-time, per-diem contract or travel nurses. Taking a nod from private industry, hospitals that cannot find nurses willing to work under the conditions they offer contract the jobs out to third-party agencies who will guarantee staff. Boston Medical has started using travelers as nurses and as scrub techs. The idea of "traveling" is not new to nursing; for years, some nurses have not held steady jobs but instead have worked for short periods at different hospitals; this practice has allowed them to work on a more casual, as-needed schedule. What is new is the explosion of firms such as Access Nurses and NursesRX that contract with hospitals to provide nurses and surgical technicians. But, like offering signing bonuses or letting nurses bid on hours, using travelers is a short-term solution at best. As SEIU's Celia Wcislo suggests: "I think they hire travelers because of their inability to come up with anything more. Where do you get somebody? Fine, I'll offer them $5,000 to give me three months because I need someone today. It's just a bidding war . . . instead of them having an in-house training program, which you would think would be the logical thing to do" (2002, 15).

Traveling has increased not only because of the hospitals' needs but also because of the unreasonableness of the demands on nurses. The traveling companies have made the work attractive to nurses by offering what the hospitals themselves have been unwilling to offer—straight shifts, no nights or weekends. Jean Griffin explains why one Boston Medical tech plans to sign up to work as a traveler—though she may well end up working at Boston Medical.

> Our youngest person that we work with is a surgical tech. She's twenty-eight. She just had her first baby and twice already she wasn't relieved until 4:00, 4:30. And she lives in Marshfield. It's an hour drive and she didn't get home until 5:00, 5:30. She has a very supportive family that takes care of her baby, but she's fed up. She's been forced to take call, gets home at 5:00, 5:30, and gets called back in at 6:00. And it's happened to her too many times in the seven months that she's been a new mother, and she's leaving next week and she's going to travel. [She will] work for a

company, a private company, and they pay them comparable to what I am making in my salary. Plus they are providing them with some form of housing, beautiful housing. I know one of the scrub techs, who struggled as a single mom, who is now living in a $2,400 apartment in Boston, who is a travel tech working at Mass General. (2001, 21–22)

Suffering under the burden of the current organization of nursing in the OR at Boston Medical, Mary Katides finds the idea of becoming a travel nurse appealing:

Normal hours. Normal family life. So you can plan ahead of time. Your weekend's not going to be thrown off by something like a call. Just Monday through Friday. You can have weekends. We'll do this, that. It would be so nice to do that. Of course, it gets into every part of your life. Like I said, the family life. And then the social life, too. I mean, the weekends, I want to go out too. (2001, 11)

Nurses in the OR at Boston Medical have two major issues with the increasing use of travelers for scrub techs. First, as John, a nurse at Boston Medical, points out, "They're not mandated to stay and, on top of that, if the situation is bad they don't have any commitment to the institution and can leave." So, in an important way, the traveling arrangement has broken down nursing's culture of caring; as simply employees, travelers come and go as they please. Second, the use of travelers adds a new level of uncertainty in the OR, especially when a traveler is new. John suggests, "You don't know their skill level. You don't know where they're coming from. They're not familiar with what you're familiar with" (2002, 6). In the fever pitch of the OR, where every second matters, this can be a problem. Mary recounts a difficulty she encountered working with a traveler:

We were doing a back case. . . . I was nervous. First of all, it's a back. It's a big case, very specific. And [the traveler] was supposed to be on the case cart, checking out all the items. So, that's what I thought he was doing and I went back there and I saw there wasn't even a back kit on the case cart. And I said, "There's not even a back kit here." And then, he says, "Oh, yeah." So I went to the front desk and told them. I called downstairs, and the back kit was still being processed downstairs. It wasn't even available. And the person downstairs did not even relay it to the front desk. And then, thank goodness, by the time the surgeon got there, I did have my act together. I said, "Listen, they're still processing the back kit downstairs. It's not ready." He went jumping around and everything. But if we'd ever started that case, with me relying on this person, then I would be in a lot of trouble. (Katides 2001, 15–16)

The use of contingent labor in the OR has created new challenges for the nurses at Boston Medical, who must pick up the slack when a traveler does not bring the appropriate skills or experience to the job. Furthermore, Boston Medical is a teaching hospital and responsible for training interns and residents. John describes how an inexperienced traveler in a teaching hospital may put a patient at risk:

If a doctor writes a ridiculous order, we'll tell them, "Go back, please speak to your attending [physician]." A traveler, on the other hand, will carry it out, not knowing it's a ridiculous order because they're trained to think in the model that you don't question a doctor's order. This is entirely different, because it's a teaching hospital. You're not only supposed to question them, you're supposed to correct them. . . . Because, ultimately, if a doctor orders something that's totally ridiculous and you carry it out, the doctor is not responsible, only the nurse. So if you were to give a dose that's ten times the normal dose and you carry it out, it's your license and you're responsible. (2002, 6)

Boston Medical is using a similar contracting process with anesthesiologists. Rather than contracting with individual physicians, they contract with a large physicians' group that provides them with an anesthesiologist whenever one is necessary. As with travel techs, this process solves problems for both the hospital and the physicians on call. But what are the long-term implications of these changes? And how will they affect patient care? One of the characteristics of the ORs at Boston Medical used to be the stability of the OR staff. They knew each other, their strengths, their weaknesses, and their working styles. This familiarity can be critical during surgery, when seconds may make the difference between life and death. Or, as Janet has observed of the anesthesiologists:

You may see one of these guys every nine months, so you have to really pay attention to what he's doing. You want to make sure the patient is safe. You don't know these people from Adam. So, here comes your patient into the room and you don't whether this anesthesiologist is good or indifferent, so again you really have to advocate for the patient. (Killarney 2001, 12)

What happens when everybody is new? As Jean says, "I really feel, I mean, you can't have every OR person travel. You can't have it. It's like having a Police Department with all rookies" (Griffin 2001, 24). With the real shortage of nurses willing to work in and the flight of nurses from the impossible situations they're offered, managers efforts to buy themselves out of the crisis feel like little more than a finger in the dike. Celia Wcislo suggests that what the hospitals are doing is "throwing money to keep people for a little while longer to see if it'll keep them from breaking. . . . At some point they're going to break. The system's going to melt down. I'm more convinced of that than ever." She continues, "You're Band-Aiding as it's breaking out in another hole and you're running there as your other Band-Aid blows off" (2002, 9, 18).

Solving the Nursing Crisis

The nurses who work in the OR are very committed to their nursing profession and to their jobs at Boston Medical. Despite the merger and the intrusion of more corporate practices, they remain compassionate and committed to serving the poor, the homeless, and the victims of the worst that society has to offer. But, the hours, the night and weekend work, and the overtime are just too much. These nurses have in some miraculous way managed to handle the stress on their bodies and their minds, but at no small cost to themselves. They are exhausted and they are not sure that they'll ever really recover.

And despite the nurses' dedication, the impact of this corporate form of health care on patients is undeniable. As one Boston Medical nurse confesses: "I'll tell you, it's a scary thing. I hope I die at an early age because I don't want to be in the hospital. I don't know who's going to be left to take care of us. I'm looking at ten years and I figure, I'll fall and break my hip or something. I don't know who's going to be around—a whole bunch of nurse's aides with one nurse on the floor?" (Esther 2002, 6).

As both the experience of the nurses at Boston Medical and national research reveal, the health care industry has been moving in the wrong direction to solve the crisis in nursing, which is at the heart of the larger crisis in patient care. The fundamental flaw in the industry's effort to buy its way out of the nursing crisis with the use of techs, per diems, internationally trained nurses, and travelers is that such measures deeply undermine the culture of caring that stands at the core of nursing. If hospitals pay enough, they may be able to get enough staff in place to fit some corporate plan, but the question is, who will this staff be? If health care continues on the road it appears to be heading down, the staff will likely consist of a smaller and smaller group of RNs who have been pushed to exhaustion by the schedule and the overtime, and an increasing number of contingent workers who are less invested in the actual working of the hospital, its staff, and its patients. Even though actual bodies may be in place, and the books may balance, what kind of care will this staff provide? And will these efforts move toward solving the crisis in health care in some fundamental way?

Any real effort at reform will need to start by embracing and valuing the work and dedication of nurses like Jean Griffin, Janet Killarney, and Mary Katides and their commitment to caring. Hospitals need to develop ways to reward their commitment to their patients and their profession, rather than taking advantage of them with a corporatized system that is out of control. This reform must begin by instituting restrictions on work hours and overtime, at least to the level suggested by the National Academy of Sciences. It will also require the safe staffing levels which, as in California, will bring nurses back to the profession. If employers themselves do not institute these provisions, there will likely be more legislative action at the state level.

But more than just mechanical regulations, true reform involves engaging the nurses themselves in a process of change—a process from which modern corporate hospitals marginalize them. As Celia Weislo suggests:

> I think there is a lot they could do to sit down with their nurses and talk about the functioning of a floor, but there's so much chaos and so much to do, they don't take the time to do that. Not like labor management [formal cooperative programs] with all their hokey stuff, but just getting people's opinion about what would go smoother and how to do it. They are so driven by budget and overtime line items. (2002, 11)

At the same time, we do need to bring more women and men into nursing. Clearly, changing hospital practices that would keep Jean, Mary, and Janet in the profession would also help attract and keep younger nurses. But we also need to consider who will be entering the nursing profession and how they are getting there. Increasingly, hospitals and health care facilities want nurses who have a bachelor's degree. "They're pushing RNs to be not two-year diplomas but to be four-year employees," says Celia Wcislo. "So, on one hand, you're saying we will narrow what we are producing because it requires four years. With college monies, they're in debt and they are going to want higher wages. You're eliminating all the entry level jobs because, before, you could be a CNA [Certified Nursing Assistant] or an aide, go to school for a year and become an LPN" [Licensed Practical Nurse] (2002, 4–5).

One of the things that made Boston City Hospital work is that it was a community where staff could advance within the system. Women like Mary, who came from the community that City Hospital served, could start as an EMT, become an LPN, and end up as a highly skilled and trained surgical nurse, making a journey that is a large part of her commitment to the hospital and its patients.

It is not easy to replicate this level of commitment with a traveling nurse or a surgical tech who has a bachelor's degree. There is more to working in a rough urban hospital like Boston Medical than applying the skills of a newly graduated BAs. Celia Wcislo reports that with the new emphasis on BA nurses at Boston Medical, "We get these young girls from the suburbs who never really hustled their butt. And they get here and they're like, 'My dad never talked to me like this. What is this craziness out here?'" (2002, 9).

The evolving education of nurses provides many fewer opportunities for staff to move up the ranks, building their skills and their commitment. Nursing is increasingly becoming an "industry without a middle," as Bluestone and Harrison (1982) once described the computer industry. They pointed out that, unlike workers in manufacturing who could move from unskilled to semiskilled to skilled positions, the vast majority of people doing data entry in the computer industry had few opportunities to advance to programming. Nursing is beginning to look very much the same, with precious few opportunities for the increasingly deskilled techs and nurses to move up into skilled nursing positions.

"One thing I would do," Wcislo suggests, "would be to recreate some of the career ladders that they've gotten rid of over time. It would probably cause fights on the floors, but I'd probably say we should reinstitute LPN programs in certain places. We should be hiring from within and moving people up in a very steady, systematic way" (2002, 11).

The real challenge for the health care system is to figure out how to re-create the best of what happened at community-based hospitals like Boston City. Because of the economics of the industry, there is no going back; Boston City Hospital is no more. Yet, in its legacy and in the lives and work of nurses like Mary, Janet, and Jean, there is something yet to be learned.

Altar of the Bottom Line

TOM JURAVICH

I grew up at a time when a man could make his own fate
By the sweat of his brow, by the work he'd do, by what his hands
   could make
Now my life it hangs in the balance of deals brokered, made and signed
Far from this town my fate is sealed, at the altar of the bottom line

I should have seen it coming, how was I supposed to know?
Record production coming out of the plant, past three years in a row
They bought that place in New Hampshire, it wasn't much of a find
But what are we workers supposed to know, about the altar of
   the bottom line?

Though their debt kept on rising still they were not afraid
They built a series of overseas plants using all the machines we made
But as greed clouded all reason, start-up fell way behind time
Next quarter they'd have to ante up, at the altar of the bottom line

They fell into Chapter 11, there was not much more they could do
A couple of top brass lost their jobs, but we all lost ours too
Though we always made money, there was no way to buy time
They shut us down to raise the cash, for the altar of the bottom line

No it's not finished, no it's not through
How much more will we let them ruin? What will it all come to?
Though time it now passes, no, everything is not fine
How many more will be sacrificed, at the altar of the bottom line?

I grew up at a time when a man could make his own fate

4

ABANDONED

The Closing of Jones Beloit

They just came in one day and said they were going to close. They marched in security guards like we were a bunch of wild animals and posted them around the room and said they were going to close. Boden (2001b, 3)

As a matter of fact, I heard that we were closing . . . out riding in the car. I took a day off, and we were out riding in the car, and it come over the news station that Beloit was closing. . . . On the radio station, that's how I heard about it. Sargent (2001a, 6)

MACHINIST GLEN BODEN worked at Jones Beloit for thirty-four years. Thin and wiry, he has the intensity and focus of a man who has spent his life working in thousandths of an inch. Bob Sargent, "Sarge" as he was known in the shop, is quiet—reserved in a way. A welder at Jones Beloit, he was just a few months shy of having worked there thirty-four years. When on August 20, 1998, without warning, a plant that was a regular moneymaker, that earlier in the year had posted record profits, closed. In the final analysis, the decision to close Jones Beloit had little to do with the workers in Dalton, who had proved their skills and productivity; or with the condition of the equipment in the factory, which was excellent; or with the market for their product, which continued to be strong. Instead, the closing was the result of a global corporation's drowning in debt because of irresponsible decisions made by the CEO and asking the 300 workers in Dalton, and their families, to pay the price. After all they had contributed to their company and their community, they were simply abandoned.

Plant Closings and Job Loss

In the early 1980s, plant closing hit America hard. As Barry Bluestone and Bennett Harrison write in *The Deindustrialization of America*, "By the beginning of the 1980s, every newscast seemed to contain a story about a plant shutting down, another thousand jobs disappearing from a community, or the frustrations of workers unable to find full-time jobs utilizing their skills and providing enough income to support their families" (1982, 4).

The nation watched as whole industries disappeared, their ancient buildings and equipment left standing idle or torn down, leaving gaping holes in the industrial landscape. Michael Moore chronicled the devastation in his independent film *Roger and Me* (1989), and Bruce Springsteen sang about it on his chart-topping "Born in the USA" (1984):

> Main street's white-washed windows and vacant stores
> It's like nobody wants to come down here no more
> They're closing down the textile mill 'cross the railroad tracks
> Foreman say these jobs are going and they ain't coming back
> To my hometown.

Even Washington listened. In 1979, when Chrysler ran into the red and was facing bankruptcy, the Carter administration stepped in with more than $1.5 billion in loan guarantees in what was dubbed the "Chrysler bailout." *Time* magazine reported, "It was designed to prevent the nation's No. 3 automaker from sliding into a bankruptcy that could have put thousands out of work and send a shudder through U.S. financial markets" (1979, 1). In the wake of continual plant closings and catastrophic job loss there was growing talk about the development of an industrial policy in the United States. One of the strong voices was that of Robert Reich, whose book *The Next American Frontier* (1984) was widely circulated in policy circles. Congress debated the idea of an industrial policy late in 1983 and again in 1984. But the Reagan administration's devotion to free-market principles left industrial workers empty-handed. Despite Washington's failure, however, a public dialogue took place about the wreckage that plant closings brought to American families and communities.

By the mid-1990s plant closings had largely fallen off the radar screen. Did we believe that they no longer happened? Did Americans think that most factories had already been shut down? Or had they just become calloused, so that one more camera shot of workers leaving on their last day had become old hat. But as Louis Uchitelle reports in his *Disposable American: Layoffs and Their Consequences*, plant closings and layoffs were a regular feature of the U.S. economy. He writes, "At least 30 million full-time workers have lost their jobs since the early 1980s." Beyond this official statistic, he goes on to suggest, "a more comprehensive survey would have very probably found that 7 or 8 percent of the nation's full-time workers had been laid off annually on average—nearly double the recognized layoff rate" (2006, ix).

By any definition this was a massive social problem affecting millions of Americans annually. Yet you would not know this by reading the press or examining public policy or congressional debate. "Why," Thomas Kochan asks, "is there no public uproar and reaction to the economic devastation so many working families and communities have experienced in the wake of layoffs, restructuring, corporate scandals, and government indifference?" (2006, 377). In 2006 all three of the major U.S. auto manufacturers faced economic situations much more dire than those Chrysler went through in 1979, but the government showed "no signs of hurrying to the auto industry's rescue" (Porter 2006, 1). It was not until the Big Three were weeks away from bankruptcy in December 2008 that President Bush, under great pressure, reluctantly stepped in with a partial bridge loan.

We have seen concern about job loss only in the plight of white-collar and professional workers. As long as plant closings affect only blue-collar workers in manufacturing, they are treated as old news. Only when outsourcing and offshoring began to affect middle-class white-collar and professional jobs—as programing and technical work were sent to India and other places around the globe—did the practice engender a public outcry. Bronfenbrenner and Luce point out that "although the media has focused a great deal on the outsourcing of IT [information technology] and customer service jobs to India and, to a lesser extent, China, *manufacturing firms continue to be the primary source of exported jobs*" (2004, 79; emphasis added).

It is also important to recognize that the factors behind plant closures changed over some twenty-five years. Early in the 1980s, in industries such as steel and auto, companies closed facilities that had outlived their productive capacity because management had failed to modernize and update equipment and the production processes. This was documented in volumes such as Bensman and Lynch's *Rusted Dreams* (1988), Hoerr's *And the Wolf Finally Came* (1988), Buss and Redburn's *Shutdown at Youngstown* (1983). In other cases productive plants were shut when product lines changed or the market for what they produced disappeared (Dudley 1994; Milkman 1997). Although these closings were still devastating to workers and their communities, many were justified in terms of shedding unproductive and outmoded industrial facilities. As the economy played out in the new social

Darwinism of the Reagan administration, there would be winners and losers (Dudley 1994), and "the fittest would emerge, trim and tough from the harrowing rigors of economic competition" (Bensman and Lynch 1988, 2003).

In the leveraged-buyout mania of the late 1980s, however, something about plant closures changed. Bartlett and Steele, in their award-winning series of articles in the *Philadelphia Inquirer*, later published as *America: What Went Wrong?* (1992), document how a series of corporate raiders, including Carl Icahn, plundered more than $200 million over eight years from the Simplicity Pattern Company. In the end it was the huge debt from a series of leveraged buyouts that led the company to close facilities and shed jobs—not unproductive workers, the condition of the facilities, or the loss of demand for their product lines. As Seymour Melman wrote at the time, American business was now generating "profits without production" by buying and selling companies (1983). We watched as Icahn, "Chainsaw" Al Dunlap, and a host of other "vulture capitalists" in firms from Eastern Airlines to Sunbeam made millions, while productive workers were laid off by the thousands—collateral damage of the corporate raids. This was the beginning of a new era of plant closings.

With the financial meltdown in the fall of 2008 we have seen these kinds of plant closings mushroom, more connected to the finances of the firm than to their productivity or the quality of their work. This reminds us that we must be cautious of looking at today's plant closings through the images and stereotypes that emerged almost three decades earlier. In this way the closure of Jones Beloit is a thoroughly modern tale.

The Legacy of E. D. Jones

Approaching Dalton from the east on Route 9, you descend from a cluster of buildings at the top of the hill which make up Windsor, Massachusetts. As you enter Dalton, Route 9 turns into a wide, shaded lane with houses set back off the street. Once in town, you can't help noticing stately maroon signs hanging from white wooden signposts. Gold letters beneath a white triangular "roof" could be an advertisement for a colonial inn, a fine restaurant, or an exclusive college. They read "Crane and Company," with smaller white letters identifying various plants, parking, and property owned by the Crane paper company. Crane is famous for its heavy, high quality, high-cotton-content stationery that for generations has been "the choice of people wanting to make the best impression." Crane also makes paper for U.S. currency in one of its mills in Dalton.

Dalton is Crane and Crane is Dalton. In fact, the sign for the town hall, a brick and stone building with a tall clock tower, is almost indistinguishable from the Crane signs. Even after you glimpse brick factory buildings, mostly hidden discreetly behind trees and hedgerows, Dalton still feels like a classic small town. This is how the community thinks of itself:

> The residents of Dalton firmly believe that their community is quite simply the best community in Massachusetts in which to live and raise a family. Nestled in the incomparable beauty of the Berkshires, Dalton has an array of cultural and natural attractions. The town is home to two world-class papermakers, the Crane and Byron Weston companies, but cherishes its small town atmosphere. Dotted with schools, churches and athletic fields, Dalton is focused on family life. Its seven thousand residents are friendly and prosperous. (Dalton n.d.)

As you descend the hill from the center of Dalton heading toward Pittsfield, several large factories appear at the bottom of the hill along the Housatonic River. Pittsfield, the largest city in this part of the state, is a dozen or so miles north of Lee and Lenox, more fashionable spots in the Berkshires, a dozen miles east of the New York state line. Off the main street is the former Jones Beloit facility.

E. D. Jones started his original machine shop more than 150 years ago in the center of Pittsfield, which later also become home to a major General Electric plant.[1] Jones's machine shop slowly evolved into repairing and later building machinery for the nearby paper industry, including Crane and Company, the mainstay of Dalton. In 1959, E. D. Jones and Sons Company, as it was officially known at the time, was acquired by the Wisconsin-based Beloit Iron Works. Beloit also produced papermaking equipment, so it was an excellent fit. In the days before multinational corporations, Beloit, like Jones, was a family-owned firm. Beloit and its owners, the Neese family, created a wholly owned subsidiary, the E. D. Jones Corporation. It soon outgrew its Depot Street facility in downtown Pittsfield, and the new Jones Beloit company broke ground for a new plant on land bought from the Crane paper company in Dalton, right on the Pittsfield line.

"This parcel was ideal in that it was relatively flat and accessible from two sides, South Street in Dalton and Hubbard Avenue in Pittsfield," writes

Henry (Terry) Williams III, a third-generation management employee at the Dalton facility, in *From E. D. Jones and Sons to Beloit Fiber Systems*, a company publication marking the 150-year anniversary of the company. "It adjoined the Boston-Albany rail line, which allowed the New York Central railroad to lay a spur line into both the Receiving and Shipping bays" (1995, 39). Williams remembers attending the laying of the cornerstone at the new facility, which also serves as a kind of time capsule containing "various memorabilia of the business as it came along at that time. I'm actually told my picture is in there as a kid" (2001, 3).

The Jones Beloit plant made machinery for the "wet end" of the papermaking industry, turning wood products into pulp. This machinery included large tanks, agitators, and beaters, but the plant was best known for its huge torpedo-shaped refiners. "Our biggest machine used to be a 54 double D. It used to go 39,000 pounds, so almost twenty tons, maybe thirteen foot across and taller than me, so maybe seven foot tall," recalls longtime Jones Beloit employee Joe Zatorski (2001, 12). Glen Boden machined the disks that these machines used to grind pulp. "They're a round disc," he explains, "and anywhere from 20 inch diameter to 42, and they have machined slots. Some of the slots would be, let's say, 3/32nds, some of them would be 3/8 inch wide. They would rub against each other," much like the action of old millstones that ground grain (2001b, 2).

The machinery made at the Dalton plant was gargantuan, dwarfing the men who built it. Joe Zatorski describes the tanks they made: "We had to take them apart in sections to get them on tractor-trailers. I'm going to say . . . roughly a good thirty foot long. Maybe fifteen to eighteen foot wide [and] . . . ten to twelve foot tall. I always said I'd like to have one in the back yard for a swimming pool!" he says, laughing. "It would last you a lifetime" (2001, 12). Dave Cohen, a union representative, explains further: "A railroad ran through the plant to load the machines to ship to customers. The shop had very high bays. It had some of the biggest cranes to move the equipment of any machine shop in the entire area" (2001, 13).

Jones Beloit had an international reputation and a world market for its high-quality, durable machinery. You didn't buy a Jones Beloit machine for just a few years of use; you bought it for a lifetime. Boden talks about rebuilding an old Jones Beloit refiner:

I took one apart that was built probably in the 1940s. Came in there and I was kidding the guys, I said, "Here it is, something in here that's older than I am. . . ." It was an old 2,000 forty-two-inch refiner, the old style. They sat that thing down . . . had brass tags on them, real brass. They didn't put any plastic stickers on these things. The brass tags with serial number, the whole nine yards. You've got to admire this. These people were very proud of what they did. Very proud. And I want to tell you, when that machine left on the trailer truck to go to its new home, it was as good as the day it went out of the old Jones plant. They put those brass tags right back on it. It would be criminal not to do that. (2001b, 10)

"We used to have what we called loaners. So a company says, 'My double D refiner's gone bad.' We'd send them a loaner," explains Michael Messina, a former manager from Dalton. "They'd put it in the line and then they'd send us the other one and we'd repair the thing completely" (2002, 2–3).

Although some of the machinery in the shop was old, it was in excellent condition, and Jones Beloit owned many millions of dollars' worth of the latest CNC (computer-based numerically controlled) machining tools. "We had 7 inch horizontals, 6 inch, 5 inch, 4 inch horizontals," Messina explains. "We had verticals running from 24 up to 64 inches in diameter. We had all kinds of equipment and it was extremely updated, and a very sophisticated, highly-trained crew" (2002, 5). Terry Williams describes longtime Jones Beloit machinist Glen Boden:

> That guy was an extremely capable machinist. The guy could really do the type of work that many of the employees there could do because they were there for their working life and so they knew this equipment backwards, forwards, upwards, downwards. They could take the drawings and in some cases, it wasn't something you could just read off the drawing and be able to manufacture. You really had to have more than that. You had to have knowledge of how the whole thing fit together. (2001, 10)

Boden recalls his experiences growing up in a family-owned machine shop. "I was cutting bars back for my grandfather when I was about eight, nine years old. I was always fooling around in the shop. On a true mill route, I guess. Yes, I was always in the shop. I was lucky because my grandfather was a really good toolmaker" (2001b, 16), and Jones Beloit was a small-town plant that hired relatives and friends from the local area. As Boden explains:

My godmother's brother was a foreman over here for years. My next door neighbor when I was a little, little kid worked there. . . . My oldest boy is named after a toolmaker that I worked for when I first got here. My godchild, who I gave away last summer at her wedding, was one of the guys I worked with's daughter, and he passed away at a young age . . . and I gave her away. And it goes on and on and on. I mean, the girl in the office in Personnel, she and I went to kindergarten and through all of school together. In this plant, everybody had those interactions. These weren't just people you worked with. They were sometimes your relatives, they were mostly your friends. (2001a, 10–11)

Jones workers report that management, until near the end, contributed to this small-town feeling.

Those people you know you differed with, you respected. You knew that they knew what they were doing. You might not like what they were doing, but you knew they knew what they were doing. They were company people, the management. The old-time management. Company people. In other words, the company came before they did. . . . These were the kind of people that if your father or your mother died, they show up at the wake and genuinely feel bad for you. Come over to you when you were sick and say, "Hey look, if you need more time off than that, take it." Or go bail somebody out of jail. . . . When I first started there, the personnel manager went down and bailed this guy out, getting him back to work under the pretense, "I've got to get down and get this dope because I need him at work. . . ." The guy didn't really have any family and I know the personnel manager liked him, and he went down and he bailed him out. (Boden 2001a, 11)

Boden remembers that it was a close-knit group that shared their lives and their pain. "[Bob] Sargent and I had the same length of time there. I remember the day he cut his fingers off" (2001b, 13). Bob Sargent tells the story:

September 9, 1966—about 10:20 in the morning. I was working on a large, I think it was a pulper tank, I'm not sure. We were putting what they call a flange around the top of it and we had welded a couple of pieces on the flange and the guy I was working with picked it up with a crane. I was climbing up the ladder to put it in place and tack it up there and weld it. I was just getting up the ladder, he was bringing it over, I put my hand up on the top of the tank, just about ready to get to the top of the ladder and swing over so I could grab hold of it, and the thing came loose from the crane and come right down. I had my hand on the edge of the tank, like that, and it just hit it. At the time I didn't know it had happened. I just shook my hand. I climbed down and by the time I got down to the bottom of the ladder I noticed they were gone. (Sargent and Sargent 2001b. 28)

The workers at Jones Beloit were members of Local 212 of the United Electrical (UE) Workers and had organized back in the 1940s. They had built a reputation as a solid, honest, hard-working local. "They weren't just a good tight local amongst themselves," UE District President Judy Atkins recalls. "They participated in district council meetings quarterly. They participated. Whenever we called a rally, or an organizing drive, or a strike, or a contract, they always showed up. And in political action, we probably had more Labor Party members signed up in that plant than in any plant in the country at that time" (2001, 3).

It was a solid local union that stood up for its members. There were strikes in 1965 and 1978, and more recently a dispute involving a major restructuring of the incentive system. But because of the stability of the workforce, the locally based management, and its roots in a local family-owned business, the labor relations in the Dalton plant were, overall, positive. Former manager Michael Messina recalls that management and the union had "a pretty good working relationship. We had some union problems like everybody has, and there are always some bad apples in the barrel that really screwed up the situation as much as they could, but on the whole I would say it was a very good working situation. Most of the guys there were really good guys and they were fair about what they had to do" (2002, 3).

Through an interesting chain of events, in 1989 the Beloit company, including its subsidiary, E. D. Jones in Dalton, was acquired by the Milwaukee-based Harnischfeger Corporation. In 1967 William N. Goessel, who had started out in the Dalton plant, was promoted to vice president and general manager of Beloit. But by 1980 Goessel "was at odds with some of the high muckety-mucks and he quit" (Messina 2002, 6). He ended up as CEO at Harnischfeger, where he was responsible for a major turnaround of the firm, which had teetered on the edge of bankruptcy.

After Goessel left, Beloit hit some tough financial times. "There came a point in the mid-80s," Terry Williams explains, where the Neese family—I think it was kind of a transitional, generational thing—had gotten to the point where there was no one really interested in pursuing the business.

I think there was some interfamily squabbling about the whole thing and the business was sold" (2001, 4). Goessel, then at Harnischfeger, knew a bargain when he saw it and bought Beloit—a much larger company than Harnischfeger—for $175 million. Williams, whose father was a close friend of Goessel's, says, "It must have been sweet revenge for Mr. Goessel at the time to basically reacquire the business, and it became a subsidiary of Harnischfeger Corporation" (2002, 5).

From a corporate standpoint, this new merger was an excellent fit. Harnischfeger's product line of huge machinery for the mining industry was similar to Beloit's papermaking equipment. Restructuring after the Harnischfeger takeover slowly shrank the workforce at the Dalton plant to around 300, and management began to change. But overall, Jones Beloit continued to be a good place to work. Demand for Beloit products was high, and the plant continued to make money.

From Indonesia to Dalton: The Harnischfeger Boondoggle

In 1993, after Goessel retired, Jeffrey T. Grade took over as CEO of Harnischfeger. He was not the typical CEO for a heavy-equipment manufacturer based in the blue-collar town of Milwaukee. As *Barron's* reports, "He was the talk of the town. Folks gabbed about his fancy Italian suits, his dyed blond hair, and his affinity for expensive jewelry. By Milwaukee standards, he lived like a pasha, with a corporate jet and three company-leased cars, including a Range Rover 4.0 SE and a sporty 1998 Jaguar XJR."

Beyond the dress and the lifestyle, Grade was obsessed with his image. His official company biography reported that he had served as a Navy pilot in Vietnam. He regaled his subordinates with stories about his military heroics. "A former Harnischfeger executive remembers Grade at a dinner for the company's board of directors describing how he'd been shot down while on a classified mission deep in enemy territory and was forced to fight his way back to freedom Rambo-style" (Laing 1999, 25).

When the investigative reporter Jonathan R. Laing began looking into Grade's service record, however, inconsistencies began to mount. The timeline was all wrong. He was actually pursuing a graduate degree during much of the time he said he had served, and the plane he purportedly flew was not operational until long after he had left the service. Having been caught lying, he came clean to Laing, who reported in *Barron's*: "He admitted he hadn't been in the regular Navy, nor had he flown combat missions in Vietnam. Rather, he claimed that as a Navy ROTC cadet during college he'd been assigned to aircraft carriers during the summers of 1964 and 1965, going on training cruises" (1999, 25).

But Grade's lavish lifestyle and tendency to embellish his past were the least of Harnischfeger's problems. Despite his bravado, or maybe because of it, he turned out to be a very ineffective manager. According to Laing's analysis, "During Grade's six years in the top spot at Harnischfeger, he drove the company's debt to untenable levels with a number of high-priced acquisitions, a large stock buyback, and a poorly-timed diversification into the service and machinery parts businesses" (Laing 1999, 26). But the straw that broke the company's back was his deal to build a series of papers mills in Indonesia. Union rep Dave Cohen provides the background:

> Harnischfeger made every type of machinery; . . . they made machinery that chewed up the trees all the way to the machinery that made the paper. So they started looking at the forests, rain forests, because the trees would reproduce quicker. . . . So Harnischfeger and a lot of paper companies started looking at Indonesia. And that was when the Asian market was booming. (2001, 5)

In 1996 the Beloit division made a deal with an Indonesian firm, Asia Pulp and Paper, to supply four papermaking mills at the cost of $600 million. But this was not just a simple purchase and sale. Harnischfeger agreed to act as the general contractor building the plants. The agreement turned out to be a disaster. First, Harnischfeger failed to get financing quickly, and that put it behind on the agreed-upon timetable, which included high financial penalties for not finishing on time. The company also had no experience acting as a general contractor, and the plants were located in remote jungle areas. As a result, "cost overruns mushroomed. Harnischfeger badly underestimated the cost of pouring concrete, erecting buildings, bringing in utility services, and building roads to the mills. Smoke pollution from raging forest fires throughout the archipelago wreaked havoc on the construction crew" (Laing 1999, 27) Construction fell hopelessly behind, with no cash coming in and hundreds of millions of dollars of machinery, much of it made in Dalton, clogging the Harnischfeger warehouses.

Although an enormous blunder on Grade's part, the fiasco did not necessarily have to lead to the demise of Harnischfeger. But rather than dealing straightforwardly with the crisis, Grade tried to hide the cost overruns from stockholders. He used every accounting trick in the book to conserve cash and minimize debt, including stretching out payments to suppliers and selling receivables at the end of each quarter. As Cohen points out, "Instead of putting up warnings, saying they were in trouble over this, they were lying. [They] kept putting out press releases that everything was going fine. So that precipitated the big crisis at Harnischfeger" (2001, 7).

Citing data from Zachs Investment Research in Chicago, Laing explains, "Harnischfeger established a modern-day record of falling short of analysts' earning expectations in 14 out of 24 quarters since the beginning of 1993, when Grade assumed the dual posts of chairman and chief executive" (1999, 26). Company projections of earnings had no more basis in reality than Grade's escapades in Vietnam. Grade's compensation, as well as that of the rest of his management team, was tied to the stock price, so sheltering the bad financial news from the public allowed him to pay himself and his management team huge bonuses in the midst of this economic chaos at the company. Once the crisis became public, Grade responded by slashing 20 percent of the company's workforce, more than 3,400 workers in the United States. But management did not follow a rational process of shutting down the least profitable facilities. Because of the dimensions of their financial crisis, they were looking only at the short term—closing facilities to help balance their books.

Several years back the Beloit division had bought a plant in Nashua, New Hampshire, and two in Canada that had formerly been part of the paper division of Ingersoll Rand. These made a different set of products for the wet end of papermaking, including large stainless-steel drums and holding tanks. Although from a product standpoint the purchase may have made sense, many questioned the economics of the deal. "I think," Messina recalls,

> they paid $125 or $150 million for that one plant [in Nashua]. When I talked to Bill Goessel about it, he couldn't believe it. He said when he was there and they were going to buy that plant, they wanted $75 million. "I wouldn't pay $75 million because I didn't want these other buildings that they had, the satellite companies that were with them. . . ." A few years later this guy [Grade] comes along and pays almost double that for the same thing. (2002, 6–7)

Very quickly after buying the facilities from Ingersoll Rand, the Harnischfeger management shut down both of the Canadian plants and focused on the Nashua facility. Rudy Pfeiler and another Jones Beloit union official had traveled to the New Hampshire plant some years earlier to explore the possibility of organizing the facility. They were shocked that a manager let them tour the plant—an infraction he was later fired for. They were also shocked by the condition of the plant. For one thing, "They didn't have a paint booth," Pfeiler reports, "so everything was getting sprayed out next to the open-air cafeteria" (Pfeiler et al. 2001, 9).

Everybody on the shop floor in Dalton knew that buying the New Hampshire plant was a huge mistake. "We told them," Glen Boden recalls, "what, are you crazy? What are you buying that for? It's been running in the red for twenty years, they're almost going under, and you want to buy it and pay top dollar for that place to make tanks? What are you, nuts?" He pauses and adds, "We didn't realize that those people were going to end up in control of us" (2001a, 5).

Despite continued questions about the economic viability of the Nashua plant and the profitability of its products, the Beloit division moved its head-quarters out of Dalton to Nashua, and resources started flowing out of the old Jones plant. Pat Hubban, a Dalton employee and the union president, describes the situation they were facing:

> They wouldn't give us the resources we needed to do our day-to-day functions. You know, drafting operations. They started to downsize ours and move them up there. Engineering became centered up in Nashua, and we had . . . two or three engineers left in our plant. And we had some intricate parts. You had to have day-to-day engineering on our floor. And we didn't have it. All the resources went up north, even though they weren't making a profit. So, little by little, you could see that they were threatened by us. And I think they had a big empty plant up there. They had two big buildings and one of them was empty. (2001, 5)

As Jefferson Cowie points out in *Capital Moves*, "The firm that abruptly closes down and abandons its workers to the street, although perhaps the dominant image of the problem, is actually much less typical than the plant that undergoes a more subtle process of cutbacks, attrition, and the gradual relocation or elimination of industrial jobs" (1996, 6). The workers in Dalton knew very well that their facility was being bled for resources, but they had no idea that the consequences would be so dire.

To stave off bankruptcy, Harnischfeger undertook a major corporate re-structuring. Part of the plan was to keep the New Hampshire plant open while closing Dalton. According to Dave Cohen, it was all about money. "If they shut down the New Hampshire factory," he explains, "they would have to write that shutdown as a $120 million loss, because that was what they paid for it. If they shut down our factory, since it was fully paid for and it was making a profit, they could write it off as a $20 million loss. So it would show good faith to the shareholders" (2001, 9). With Grade's reputation so thoroughly sullied, shareholders would soon play a significant role in the reorganization of the company, in what Useem (1996) has referred to as "Investor Capitalism." And what was in their short-term self-interest had little to do with a rational assessment of the product line, its facilities, or its workers.

On August 20, 1998, union representatives received a letter from the Harnischfeger vice president for human resources, informing them, "Beloit has made a tentative decision to close the Dalton, Massachusetts, manufacturing facility." The letter gave no specific reasons, saying only that "the tentative decision to close Dalton is wholly unrelated to labor productivity or quality issues." That statement infuriated the Dalton workers. They knew they were an incredibly efficient plant making an excellent product that made money for Beloit.

The company attached "the required WARN notice for a complete shutdown of the facility by October 23, 1998," leaving little doubt among the union members that the decision was already final and that the company was moving quickly to close the plant (Beloit 1998a). The Worker Adjustment and Retraining Notification (WARN) Act is a piece of federal legislation passed in 1998 to offer "protection to workers, their families, and communities by requiring employers to provide notice sixty days in advance of covered plant closings and covered mass layoffs" (U.S. Department of Labor, 1).

In a press release the same day, the company pushed a theme that pervaded much of the public relations coming out of Beloit at the time, suggesting that the financial difficulties of the company were a result of a downturn in the industry. "The tentative decision has been made following two years of the most severe downturn in the history of the pulp industry, in which pulp prices dropped to nearly 50% of what they were in 1995" (Beloit 1998b). Undoubtedly, the paper industry was in a downturn, but this press release and the rest of the company public relations failed to point out that the crisis at Beloit was not primarily the result of market forces. Grade had recklessly diversified and expanded the firm, ballooning its debt, particularly with the Asia Pulp and Paper project, leaving Beloit unable to weather the market, as other firms in the industry were able to do.

It must have been a particularly bitter pill for Bill Goessel, who had navigated Harnischfeger through an extremely tough financial situation a decade earlier. "I'm terribly saddened by it all," he told Harnischfeger's hometown paper, the *Milwaukee Journal Sentinel*. Goessel had a particular affinity with the plant in Dalton and its workers there, having bought a house in the area for his retirement (Savage 2000a, 1D). As one rank-and-file worker tells it: "Years ago we had Bill Goessel, who was the CEO of the whole place. He told me a couple of times, 'As long as I'm in charge, this plant is going to be here. This is a productive plant.' Well, he finally retired and he put this other fellow from out West in charge and he just sunk the whole place. It was the beginning of the end" (Pfeiler et al. 2001, 11).

The day following the union's receipt of the notice of the "tentative" decision to close, company officials held a meeting in the plant to announce the shutdown. They came with a security force. Bob Sargent describes management's demeanor toward the workers: "It was like their mind was set. Like they were talking to wooden statues. They weren't even listening to them or communicating with them at all" (2001a, 16).

Fighting the Closing

The first few days were tough. Joe Zatorski remembers talking to his wife as soon as he heard the news. "I called her on the phone and I says, 'I got some bad news. They're closing.' She couldn't believe it. I just started thinking, 'Where are you going to apply for a job around here?' Because this ain't exactly a booming community, you know" (2001).

Despite his calm exterior, Bob Sargent's mind was "whirling":

> I'd say it didn't bother me, but it did bother me, and it still bothers me today if I'm just sitting and thinking about what happened. I had a lot of things going through my mind. I says, "What am I going to do about this and that—the insurances and stuff?" I never said nothing to anybody but I was really worried. I didn't know what was going to happen, you know? I was worried and mad all combined into one. It was a very frustrating time for me. I really didn't know what to do or what I was going to do. It took me quite a while to more or less calm down and start thinking straight, really. (Sargent and Sargent 2001b, 23)

For the first time in a long time Bob's wife, Gae, was also worried.

We certainly went into a downspin. We let a lot of things slide. I think we just went through an emotional turmoil. I thought [Bob] was going to have a heart attack before it was over. When he said, "I'm leaving in October instead of waiting until they kick me out in January," I said, "Well, jeez, I don't know!" Because, see, I was trying to figure out the bills for the year. What happened with me is I hurried up in September and tried to start to get all the money for the whole five or six months to live on, you know? It was kind of a bad thing trying to get the car insurance and fire insurance situated. Oil money. I tried to fit four years into two months' worth of pay, I guess. (Sargent and Sargent 2001b, 23)

Like the rest, Pete Peras, who started in the plant in 1974, was shocked when he heard about the closure. "I'm 49 years old. Where the hell am I going to find another job to make this kind of money. . . . I've got to start looking for a job. I worked at this place for 24 years." His wife, Kathryn, worried about the families and the children: "It's not just like the luxuries. It's the necessities. Will they eat? Will they be warm? I mean, you're talking about the Northeast up here. We have to heat our homes, and our gas and electric and stuff like that is more expensive than the rest of the country in the wintertime for us." She continues, "He worked hard for his job all those years and to get kicked like he did and here I am, I can't help him, I can't go out and get him his job, he's got to do that, but I've got to stand by and watch it. Yes, I'm bitter too for what they did to him (Peras and Peras, 2001, 8, 29–31).

Pete and Kathryn were hardly alone in their fears and anxieties. As Uchitelle points out, "Even if a person is accurate in saying, 'I did a really good job, and I can see the company is in a bad way and they have to lay off a lot of people and it's really not about me,' there is seldom an escape from the inner sense of 'why me?' In other words, one has the sense that one has failed and the outside world has made that judgment" (2006, 7–8). In *The Dignity of Working Men*, Michele Lamont traces these feelings back to working-class values. She writes, "Morality is generally at the center of these workers' worlds. They find their self-worth in their ability to discipline themselves and conduct responsible yet caring lives to ensure order for themselves and others" (2000, 2–3). When the plant closed, all this was put in jeopardy.

Union staff person Dave Cohen remembers that at the announcement of the closing, "you instantly had people going through eighteen different emotions. Some people want to strike them right on the spot. Some people just want to get it over with, you know, they're expecting something. So you've got to try and get people together and explain, 'Here's what's going to happen.'" But the union's approach was not just to fold and start negotiating a severance package. Cohen told the membership: "We don't just want to bargain severance pay. We want to put up a fight to stop it if we can, and here are all the options on that. And right from the beginning there, we looked at taking the factory over by eminent domain, doing some sort of workers' buyout, something like that" (2001, 15).

The UE has a history of fighting plant closings, but it had to move quickly. The WARN Act gave the workers and their union only sixty days' before the plant would close. It wasn't much time. They began by mobilizing the political community. U.S. Congressman John Olver and a number of state senators and representatives sent a letter to Beloit headquarters: "We, the undersigned, representing the workers affected by this decision, wish to state our great disappointment and protest your company's recent decision. We hope to meet with you in the near future to discuss ways in which we can support Beloit's future in Dalton" (Olver 1998, 1).

But the union knew that it would take more than just a letter to the company to keep the plant open. Beginning with the fight in 1984 in New Bedford, Massachusetts, to save the Morse Twist Drill company after it was bought by Gulf and Western, UE had explored using eminent domain to keep plants open. During a later campaign to keep the J. C. Rhodes plant open in New Bedford, the UE had worked with a top Boston lawyer to sort out the legal provisions of eminent domain. Dave Cohen explains:

> He did a lot of work, and turned out to be very excited and interested in this, because he determined that in Massachusetts, according to the constitution, a union, an estate, or a city or a town could seize the factory, not only the building and machinery, but seize the goodwill and the product name, which is key to doing any of this. You don't want just the equipment, you need the business lists, what they call the goodwill. (2001, 15)

In his six-page letter to the Dalton Select Board on September 14, 1998, UE attorney David S. Nalven laid out the legal underpinnings of eminent domain as it applied to Beloit. Both federal and state law, he wrote, allow for government "to take private property, but only on two conditions: that the taking be supported by a sufficient public purpose, and that just compensation be paid. There is little doubt," he continued, "that the taking of the Beloit plant would be supported by an appropriate, if not urgent, public purpose. Over the last decade, western Massachusetts has lost many thousands of good-paying manufacturing jobs. The Town has lost its share and cannot afford to lose any more" (Nalven 1998, 2).

Meanwhile, the Dalton Select Board sent a letter to Beloit, stating, "We were shocked because this decision seems at odds with both previous corporate statements indicating plans to grow this business locally and the fact that your local operations have been consistently profitable." The letter goes on to speak about the "business-friendly" climate in Dalton and notes, "Although permitted by state law and despite pressure on the local property tax, the Town of Dalton has consistently resisted the temptation to assign a higher tax rate to commercial and industrial properties." Furthermore, the letter suggested, "these decisions were made deliberately in order to help secure the health of our businesses" (Gingras 1998, 1).

The Select Board also authorized a trip to meet with officials at company headquarters to discuss the future of the plant. "The mayor of Pittsfield, Jerry Doyle, . . . talked to the City Council and the City Council approved funds for a Cessna jet," recalls Pat Hubban, the union president, who was invited along. On Friday, September 25, 1998, "We flew out of Pittsfield airport, the mayor and myself, several of the politicians, and [the union representative] David Cohen. We went over and made our pitch to try to keep the plant open in front of all the big shots at Harnischfeger. Told them that our plant could do the drums, why not shut down Nashua. We were productive. We were more profitable and so on." But as Hubban laments, it was clear that their argument "wasn't going anywhere" (2001, 12). Mayor Doyle was disgusted: "We offered them a lot of incentives to stay, but it was like they gave us an hour of their time and that was it" (quoted in Tastad 1999, 1). Six days later, 153 years after E. D. Jones had opened his first shop, company officials announced that the Dalton facility would close permanently.

The union held a massive rally on October 1, 1998, marching from the Beloit plant to the center of Pittsfield. As Dave Cohen reports, "It was a three or four mile hike; . . . [we] took over the road, stopped all of the traffic. I think the line of march was probably a quarter mile long or so; . . . everybody came out of the businesses and waved and cheered, and police escort all of the way, and there we had a really good rally" (2001, 18). Several local politicians and union officials spoke. As one worker at the rally said, "Restructuring the company? They're restructuring a community. They're restructuring everyone's lives" (Stein 1998, A4).

It was an emotional day for many of the workers in Dalton and their families. "For a grown man to stand up in Park Square with tears running down his face and say, 'Guys, I love every one of you.' Hey, look, this is a machine shop," remembers Glen Boden. "These guys are all tough guys" (2001a, 12).

Bamberger and Davidson reflect these sentiments in their *Closing: The Life and Death of an American Factory*. A plant closing, they point out, "is not just about economics. It is about personal loss and family tensions. It is about the joy of work and the tragedy of being deprived of work. It is about the sense of self that comes from pride in one's craft. And it is about the sense of community that develops when people who might otherwise have little in common . . . work side by side, depending on one another to get a job done right" (1998, 19–20).

Union officials met the following week with a number of legislators to discuss the remaining options, including using eminent domain. Despite pledges to help, it soon became clear in this small Republican town that local officials had little will to act decisively. Union rep Dave Cohen suggests, "The selectmen were clearly terrified by the idea that we were asking them to use their power of eminent domain to seize part of Harnischfeger Corporation" (2001, 20). So the union and its members moved to Plan B—a worker buyout of the plant.

Jones Beloit was the perfect target for a buyout. The factory and its equipment were in excellent shape, and the demand for their product line was high. The union brought together an impressive team to make a run for a buyout of the plant. Bill Goessel, former head of Beloit and Harnischfeger, now retired in the Berkshires, signed on, as did Michael Messina, a top management official at the Dalton facility who had also retired a few years before. This was no ragtag group of union supporters but included senior management who brought tremendous experience and clout to the table. Goessel in particular had important fund-raising connections.

The union floated several offers to Harnischfeger, including leasing the plant, acting as a subcontractor, or buying it outright. They were surprised when, as Dave Cohen remembers, "We got the message that we should fly out to the Beloit headquarters. . . . We were going to meet with the vice president in charge of paper manufacturing. And so we got all excited. We thought, 'Maybe they're going to listen to our argument about leasing'" (2001, 21).

So Pat Hubban, Dave Cohen, and Michael Messina flew out to the Midwest, hopeful that there might yet be a future in Dalton. This was the first time Cohen and Messina had spent any time together. Cohen recalls, "He was not a pro-union guy. I sat with him the whole plane ride and he told me how he hated the unions, but in order to save the factory, he'd work with us" (2001, 21).

Messina describes the meeting at Beloit headquarters. It got off to a bad start.

> We met with this Bill Hacket and he was just an uppity kind of guy. The first thing he did was he threw out a sheet of paper that was faxed in to him that was copied off the *[Berkshire] Eagle* that morning that somebody, I think the personnel manager in Dalton, sent him out, a fax of what was in the *Eagle*. And it was something about Pat Hubban saying, "We're trying to do this. We're trying to do that." "Listen,' he said. "We don't need this kind of publicity because this plant is going to shut down and I don't want to give these people a lot of high hope or anything like that." (2002, 9)

The conversation then turned to the possibility of a buyout or leasing of the company's facility. Their hopes were dashed before they even got a chance to make their argument. Hacket was brusque and to the point. "He said, 'Let me make this clear,'" Messina recalls. "'We're getting rid of all the machines.' He says, 'We're going to sell everything.' He wouldn't hear any of it. 'I just wanted to tell you straight to your face, go fuck yourself. We'll never do it'" (2002, 9).

"I thought that Messina was going to have a heart attack," Cohen remembers. "I thought his head was going to explode, he turned so red. No one had ever talked to him like this. [Then Hacket continued] 'You're not getting my message. I figured I had to tell you straight to your face. Otherwise you'd never stop trying.'" And he went into a long speech, explaining that they were going to get rid of every worker they had in the United States, that it was a waste of money to hire workers who were going to be only assemblers. The company's plan was to subcontract the work that had been done by the Dalton plant. As Cohen reports, "He put up big charts on the wall.

And their plan was, they said, since they had all the blueprints, they were going to create mom and pop, that was the term he used, 'mom and pop,' fifteen-person machine shops throughout the United States. . . . When they needed to build a pulper, they would send blueprints to each of these machine shops, and they would make the different parts, and then they would send them to whoever wanted a pulper, and they would assemble it" (2001, 22, 11).

This plan sounded ludicrous to workers who had honed their skills over a lifetime creating the products that had made Jones Beloit products famous around the world.

> You don't take thirty years of experience and replace it with some kid who just went to technical school. . . . Our guys could tap a hole and look inside the hole and tell if the gauge would go in. . . . We used to take our scales and measure things and see how close we could get and check it with a mike. I mean, we could get to a point, of course, with young eyes you can get within ten-thousandths with a scale. Those are things you bring with you for the rest of your life. (Boden 2001a, 26–27)

A lot of the men on the shop floor saw Harnischfeger's recalcitrance over making any deal with the union the same way Pete Peras saw it: "They didn't want us to make it. . . . They're not going to do it because the only thing this is going to do is show everybody that this company blew it" (Peras and Peras 2001, 26).

Time was running out, and the union continued its negotiations over the severance package. The final agreement would provide one week's pay for every year that an employee had worked, capped at twenty-six weeks. For many, this was a substantial amount of money, which they would start receiving weekly. Some workers left as soon as the agreement was signed. Bob Sargent was one of them.

> I was fairly close to one of the head people over there, and I got really ticked. That's why I left right at the beginning, when they said they were going to close. I could have worked longer, but I didn't want to because I really had hard feelings. I had just talked to, about three weeks earlier, one of the higher-ups there—I don't want to mention his name—and I was asking him "What's it look like?" He says, "Oh, it's great. We ain't got to worry, we're going to be here for a long time." (Sargent and Sargent 2001a, 5)

Others, like Joe Zatorski, stayed to help out with the transition:

> I worked in the shipping department the last six months because they closed down all the other departments. We loaded I don't know how many trucks to go off to Nashua, of our own stuff. And I said to my shipping boss, "They put me loading the trucks. That's like putting a fox in the henhouse." Because I knew what I could do to these machines to damage them. But we walked out of there without doing anything. Yes, we did. To me that's a plus. (2001, 4)

Meanwhile, since the union couldn't buy the plant or lease the facilities, the members moved to yet a third plan—to start their own company. They had an excellent workforce and a solid reputation in the industry. Messina's experience was invaluable here:

> I was also manager of what they called subcontracting. And what that involved was, when our company was low on work with our own product, it was my job to go to different companies to see if I could subcontract some of their work to keep our company going. And through that effort I had built up quite a stack of companies that I used to call and get work from. (2002, 9)

They drew up papers to form a new company, Dalton Machine and Associates, and started soliciting work. Pat Hubban threw himself into the process: "Bill Cardy, who was our former head of sales and engineering at Beloit, became president of our new company. He was sixty-eight years old and he was just fired up about it. So he would go with me on these different trips." Hubban reported: "I actually personally put in about six thousand miles of driving, just to try and drum up business, potential business, and ended up setting up fifteen customers with letters. Yeah, it was something like $3.2 million worth of potential business" (2001, 15, 13).

The next hurdle was finding equipment, because the company was committed to selling everything in the Dalton facility or moving it to New Hampshire. "A guy that worked for me for years, his name was Bernie Olds," Messina remembers, "we sent him down to North Carolina, I think. They had a huge machine auction at that time, and he was supposed to look it over—he was a crackerjack with machines—and pick out machines that we needed, what we had to pay for them to get them up here and everything. We even went that far" (2002, 13).

The last remaining issue to resolve was the building. Despite Harnischfeger's refusal to sell the business, the union still held out hope they could lease the mothballed building. "We already had the business plan going. We had the machinery going. We had the work already signed up and ready to go. Our biggest stumbling block was the building," explains Pat Hubban (2001, 14). Because they planned to continue the large-scale work that had been done at Beloit, no ordinary factory would do. Outside of some very rundown former GE buildings in Pittsfield, the Beloit plant was the only facility in Berkshire County tall enough, to provide adequate crane capacity.

The Crane firm, which had originally sold the land to Beloit, expressed interest in buying the building. According to Hubban, "We entered into an agreement with Crane and Company that if they bought the building, they would lease us the manufacturing space. But then Harnischfeger . . . filed for Chapter 11, Reorganization. Froze all their assets" (2001, 15). All Grade's financial manipulations ultimately could not save Harnischfeger, and on June 7, 1999, it filed a Chapter 11 bankruptcy petition.

Earlier that spring it had begun to be clear that because of the trajectory on which Jeffrey Grade had placed the company, he could no longer save Harnischfeger or himself. Stock prices, according to the *Wall Street Journal*, had plummeted from more than $30 per share to "as low as $5.35 in March." Investors were not happy, and the Trinity Fund, who controlled 8 percent of the stock, "started putting pressure on the Milwaukee-based company to revamp its management." On May 26, 1999, Grade resigned under pressure. With typical Grade grandiosity, he told the press that he had been planning to resign anyway within the next year. Perhaps for the first time, though, he did admit to some remorse, telling the *Journal*, "Hopefully I retire taking all the sins and evils that people have ascribed to us with me" (Quintalla 1999, B8). But that was not the case. By the time the new management team took the reins, bankruptcy was the only option.

The bankruptcy had a direct and immediate impact on the workers in Dalton. First, the option to use the old Beloit building was gone, effectively terminating any possibility of a new firm growing from the ashes. The team explored other spaces, but as Pat Hubban recalls, "It just kind of faded, you know." Months later he was contacted by the Massachusetts Workers Compensation Board, seeking to bill the fledgling company, even though it never had any employees. With no options in sight, Hubban says, "we dissolved it" (2001, 17). He had spent six months working almost full time to make something come out of the closing for the workers. It was now over.

In a shock to the Jones Beloit workers, the bankruptcy also stopped all severance checks, despite the severance agreement and the signed contract with the company. The workers would now have to line up with all the rest of Harnischfeger's creditors. Joe Zatorski, one of a few workers who didn't have direct deposit, was stunned when the bank returned his last Beloit severance check marked "insufficient funds." They still owed him more than $8,000. "The few of us that did leave right away, we collected our whole thing," reports Bob Sargent. "But there's a lot of people out there that they owe money to. I'm not talking a hundred dollars. I'm talking about thousands of dollars that they owe some of these people. It's really sad" (Sargent and Sargent 2001a, 13). Pat Hubban, who lost $3,000, was angry. "So that's how they rewarded people for working all those hours and helping them close the plant. They ended up cheating them out of the severance" (2001,15). Glen Boden was angry, too:

> Two of the girls in the office literally ran the place by themselves up till the very end. Neither of them received a penny in severance pay. One girl worked till the Friday before they declared bankruptcy. She was one of the last people to leave. . . . Now if the personnel manager didn't know, that's criminal. Would you treat a human being like that? Somebody that worked twenty-five, twenty-six years for a company. Things like that made me sick. Make me sick. How can people do a thing like this? They ought to be in jail, that's where they ought to be." (2001a, 4)

The workers at the Dalton plant weren't the only ones affected. In Milwaukee, state officials were quoted in the local paper saying that "the former Beloit Corp. owes about 200 of its ex-employees $3.6 million in severance pay" (Savage 2000b, 3D). As if to add insult to injury, as part of going into Chapter 11, Beloit cut off all health care coverage to retirees. Glen Boden remembers:

> When I was a kid, when they were down on Depot Street, . . . I used to see the old-timers down there that used to come out at lunch and used to sit on the sidewalk there and have their lunch. I knew some of the people that worked down there came up to the new plant. There was a lot of them I knew that worked down there. And the thing that makes me sad is because, even those people, they lost their insurance. (2001a, 22–23)

Life after Beloit

Joe Zatorski was one of the last to leave. He related the conversations workers had as they finished their last days and talked about life after Beloit. "That was almost a slogan. 'Life after Beloit' " (2001, 30).

> I worked right up until February of 1999. It was a Sunday, the last day we were working. There was like, I forget how many of us they had out there. I want to say 26 to 36 of us, something like that, at the end. Because the guys were still stuffing crates and everything. And that was it. They said, "Next Sunday's your last day." And it was. There was a very small skeleton crew out there. I want to say four or five guys left out there. . . . We just walked out and drove away. (Zatorski 2001, 4–5)

Finding work was not easy. GE had had major layoffs over the previous few years, and most of the industrial companies had closed shop and moved away. Bob Sargent was a highly skilled welder with more than thirty years' experience.

> I was disgusted. I did look. I looked in the papers, but there was nothing. Like my wife said, there were $7-, $8-an-hour jobs and I wasn't about to start all over like that. . . . In order to get a job where I got paid, I probably would have had to go up to New Hampshire, or some place away from here, and I didn't really want that. Not at my age. I didn't want to start over again (Sargent and Sargent 2001a, 14).

It was a new experience for Sargent, who had spent the previous thirty-four years of his life in a secure job as a welder. "Bob Sargent is a real genuine person," declares Glen Boden. "This almost killed Bob Sargent, I want to tell you" (2001a, 12). Looking for work was new terrain. As Kathryn Dudley suggests in *The End of the Line: Lost Jobs, New Lives In Postindustrial America*, "For dislocated workers trying to find work in the new labor market, experience is no longer a guide to what the future may hold." And describing the process that workers like those at Dalton faced, she writes, "The relocation of workers in today's economy is not a straightforward process of people moving from one fixed location in the labor market. As workers are pushed out of vanishing slots in the occupational structure, the structure itself is shifting and in flux" (1994: xxiii).

Bob Sargent ended up a long way from the job he had held at Beloit.

> I went and got this part-time job that I got right now, just to hold me over until I sign up for Social Security this September. . . . I deliver dry cleaning clothes. I work on a percentage basis. How much I deliver, I get 20 percent of whatever I deliver. It's four days a week. It averages out probably about maybe twelve hours, thirteen hours for the whole week. On a good week, I get $200, maybe $220 out of it. Bad weeks are down, a hundred-fifty, a hundred-forty. But it's enough to hold me over. I'm collecting my pension. We make do. My wife went out and got a job. (Sargent and Sargent 2001a, 11)

Like many of the other men in the shop, Sargent comes from a time when wives did not need to work. But times had changed. Gae found work, but far different from the kind that had defined their generation. "I got a job the week after he did," she reports.

> Mine is $7 an hour. I mean, that's all I could get anyways. I'm in a cleaning service at GE, and I work twenty hours a week, and I bring home about a hundred twenty-two, twenty-three. And I use that to pay the property taxes, the car insurance, the fire insurance, and it's all gone just for those things. We had to go to savings to pay the oil bill. (Sargent and Sargent 2001a, 11)

For the Sargents, and many of the other families of the workers laid off at Jones Beloit, transitioning into retirement was a major concern. The transition into retirement is challenging itself, but now the process had been accelerated. Gae Sargent explains:

> Yeah, because I used to think—women talk about this stuff—"What will we do when they all come home, and they retire?" But when you're thrown out of work three and a half years early and things have changed and you don't even have half the money you expected to have. . . . That kind of stuff is really rough. It was a hard adjustment. I hope our furnace doesn't quit, and I hope our roof doesn't quit, because we planned to do those things before retirement. We were planning to try to get a car and a truck and the roof and the furnace done before the three years were up. That's all on hold now. Now we do have to do the porch roof and the garage roof desperately. (Sargent and Sargent 2001a, 18–21)

Once the severance pay stopped, health insurance became a real issue for those who hadn't found work and for those whose new work didn't have benefits. It was particularly hard on the older men who had never expected their wives to work. As Joe Zatorski tells it:

I went to one trucking outfit and I says to them—at that time my wife wasn't working, that was when I first got my license [for driving trucks]—"You got any benefits?" He says, "No, we don't." I says, "How about health insurance?" He says, "No, we don't." I says, "You can't even buy it?" He said, "Nope." I said, "Terry, I can't work for you then." I says, "I need health insurance." To me that's a major. Salary is good but health insurance for me is a key factor. Because, like I say, you and I know, you go into the hospital for one day, two days, and your weekly pay is going to be—forget it. (2001, 8)

The company did provide health insurance for three months after the closure, in accordance with the severance agreement with the union. After that, those who wanted to stay on Beloit's plan under the Consolidated Omnibus Budget Reconciliation Act (COBRA) would have to pay. But, Bob Sargent points out, "The insurance that I was getting would have cost me almost $600 a month to keep if I wanted to keep it" (Sargent and Sargent 2001a, 22–23).

Many of the older men faced age discrimination; though employers wouldn't come out and say it, it was clear. Joe Zatorski tells of looking for work:

I applied to one place, I won't say the name. They had an ad in the paper for a driver. So I go down there and apply. About a month later the ad's in the paper again. I go back down there and said, "I'd like to apply for that job." They said, "Fill out an application." I said, "Okay." So I filled out another application. They never called me. . . . A week later I get a letter, "Sorry, we don't need you at this present time." Okay, I know what it is. It's my age. (2001, 6)

Joe finally found a casual job at the Post Office for $8.00 an hour. He left when he got a better job as a custodian at the school, but he was laid off at the end of the school year.

Younger workers faced a different set of challenges. Mike Blair was thirty-six at the time the plant closed. In addition to having a three-year-old daughter, Blair reports, he and his wife had bought a house just "three or four years before. It was tough. It was something we didn't plan on, because when you went to Jones Beloit you planned a retirement just like everybody else did. But not with the new corporations. You don't see that anymore. They make their profit and move on" (2001a, 4).

Because some of their work was moved to Canada, the workers laid off from Jones Beloit were eligible for education and training at little or no cost under NAFTA (North American Free Trade Agreement) training assistance. Several men signed up to become certified as truck drivers. Others learned heating and air conditioning. A small number of mostly younger workers returned to community college. Mike Blair was one of them. "I was thirty-six," he says.

> See, I was in the medical corps for four years in the service. I had a background in nursing. I went up to Berkshire Community College. . . . The worst part about it was getting prerequisites for English, math, and all that stuff. I had to start all over. I haven't been to school in twenty years! It was scary. Not only do you come home to a three-year-old son and a house you just bought, but also you're out of a job and it's scary. I had to make my mind up. I just was going to do what I had to do. I went to school and got my prerequisites. It took about eight months. Then I did the year program. That's when I made up my mind I wanted to at least make the same money as I did when I left. (2001a, 3–4)

He was not alone at the local community college: "I found out at BCC there are so many people that don't have jobs around here. It's amazing the number of people that were in their fifties who were in class with me" (2001a, 6). Pat Hubban, who had worked so hard on the buyout, also went to study in college:

> I always wanted to do something different. I'd always tell my wife that. I wanted to do computers or I want to do something different. And I never had the opportunity because you're making good money and you have a family and, you know, you just can't do that. So this did open a different opportunity for us. (2001, 9)

Hubban went on to become a salesman for the Yellow Pages, traveling all over New England. Mike Blair finished his schooling and became a licensed practical nurse. He got a job at Berkshire Medical Center in Pittsfield.

At fifty, Pete Peras was between the older workers like Sargent and Boden, who had just a few more years to go before retirement, and the younger ones like Blair and Hubban, who still had much of their work life ahead of them. The severance pay would have been a cushion, but when those checks stopped, the company still owed Peras $6,500. The plant closure also froze pensions. And so, Peras points out, "At $700 a month or $701 or something like that, that's what I'll get. But I'll get that in the year 2015, that won't even buy me a couple of six packs" (Peras and Peras 2001, 13). So Peras needed to find work that would provide both health care and an opportunity to get vested in a retirement plan.

He put his name in a few places. "I was a welder by trade," he says, "and I'd worked in the woods driving a skidder and logging. So finding a job in construction or something like that, I could have done that, but fifty years old is no time to start shoveling. . . . But I knew I'd find a job. I went down and put applications in—$9.50, $9.75 an hour, I mean that's an insult as far as I was concerned." He heard that there were openings at the Berkshire County House of Corrections. "I put in an application and they hired me, so I was real lucky." But then he learned that he would have to go through a ten-week training course at the police academy. "It was like boot camp and I've never been in the service but we were running and physical for four hours in the morning, and classes" (Peras and Peras 2001, 16, 9, 10). Peras, who has a barrel chest and a powerful build, had kept himself in good shape, but he was by far the oldest recruit in the police academy. The training, he recalls, was grueling.

> I'd get up at 5 o'clock to go there for 7 o'clock and ice down before I went, to make sure there was no swelling or anything like that. It was pretty rigorous. We were running four miles in one pop. . . . I was never in boot camp but we had these guys come down from another jail for tactical training and if you weren't doing exactly what they said, "Everybody get down, give me fifty push ups." Leg lifts and raises. Your back is up in like a sit-up position and they hold you there until you fall. They just make you sit up like that until you collapse. (Peras and Peras 2001, 37)

Peras's good friend Mike Blair reports: "This is a great story because he's fifty years old and he had to go through the academy for the state to be a guard. They were calling him 'Grandpa.' 'Old man.' But he made it" (2001a, 22).

Glen Boden worked for twenty-five years right next to Pete Peras. He recalls: "Actually Pete worked in an office, but it was right behind my machine so I could bang on his window. His window was right there, and my machine actually traveled back and forth, and so when I'd be down at this end I'd be right in front of Pete's window and I'd always bang on it. Pete's a good man. We were together a lot of years" (2001b, 5). A highly skilled machinist, Boden was luckier than most. At fifty-eight he was hired right from the plant by a small operation making many of the same parts he had been making at Beloit. They are located in the old Beloit laboratory building. But he saw others still struggling.

God bless them. 'Cause I'm going to tell you something. Those people are hurting. I'm one of the lucky ones. You probably shouldn't even be interviewing me because I'm the guy that got out of there with thirty-five years' pension. Sure, it was reduced, but I'm getting it for ten years early. . . . I got out of there with a job with a four-week vacation to start. Not quite the money, but much better benefits. I want to tell you something, I'm the luckiest guy in the world. And if you can relate to this, a lot of times when things happen you almost feel guilty, because you made out and you watch others that didn't. Sort of like the guy that went to Vietnam and didn't get killed, he came home and was screwed up because all his friends didn't come home. There's something about that. My wife once said, right after this happened, that guys all go see a psychiatrist and talk about this and I pooh-poohed her and told her, "What are you, nuts?" She was right. Because I know it has affected me and it was affecting all my friends. And it's devastating, that's what it is. 'Cause we weren't a business, we were a family. (2001a, 9–10)

Terry Williams ended up as the last official Beloit employee, leaving June 25, 1999. For the previous several months he had been working largely at the Nashua, New Hampshire, facility, sorting out company billing. He was unimpressed with the integration of the work and equipment from Dalton. "You can't just suddenly click your fingers and suddenly move something that was here for 150 years." He continues, "This equipment is not something you just throw on a truck and bring it up and unload it and plug it in and go. You have to build foundations that are quite intricate. If you see these foundations, they're all these different gradients using tons of concrete" (2001, 20, 23). Glen Boden adds, "They stole all our equipment and moved it up there and never could run it. They destroyed most of it. We had a turning center that was well over 3 million bucks probably. And they brought it up there and they could never make it run" (2001a, 5).

Much of the equipment had yet to be set up when, early in 2000, as part of their reorganization plan to emerge from bankruptcy, Harnischfeger sold its Beloit division. The integrated firm brought together by the merger of E. D. Jones and the Beloit Iron Works, a firm that had been one of the three top players in the worldwide market, would be no more. As too often has been the pattern since the 1980s, it was sold off in parts. The Paper Aftermarket and Roll Covers Division went to the Finnish paper machinery giant Valmet Corporation. The Paper Technology Division was sold to Mitsubishi Heavy Industries. The Pulp and Finishing Division, including the Nashua, New Hampshire, plant and the remnants of the Jones legacy from Dalton, was sold to the Montreal-based Groupe LaPerriere and Verreault (*PR Newswire* 2000).

In July 2000, having jettisoned a major part of its operations, Harnischfeger, renamed the Joy Global Corporation, was released from bankruptcy protection (*Mining Journal* 2001, 51). The new name was taken from one of its remaining divisions, which made machinery for underground mining. Its only other division was P&H Mining Equipment, which makes equipment for surface mining. Harnischfeger's connection with the papermaking industry was over.

Industrial Workers in a Global World

Far from the shop floor in Dalton, decisions were made that irrevocably changed the lives of Glen Boden, Bob Sargent, and Joe Zatorski and their families and community. It was a changed world. A generation of experience in the postwar era had taught industrial workers, and their unions have long believed, that what happens on the shop floor determines their viability and job security. Based on a generation of experience in the postwar era, the assumption was that if they produced high-quality goods that were profitable, their future was secure. Or so the workers at Jones Beloit assumed. They believed that the larger business strategies of corporations were aligned with their human resource policies and practices on the shop floor.[2] This belief fueled the movement by unions in the 1980s to agree to concessions for the good of the company. If by cutting wages they could return their factory or product line back to profitability, then they could hold on to their jobs.

The wreckage of the 1980s and 1990s showed just how insidious business had become. With the growth of multinationals and the globalization of production, macro decision-making was often entirely independent of what made sense from the view of the shop floor. Factories and operations were closed or sold in the interest of stockholders, often in complete disregard for the economics of shop-floor production. In some instances the larger corporate strategy directly contradicted what was being communicated by management on an operational level. For example, at the Bridgestone/Firestone company in the early 1990s, at exactly the same time that the company was pursuing an ambitious employee involvement and partnership program, heralded by many in the industrial relations community as an important new model, the company was implementing a larger corporate strategy to break both the union and the pattern agreement in the rubber industry (Juravich and Bronfenbrenner 2004).

Although the closure of Jones Beloit was less the result of deliberate corporate design, it was nonetheless independent of the productivity of the workers in Dalton, the quality of their products, or the bottom line of their facility, which by all reports was strongly profitable. Ironically, as Grade's boondoggle in Indonesia and his effort to hide his losses from stockholders caused Harnischfeger to tumble into Chapter 11, the profitability of the Dalton plant made it more, rather than less, likely to close.

From an economic perspective, the closing of Jones Beloit destroyed a highly productive business and a world-renowned product line that supplied high-quality products to a worldwide market. The closing also wasted the skills and talents of people like Glen Boden and Bob Sargent, as well as disrupting their families and communities. Making the situation even more difficult was the refusal of the company to sell or to facilitate any kind of worker buyout or worker-controlled firm. As one of the Dalton workers noted, to do that would have publicly revealed how irrational the closing was in the first place.

This widening disconnect between shop-floor operational practices and larger corporate strategies leaves American workers like those employed at Jones Beloit incredibly vulnerable. As Ruth Milkman puts it in *Farewell to the Factory*, "Once among the most privileged section of the working class, non-college-educated men have borne a disproportionate share of the costs of economic restructuring" (1997, 94–95).

What is stunning about the closing of Jones Beloit in Dalton, Massachusetts, is the absence, on a number of different levels, of any legal or regulatory mechanisms to protect the workers from the ravages of global capital. A decade or more has clearly demonstrated the failure of the regulatory framework governing corporate behavior. As the Enron, WorldCom, and more recently Bernard Madoff scandals made clear, the regulators in the Security and Exchange Commission, the stock markets, and the accounting community were in many ways complicit in the wrongdoing that brought down these major firms (McLean and Elkind 2004; Pavlo and Weinberg 2007). The net result was the loss of hundreds of thousands of jobs and billions of investment dollars. Many workers watched as both their jobs and their pensions disappeared.

At Harnischfeger, the repeated failure to meet quarterly projections should have set off alarms among the auditors and regulators. One also has to question their accounting firm's oversight in the light of Grade's efforts to hide financial difficulties from stockholders. Early intervention could have staved off the collapse of Harnischfeger, saving jobs, stock values, and a firm known around the world for its high-quality products. Tragically, by the time anyone outside Grade's inner circle learned of the financial morass, it had gone beyond the point of no return.

On the macro level we also need to acknowledge the role of U.S. trade, investment, and tax policies that promote overseas investment and job shifts, as in the example of Harnischfeger's Asia Pulp and Paper project in Indonesia. The effect of these policies on American manufacturers and their workers has been devastating.

When Bill Clinton took office in 1993, from his base in the Democratic Leadership Council he abandoned much of the New Deal framework, including the plank regarding full employment. "The president soon signaled after he took office that 'layoffs would be allowed'" (Uchitelle 2006, 154). As Clinton marched forward with his "new" Democratic agenda to gain passage for NAFTA, his concern was not for the workers who would be laid off as American manufacturers found it much easier to relocate in Mexico. He rejected any institutional governmental approach that would either constrain firms from moving jobs or provide additional assistance for laid-off workers. Instead, he individualized the solutions, looking for employers to act responsibly and for workers themselves to become better educated and trained to be able to find new work.

In this arena Clinton relied on the thinking of his classmate Robert Reich, whom he had met at Oxford when they were both Rhodes scholars. Reich's *The Work of Nations* argued that work in the "old economy" was destined to leave the United States, and therefore, he believed, Americans instead should be trained and educated as "symbolic analysts" (Reich 1992). Rather than trying to keep manufacturing jobs in the United States, he argued, "the government's role in this process . . . is to subsidize education and training for vast numbers of people so they can acquire the necessary problem-solving skills" (quoted in Uchitelle 2006, 164). In this way the Clinton team transmogrified the American dream from the right to a have a job to the right to have training.

The NAFTA agreement provided rudimentary retraining provisions for workers displaced by production shifts but, as at Jones Beloit, it did little for most of those who lost their jobs. Mike Blair, who retrained as a nurse, may have been the exception, but most of the short-term training programs offered to the Jones Beloit workers—truck driving; heating, ventilation, and air conditioning—were hardly tickets to a job in the "new economy."

Training was not the issue for workers like Glen Boden and Bob Sargent; they were already highly skilled workers. At Jones Beloit, Glen operated state-of-the-art CNC machine tools. Rather, for him and many others laid off, the issue was the unavailability of good jobs. With the demise of manufacturing as a consequence of U.S. trade and investment policies, there simply weren't any good jobs left in the Berkshires in either the "old" or the "new" economy.

In *The Job Training Charade* Gordon Lafer documents that job training programs as a public policy just don't work. "There simply are not enough decently paying jobs," he writes, "for the number who need them—no matter how well trained they are—and thus . . . training programs cannot hope to address more than a small fraction of the poverty problem" (2002, 3–4). No matter how well workers are trained, as long as these larger economic policies remain firmly in place, there is little that individual workers can do to hold or get good jobs.

The only program the Clinton administration passed to address plant closings was the WARN Act, whose major provision is a requirement that employers provide sixty days' notice before closing a plant. Drawing from Clinton and Reich's beliefs, the basic assumption of the legislation is that a decision to close is already final, and thus the intent is to provide an orderly transition of workers through the shutdown to other employment. In this way the legislation is designed to manage the shutdown of an aging steel plant that has outlived its usefulness and productive capacity. Yet this model did not apply to Jones Beloit. Nor does it apply to the thousands of other workplaces where the decision to close a plant is based not on the productivity or efficiency at the plant level but on larger corporate decision-making. At Jones Beloit the sixty days provided by WARN was simply not enough time to put together a realistic plan for keeping a plant open under its current owner, securing new owners, or developing some form of worker buyout. The Jones Beloit case and the lack of any restraints on corporate restructuring of global firms makes it clear that we need more comprehensive plant-closing legislation that includes extending the timetable so productive facilities and workers are not wasted.

Joe Zatorski saw little difference between the closing of Jones Beloit and the experience of his grandparents who had worked in the woolen mills in nearby Pittsfield: "They left work on a Friday or Saturday and when they went to work on Monday the plant was closed" (2001, 18). Over the following hundred years we seem to have made very little progress.

Getting By in the Berkshires

The economists and the policymakers often look at the aftermath of a plant closing by counting how many people have found work and measuring their income levels. Many of those laid off when Jones Beloit closed have found work. Some are more fulfilled in their new jobs, and some are even making close to the money they made at Jones Beloit. Others left the area, or settled into new low-wage service jobs, or faded quietly into retirement. For a long time, several former Jones Beloit employees met for breakfast on Mondays at Kelly's Diner to reminisce.

But counting how many got work after the plant closing and measuring their income levels does not get at the costs to workers and their families. Years later, many of these workers—even those gainfully employed—are still angry about the closing and how it affected them and their families. Glen Boden, for example, declares:

> No, everything's not okay. Because somebody hasn't had their due. If I went and harmed somebody, physically or mentally, I would get arrested. Somebody would call the cops, if I beat you or drove you nuts or something. These people can do this and get away with it. They can ruin people's lives that have been good employees. That isn't the American way. (2001a, 18)

"For the victims," Louis Uchitelle points out in *The Disposable American*, "layoff is an emotional blow from which very few fully recover. . . . The laid-off are cut loose from their moorings and rarely achieve in their next jobs a new and satisfactory sense of themselves" (2006, x).

The former Jones Beloit workers worry about the future of work in Berkshire County and the ability of their friends, neighbors, and children to make a living. Several attempts have been made to bring new industry to the area, but the competition is stiff. Local officials used to brag about their highly skilled workforce, but as the years pass the skills of the workforce are atrophying. Former Jones Beloit manager Michael Messina says, "I tell you the truth, I think right now, if a big company came in and said we want to establish this manufacturing facility right here, I don't think we could supply the help to do it. I think all the skills are gone. No one is taking over the skills. No one is trained for them. I honestly think they would have a tough, tough time fulfilling their needs" (2002, 18).

Like New Bedford and many other old manufacturing towns that have lost their industrial base, Dalton and Pittsfield are desperately leaning into tourism, trying to capitalize on the success of nearby towns such as Stockbridge and Lenox and North Adams, the home of Mass MoCA, the Massachusetts Museum of Contemporary Art. But local residents are skeptical about how much tourism the area can support. "Other than Tanglewood [music center]," Joe Zatorski asks, "what do they have for attractions around here? Nothing. During the wintertime you've got Brody Mountain up there [for skiing] and that's from maybe the end of November to March" (2001, 16–17).

Even if tourism gets a foothold in the area, there is the issue of what kind of jobs it creates. As former Jones Beloit employee Mark Cole puts it, "You'll have your waiters, your waitresses, your hotel people, and stuff like that. And you're going to get the basic minimum wage, but somebody is going to be making money and it isn't going to be the workers" (2001, 17). Unlike manufacturing, where dollars get recycled in the community as people buy lunch, clothing, or a house or car, most funds from tourism leave with the hotel and restaurant chains that are based elsewhere (Phillips-Fein 1998). So far, the only impact of the move to tourism has been rising prices in the Pittsfield area. "They're making us pay the same prices as them during the summer," Gae Sargent reports. "They're building a new hotel. They said the rooms are going to be $300 a night. We can't afford that, the people that live here" (Sargent and Sargent 2001a, 12–13).

So the future of Dalton and Pittsfield, Massachusetts, like that of so many similar towns across the United States, remains uncertain. It's difficult to see what engine will drive the economy in the years to come to provide the stable work and lives that they have come to expect. As Kathryn Peras explains, it is not a question of unrealistic expectations.

> I really believe that the vast majority of people such as ourselves, we're not looking for tons of money just falling off of us, a lavish lifestyle. All

we wanted to do was maintain and have, just have a little edge so we are not living day to day. A little breathing space. I guess what we wanted was what we felt [Pete] was entitled to. He's worked all these years, we wanted what he was entitled to. What was fair. (Peras and Peras 2001, 41)

For Glen Boden and many others who spent most of their working lives at Jones Beloit, their time at the company still defines them and their lives. "So," says Boden, "they might have shut the door and threw us out. I don't think any of us will ever leave" (2001b, 18).

CONCLUSION

Beyond the Altar of the Bottom Line

IN EACH of the four sites detailed here, workers watched as larger corporate decision-making fundamentally changed the nature of their work and lives. Boston Medical pushed to maximize its revenue by adopting an assembly-line approach to surgery. Verizon increased its profits by forcing workers to perform nonstop through the workday and into many overtime hours, with no respite, no flexibility. The Guatemalans in New Bedford, whose work was nineteenth-century in character, saw it grow even worse in the aftermath of the ICE raids. The highly skilled workers at Jones Beloit were jettisoned by an employer too reckless to care. Although in very different ways, each employer's workers found themselves victims at the altar of the bottom line.

The call center at Verizon represents an archetype of bread without roses in the new economy. Verizon CEO Ivan Seidenberg's "new industry paradigm" reduces to little more than "paying people well to treat them bad," as one call center representative expressed it. The work system in the call center, the logical extension of Taylorism, delivers work electronically, without pause, without interruption, and without rest. All the horrors of the assembly line have been recast in a new form, with workers facing them alone in their cubicles—while almost constant monitoring and a shift from service to sales have turned their workplace into a pressure cooker.

Management at Verizon further intensifies this pressure through a series of rigid, arbitrary, and what at times appear to be punitive human resources policies and practices: inflexible schedules, the lack of any real sick days, and restrictions on the use of vacation and personal time. Already grueling eight-hour days are regularly extended by mandatory overtime, with Verizon making an end run around the contract provision that was meant to provide twenty-four hours' notice for overtime work.

The combination of the work process and these aggressive human resources policies and practices creates stress at two levels. First is the stress on the job, as call center reps struggle to keep up with the daily pace, with little chance to come in an hour late or take a long weekend or a few days off. When combined with the mandatory overtime and inflexibility, the stress also reverberates in their lives off the job as they struggle to have time and energy for themselves or their families. And the paradox is that in a fundamental way, the very job they desperately need to support their families makes that family life impossible.

Nurses at Boston Medical Center are also expected to work far beyond a forty-hour week. This expectation is not seasonal as it is at Verizon but a regular part of their work life. Nurses feel less stress than the call center reps do, however, because, as professional workers, they have considerably more control over their work. They are neither monitored nor timed and retain the right to make important decisions in their practice of nursing. But because of the off-shift and weekend requirements and the new corporate model of health care in operation at Boston Medical, which works counter to their culture of caring, the nurses are exhausted.

Nurses do not feel trapped in their jobs in the same way call center representatives do. Even though many call center representatives loath their jobs, they feel as though they cannot leave them. They know these are probably the best-paying jobs they will ever have and, as one rep expressed it, "they have you" (Sally 2001, 7). Nurses at Boston Medical never see their work this way. In fact, they are incredibly dedicated to their work and to their patients, and they see the corporatization as an obstacle to practicing their profession. Whereas the salary keeps the call center representatives in place, the culture of caring keeps the nurses there.

As national trends reveal, however, nurses do leave the profession in startling numbers. Unlike the call center representatives, nurses have the option of moving to part-time, per diem, or traveling work, which can limit work hours in a way that hospitals and health care centers seem unable or unwilling to do. But even with these options, nurses are leaving their profession at an alarming rate.

As we saw at Boston Medical, the crisis in nursing cannot be solved simply by training more nurses to enter a profession that is increasingly unmanageable in terms of hours and working conditions. Nor can it be solved by outsourcing the work to techs and travelers, who may have the requisite skills but rarely have the same level of commitment or the ongoing relationships necessary to provide high-quality health care. The nursing crisis will be solved only when decent working conditions are restored to nursing. Restoring these conditions would require a rollback of hours, of mandatory overtime, and of off-shift work, as well as policy changes that would ensure that the requirements of corporate hospitals like Boston Medical do not eclipse the ability of nurses to practice their profession.

The Guatemalans in New Bedford's fishing industry seem to be working in an entirely different century. There is no need for electronic monitoring or stringent human resource policies. Not unlike workplaces throughout the nineteenth and early twentieth centuries, foremen exert their direct power over highly vulnerable workers who desperately need jobs. If they work too slowly, leave too much fish on the bones, or get injured in the whirl of knives and machinery, they are threatened, sometimes hit, or just let go. Even if they survive the crushing pace in the wet and the damp of a New England winter, some workers are cheated out of their money by their employers, and others are robbed by punks in their own neighborhoods.

Yet as bad as these jobs are by American standards, because of the poverty in Guatemala they are the best jobs most of these immigrants ever had. After their work on the *fincas*, the plantations in Guatemala, even working two full-time jobs, as Juan did during his first two years in New Bedford, seems like a good deal. For Juan, who used the money he saved to buy the first plot of land his family has owned for generations, there are no expectations of good working conditions. They are a luxury for white workers who are citizens. It is enough for him to have food, to have money to buy land and send to his family in Guatemala, and to have the dream that someday he will become an American citizen.

The Immigration and Customs Enforcement (ICE) raids at Michael Bianco in the spring of 2007, however, changed everything for the Guatemalans in New Bedford. The entire community was traumatized by the brutality of federal agents, their inhumane treatment of the detainees, and the ripping away of parents from over 200 children. For the 168 workers deported, it was the end of their American dream. With their earning power now a fraction of what it had been in New Bedford, they struggle to provide for families at home in a Guatemala poorer and more violent than when they left.

In the aftershock of the raid, fear overtook the remaining Guatemalans, who had been taking small steps into the local community and public life in New Bedford. They retreated to their apartments, made their contingency plans, and ventured out only when absolutely necessary, returning to the hiding they knew all too well from their lives in the Guatemalan highlands—lives they thought they had left behind.

In the aftermath of the raid, many Guatemalans lost their jobs as regular employees and were driven deeper into the informal economy, into the shadows where there is no light to shine on worker abuse. And they watched as their hopes that Washington would finally do something about immigration reform were dashed, with the only real result the demonization of immigrants on the airwaves and on city streets. Their dreams, as Juan put it, are now "on the edge of a cliff" (2007, 2).

After the failure of comprehensive immigration reform in 2007, the country seems to have settled into a dangerous place. ICE raids, which increased in the last years of the Bush administration, did nothing to solve the immigration crisis, yet as political theater they continued to drive undocumented workers deeper into the shadows in their workplaces and their communities. It was almost as though we accepted that undocumented workers were here to stay, as long as they remained in the shadows.

At Jones Beloit we saw an example of corporate greed consuming a major company and destroying a very profitable operation in the process. In the end, it was not just the failure of the CEO, Jeffrey Grade—who tried to hide the growing crisis from stockholders, workers, and the public—but the failure of a regulatory system that somehow overlooked unmet earnings projections by Harnischfeger, the parent company of Jones Beloit, in fourteen out of twenty-four quarters. As in the scandals at Enron and WorldCom, or more recently with Bear Stearns and Bernard L. Madoff, the closing of Jones Beloit is a clear indictment of the Securities and Exchange Commission and the regulatory system whose mission is to ensure that firms trading stock are open and honest with their financial reports. Even with his poor decision-making, if Grade had been forced to come clean earlier in the process, it is highly unlikely that the plant in Dalton would have been shuttered and the firm dismantled.

Another troubling aspect about the closing of Jones Beloit is the range of obstacles the workers and their union ran up against in trying to purchase the plant, lease space, or open their own firm. These were not the actions of just a few workers desperately trying to save their jobs but solid, well-thought-out efforts by the union, in concert with high-level managers who had the ability to make something happen. Yet they were thwarted at every turn. The company actively opposed any effort by the workers and their union; the bankruptcy filing made leasing the space impossible; and the Worker Adjustment and Retraining Notification (WARN) legislation provided only sixty days for any buyout to happen. With restraints like these, it is no surprise that precious few examples of ongoing operations have emerged from the ashes of plant closings.

In the end, the story of the closing of Jones Beloit is one of monumental waste. It was the waste of a 150-year legacy that went into building a world-class product. It was also the waste of a major firm that was one of the leaders in the papermaking industry. But most important, it was the waste of almost 300 workers—a waste of their skills and their abilities to earn a living.

The question is, how long can the workers at Verizon, at Boston Medical, and in the fish houses endure? Many of the changes documented here are fairly new—what will be the impact on Martha, Janet, and Juan over the next few years, or the next decade? How long can they sustain themselves in jobs like these? What is the long-range impact of sixty-hour weeks or of unbridled stress and exhaustion and the loss of jobs on workers, their children, their families, and their community life?

It is important to recognize what we are asking of American workers. Despite the massive changes in the postwar workplace brought on by changes in the economy and in business practices, we are asking workers to make sense of these changes in private—behind closed doors in their homes. There has been virtually no public discourse about massive workplace change, and as a nation we have done nothing structurally to assist workers and their families—no restrictions on overtime or limits on the total number of hours worked. Jody Heymann calls this "society's unfinished response." She explains, "We as a nation have failed to respond, leaving a rapidly widening gap between working families' needs and the combination of high workplace demands, outdated social institutions, and inadequate public policies" (2000, 4, 6).

The financial meltdown in the fall of 2008 and the rapid rise of unemployment have driven concerns about work even further underground. Have we entered an era where what we actually do at work—the work process and the conditions under which we do our work—is no longer something we should talk about or question? Are we lucky just to have a job, so we don't ask too many questions about the work itself? Do we have to just put up or shut up? When I spoke with a top official of the union that represents the

Verizon employees about the denigration of working conditions, she fired back, "Corporate America doesn't give a shit about it." She added, "If you write about decent working conditions in this day and age, sadly, people will laugh at that notion" (Herrera 2004, 20).

No Low Road to Recovery

President Barack Obama faces an enormous challenge to restore an economy left in shambles by the prolonged war in Iraq, staggering deficits, the seizing-up of the credit market, and the collapse of Wall Street. By the end of 2008, 4.5 million Americans were unemployed, the highest number since December 1982. Employment projections for 2009 were described as "bleak" (Associated Press 2008). Delivering on a campaign promise, less than a month into his term, Obama signed the $787 billon American Recovery and Reinvestment Plan into law, designed to create 4 millions jobs in the United States, in concert with a variety of other economic stimulus measures (Stolberg, 2009).

At this watershed moment, as we develop new federal policies and a new national discourse around the job question, we must do more than just address the number of jobs. Along with keeping and creating jobs, we need to develop an agenda for good jobs. Any return to prosperity in the United States cannot be built on the creation of more poorly paid contingent jobs with little security and marginal working conditions. We need steady, stable jobs that can sustain a generation of workers.

We need to create jobs with purchasing power, so that Americans can hold onto their homes, pay down their debts, and begin purchasing goods and services that create other jobs. Henry Ford understood this process when he instituted the "five-dollar day": workers would need to make enough to buy the cars he was mass producing. United Auto Workers (UAW) president Walter Reuther also understood it when, as part of union negotiations in 1946, he pushed General Motors to freeze the purchase price of its cars.

One of the lessons from the economic meltdown is that our economy cannot be sustained with massive inequality, with prosperity enjoyed by the few while ordinary American families go deeper into debt and work more hours to try to make up for stagnant wages. Nor can it be sustained if employers are allowed to step outside the regular labor market and extract profits from millions of undocumented workers who do not have even the most basic rights on the job. Stimulus efforts may enable credit to flow once again, allowing the stock market to bounce back. But unless we make good jobs central to any recovery effort, we could easily return to the inequality of the 1990s that led to the economic meltdown. There is no "low-road" employment path to economic recovery. As Damon Silvers says, we need "to challenge our labor-market policies to encourage a high-wage economy" (2008, 25).

It is not just about the economics of work, however. As we have seen, jobs that pay well are not necessarily good jobs and may not provide models for rebuilding our economy. We cannot rebuild a sustainable economy that is based on how work is done by nurses at Boston Medical—a system that spits out 40 percent of nurses along the way and finds those who are left exhausted to the bone and barely holding on. Nor can we rebuild a sustainable economy based on the "new industrial paradigm" at Verizon, which leaves workers desperately trying to provide for their families in jobs that make family life impossible, so stressed that, as one worker reports, even talking with her daughter after work is too hard.

Undoubtedly there will be those who argue that we cannot afford good jobs as long as there are people unemployed, and making jobs better will have to wait until we are on more solid economic ground; these are tough times, and we will all have to work harder to get things back on track. I would argue the opposite: no real economic turnaround is possible if our recovery is not based on creating and sustaining good jobs. We must go beyond the narrow economic analysis framed in recent decades that sees workers only as human resources, only as units of productivity.

Out of the ashes of this economic crisis we need not just to get the economy stabilized but to get the country back on track. As shown by these four case studies, for too many Americans work is already too hard, too stressful, and too long. Building a decent life for themselves or for their families has become almost impossible as weeks and months disappear in a whirl, leaving them so exhausted that even getting out in their community to help with basketball, the food drive, or the women's shelter is becoming just too hard. Only good jobs, those with both bread and roses, will restore the foundation on which we can rebuild our economy and restore some sense of fairness and possibility again for American workers.

The national conversation about the quality of work got off to a terrible start, however, with the bailout of two of the Big Three auto companies in the waning days of the 110th U.S. Congress in December 2008. General Motors and Chrysler reported they would be in bankruptcy before the end of the year and, along with the Ford Motor Company, whose financial picture was only slightly less dire, were asking Congress for a $34 billion emergency bridge loan.

In Washington and across the news media the big story was that Big Three workers were paid $73 an hour, compared with $48 an hour that workers were paid at the Japanese transplants in the United States—Toyota, Honda, and Nissan. Although the story made dramatic news, the figures reported were misleading. First, many Americans thought that the $73 referred to an hourly wage, instead of total labor costs, suggesting that auto workers were making over $150,000 a year. To Americans whose annual incomes average near $48,000, it was no wonder the Big Three were in trouble.

Although the hourly rate of workers varies both within and among the transplants, the Associated Press (2008) reports that on average Toyota's base hourly rates overall are comparable to those in the Big Three. The Detroit-based automakers do have more generous benefit packages, and when they are combined with wages, these companies spend approximately $55 an hour, compared with $45 for the transplants (Leonhardt 2008, 3). The major difference in the "total labor costs," however, is what the Big Three pay to their retirees, often referred to as their "legacy cost." For the Big Three, with close to half a million retirees and spouses, this cost is significant, especially compared with that for Toyota, for example, which has just a few hundred retirees. Despite the real numbers, the public story remained a wage issue.

The bailout bill passed the House with a significant margin but stalled in the Senate. With Christmas fast approaching, the debate turned into a face-off between UAW president Ron Gettelfinger and a junior Republican senator from Tennessee, Robert Phillips Corker Jr. Corker, a champion of transplants in his state—Toyota, Honda, Nissan—took the lead for the Republicans. As negotiations entered the final hours, the discussion focused almost entirely on auto workers' wages and benefits. Republicans insisted that any bailout should require UAW wages to drop to the level paid by the transplants. Although Gettelfinger and the UAW agreed in principle to the concessions, they could not agree on a firm implementation date, and the bailout went down in flames.

Despite the Bush administration's opposition to using TARP (Troubled Asset Relief Program) funds—already allocated by Congress—to bail out the Big Three, when the congressional bailout failed, fearing another major economic meltdown, the administration capitulated: on December 19, 2008, the Department of the Treasury allocated $17.4 billion to GM and Chrysler, half of their original request. The agreement took a page directly from the Corker proposal, requiring

> reduction of the total amount of compensation, including wages and benefits, paid to [GM and Chrysler's] U.S. employees so that, by no later than December 31, 2009, the average of such total amount, per hour and per person, is an amount that is competitive with the average total amount of such compensation, as certified by the Secretary of Labor, paid per hour and per person to employees of Nissan Motor Company, Toyota Motor Corporation, or American Honda Motor Company whose site of employment is in the United States.

It also went one step further. Going beyond wage issues, the loan agreement stipulated the "application of the work rules to their U.S. employees, beginning not later than December 31, 2009, in a manner that is competitive with Nissan Motor Company, Toyota Motor Corporation, or American Honda Motor Company whose site of employment is in the United States" (U.S. Department of Treasury 2008, 5–6).

As important as what is in the agreement is what is not. There is nothing in the agreement requiring GM or Chrysler to make "green" cars, to reduce or rationalize their product line, or even to increase the mileage of their vehicles. Except for management at the very top, there are no restrictions on management compensation. The agreement includes unprecedented restraints, however, on all auto workers' wages, benefits, and work rules, even though these changes would result in only very modest improvements in the companies' bottom line.

Labor costs make up only 10 percent of the purchase price of an automobile, and it has been estimated that implementing changes to match wages and benefits at the transplants would reduce the cost of manufacturing a car by only $850 (Leonhardt 2008, 3), too little to have any real impact on the financial woes of the Big Three. According to AFL-CIO president John Sweeney, "If autoworkers who are members of the UAW worked for nothing, they could not save the auto companies" (Parks 2008). What is troubling about the bailout language is that it falls into an all-too-familiar pattern of blaming downward. We have tended to canonize CEOs and traders for their high salaries but demonize workers if we think they make too much, or, as Leo Gerard, president of the United Steelworkers put it, "Washington will bail out those who shower before work, but not those who shower afterwards" (Kesterton 2008).

It is difficult to see this decision by Republicans to focus on workers' wages, first in the Congress and later in the Bush administration bailout, as anything more than political. Paul Krugman reported on an e-mail message circulating among Senate Republicans that said rejecting the bailout would allow them to "take their first shot against organized labor" (Krugman 2008a). In contrast, Ken Lewenza, president of the Canadian Auto Workers suggests, "The European Union this morning announced $40 billion for aid for the automobile industry and they are not challenging German auto workers who are at a higher wages and benefit level than we are in the United States and Canada" (Lewenza 2008).

For auto workers in the United States, more than seventy years of collective bargaining in the auto industry is effectively over. The U.S. government is now imposing wage and work rules, and not just in some abstract sense; it is taking the pattern in nonunion plants and imposing it on workers in the Big Three.[1] This action seems to be based on the assumption that the downfall of the Big Three was caused by the inability of the auto companies and the UAW to discipline themselves and that the only solution is for the U.S. government to step in and impose wages and benefits from the more efficient nonunion sector. President Obama is taking a much more activist approach to the auto bailout, including demanding more management accountability, as we saw in his call for the resignation of GM CEO Rick Wagoner (Stolberg and Vlasic, 2009). Major concessions by autoworkers, however, are still very much part of the plan.

The Way Out

The Bush approach to the auto bailout got it all wrong and in the process set a very bad precedent. There is already evidence that, with UAW wages cut to the level of the transplants, the transplants will begin cutting their wages as well. A Toyota report leaked to the *Detroit Free Press* suggests that the company should start aligning wages with those in the states where its facilities are located and "not tie ourselves so closely to the U.S. auto industry" (Roberson 2008). Toyota and the other transplants set wage levels only high enough to stave off unionization, and with the UAW on the ropes, why keep wages high? What is to stop similar provisions from pegging workers' wages to their nonunion counterparts if a bailout is approved for the steel industry, for example, which is also in freefall, or for other sectors in our economy? Like President Ronald Reagan's firing of the air traffic controllers for striking in 1981, Bush's last-ditch jab at workers and their unions could have broad implications (Maher 2008).

What about in states and municipalities facing huge budget deficits? Why not apply the Bush approach and force state or city employees to work at the wage and benefit levels and under the work rules of nonunion private contractors? Although in the short term and from the perspective of balancing the current budget this approach would seem to make sense, it is exactly the wrong approach to take when the federal government is working to stimulate the economy. With this focus at the state level on deficit reduction only, economist Paul Krugman refers to the governors as "fifty Herbert Hoovers" (2008b).

The last thing our economy needs right now is to set in motion a downward spiraling of wages, benefits, and working conditions. As in the auto example, lowering wages would do little actually to assist firms, which will need much larger bailouts, but it would further exacerbate inequality, making recovery harder for families. Instead, we need to start an upswing, a tide to raise all boats.

This tide was the promise of the New Deal that came to fruition for many Americans in the postwar era. Unionized jobs in the auto and steel industries and in the garment trades were the flood that raised many boats even beyond these basic industries and brought a level of economic security to Americans that had been inconceivable a decade earlier at the height of the Great Depression. Although we must be careful about romanticizing work in the postwar era which excluded large numbers of African American and rural workers from good jobs and narrowly circumscribed women's participation in the workforce, it was a period of steady escalation of wages and benefits and steady improvement in working conditions across a wide swath of the economy.

The question is, what would an upward spiral of wages, benefits, and working conditions look like in our current economy? Even with massive bailouts there is no scenario in which the postwar giants of auto, steel, and rubber will recover and lead the economy. Because of thirty years of outsourcing, offshoring, and the globalization of production, the postwar icons cannot be the engines of the new economy. At the same time, American industry should not be abandoned. With a thoughtful industrial policy, including government procurement policies, some elements of American industry could be an important part of a revived American economy. It is unlikely that hi-tech industries will be at the center of a new economy. What the 1990s showed is that hi-tech jobs, no less than industrial jobs before them, can be segmented, outsourced, offshored. Yet with forward-looking policies and incentives, science and technology can be important pieces of a revived economy, especially with a focus on green and sustainable technologies.

For the engine to drive the U.S. economy, Robert Kuttner suggests we look elsewhere. He writes, "Suppose the new administration announced a national policy goal of converting every human-service job to a good job that pays a living wage with good benefits and includes adequate training, professional status, and the prospect of advancement—a career rather than casual labor"(2008, 147). Professionalizing those who take care of and educate our children, the sick, and the elderly, he argues, makes a great deal of sense. Kuttner also points out that the helping professions make up a significant part of our economy, one that is growing and one that cannot be outsourced. Since the human services industry is heavily dependent on government funding, directly and indirectly, new policies could be put in place quickly. Furthermore, improvements in wages, benefits, and working conditions across the human services sector would gradually pull up wages, benefits, and working conditions for American workers in other sectors.

Regardless of the policy decisions we make, we should remember that there is also a union story here. It is not a coincidence that in the postwar era, wages, benefits, and working conditions improved as unions grew. After the collapse of the economy in the Great Depression, unions emerged, through legislation and in practice, as important counterweights to business and industry and became an integral part of our postwar democracy (Lambert 2005). On the national level, supported by a more interventionist state, through collective bargaining and political action unions fought so that their members could share in the massive postwar profits, and for the first time in the United States they established a link between workers' productivity and their wages. On the local level, elected union officers and workplace-based stewards organized to constrain management rights and thus establish some measures of justice and fairness for workers on the shop floor.

As union density—the percentage of workers represented by unions—fell from a high of 37 percent in the 1950s to single digits by the turn of the century, unions lost much of their bargaining power. Wages stagnated while corporate productivity soared. With the loss of density came the degradation of work. As we have seen, without unions or unions that were part of a strong labor movement, a new bottom-line corporate ethos left too many workers stressed, exploited, exhausted, and abandoned. With fewer members and diminished political and institutional power, unions were also unable to hold back a tide of growing neoliberalism and deregulation. Thus, in the final analysis, the loss of union density was a loss for democracy as well.

As we strive to put the country right, it is clear that we need a strong labor movement again. Having seen the consequences of unconstrained and unregulated capital, we can recognize the importance to our democracy of a check on corporate interests. We need continued voices supporting not only economic stimulus and reregulation of the financial sector but worker issues such as pension reforms, fair unemployment compensation, and programs to forestall foreclosure.

The labor movement is also foundational in our efforts to improve wages, benefits, and working conditions. As the *New York Times* editorialized in the wake of the auto bailout, "Even modest increases in the share of the unionized labor force pushes wages upwards, because nonunion workplaces must keep up with the unionized ones that collectively bargain for increases. By giving employees a bigger say in compensation issues, unions also help to establish corporate norms, the absence of which has contributed to unjustifiable disparities between executive pay and rank-and file pay (2008)."

For labor to play a strong role in rebuilding America, it will need to reverse the massive employer opposition that over three decades has crippled unions in the United States. Kate Bronfenbrenner and Robert Hickey report that "the overwhelming majority of employers aggressively oppose union organizing efforts through a combination of threats, discharges, promises of improvements, unscheduled unilateral changes in wages and benefits, bribes, and surveillance" (2003, 12). In the 1950s, according to a major report by Human Rights Watch on human rights violations in the United States, "Workers who suffered reprisals for exercising their right to freedom of association numbered in the hundreds each year. In 1969, the number was more than 6,000. By the 1990s, more than 20,000 workers each year were victims of discrimination that was serious enough for the NLRB [National Labor Relations Board] to issue a 'back-pay' or other remedial order" (2000,1).

Unions have worked hard, even in this extremely hostile environment, to set the foundation for a revived labor movement in the United States. Among their efforts are some exciting initiatives in organizing immigrants, women, and people of color (Milkman and Voss 2004), using strategic campaigns to take on global capital (Juravich 2007), and linking up the unions across the globe (Bronfenbrenner 2007). The Employee Free Choice Act, (HR. 1409, S. 560) was introduced on March 10, 2009, in both the U.S. Senate and House of Representatives, with the support of President Obama (Greenhouse 2009). It would allow workers to form unions if a majority of workers at a particular workplace sign authorization cards and would then require employers either to engage in a first-contract bargaining process or to submit to binding arbitration. Passage of the Employee Free Choice Act, which would do much to restore fairness to the process by which workers can form unions, could be an important stepping-stone in the revival of the American labor movement.

The momentum will be squandered, however, if unions use it only to restore some of their past institutional glory. It is not business as usual for either workers or their unions. U.S. workers across a wide variety of workplaces face a whole new set of circumstances and a whole new series of contradictions, only intensified by the current economic crisis.

Organized labor's movement away from work and the shop floor, which came with the postwar labor-management accord, served workers poorly as the ground shifted under their feet in recent decades. Unions must reengage with workers on the shop floor, in the office cubicle, on hospital floors, and on construction sites. Labor must build a democratic movement of workers' voices, their analyses, and their ideas about the length of the workday and the kinds of stress they are confronted with at work and too often take home. It must shine a light on undocumented workers in the shadows of the economy and, with immigrant workers' voices and their participation, build a movement based not on pity but on possibility. And it must build a movement to research, strategize, and educate workers, their employers, and the public about alternatives to simply closing plants.

Unions need to pull these private struggles out of workers' homes and turn them into public issues, reaching out to their allies and the general public, to academics and policy analysts. In many ways, the last time that work was on the national agenda was in the early 1970s. As younger, college-educated, and radical youth entered the industrial workforce, the old social order became unglued, with wildcat strikes and diagnoses of the "blue-collar blues" in dehumanizing workplaces. There was academic research, media analysis, and a major study commissioned by the U.S. government, *Work in America* (U.S. Department of Health, Education, and Welfare 1973).

From today's vantage point the "blue-collar blues," which occurred during a time of great economic prosperity, seem tame compared with the issues workers are now facing. Without academic studies, government commissions, and a new discourse about what American workers face on the job today, the thinking, the framework, and the analyses of the corporate community honed since 1980 will continue to dominate, as in the auto bailout. The legacy of providing for retirees, which represents the best that our postwar industrial economy delivered—a decent and secure retirement even for those who did not have a college education—will be reduced to "legacy costs." Somehow these retirees—not their CEOs, who failed to make any bold decision about their companies despite enormous compensation packages, or the traders whose greed brought the economy to a standstill—are seen as the problem. Without real alternative explanations, corporations will continue to use time-honored arguments against workers and a labor movement that in many ways no longer exists.

To build an argument and a movement to counter corporate America, we will need to hear from more workers directly. No sophisticated analysis or media savvy can match the power of workers' voices, telling their story. Glen, Jean, Margaret, Juan, and the others I interviewed have told us only part of the story. We need to hear more and listen closely.

APPENDIX

On Workplace Ethnography

IF THIS book were based on survey research, econometrics, or even documentary history, no extended discussion of method would be necessary. All those ways of conducting research are so much a part of the mainstream of social science and so accepted that no justification of method is necessary. But I have taken a different approach. As I have shown, my desire was to go deep to learn as much as I could about four workplaces and four groups of workers through extended interviews. Interviews, however, can be employed in a variety of research methods and different "ways of knowing," so it is important to distinguish the interpretive approach I have used from other qualitative methods and from traditional positivist ones.

It is not unusual for social scientists to use workers' voices anecdotally in their scholarly writings about work. Even highly quantitative researchers sometimes use open-ended questions or focus groups to add color to an otherwise straightforward discussion of tables and figures. Freeman and Rogers, for example, take this approach in *What Workers Want* (1999). In such works, however, it is very clear that the numbers are what really matter and that the workers' voices are ancillary. To these scholars, qualitative work may assist in the construction of better survey questions or play a role in enlivening write-ups, but it is never seen as a substitute for real quantitative science.

Other social scientists gather qualitative data through interviews and similar methods and may use statistical software to code their data to create numerical categories. They then employ the same methods of quantitative research to analyze the data and make statistical inferences. Although the data collection process is qualitative, the methods are still very much in the positivist tradition.

At the other end of the spectrum is what many refer to as oral history. As perhaps best practiced by renowned author and radio personality Studs Terkel, this approach involves letting individuals tell their stories as the tape recorder rolls. One can also see this approach in David Isay's award-winning documentaries on National Public Radio, including the series he produced of two very young African American boys, later published as *Our America: Life and Death on the South Side of Chicago* (Jones and Newman 1997). Isay is also the founder of StoryCorps, a project that has recorded more than 10,000 oral histories since 2003, and the author of *Listening Is an Act of Love: A Celebration of American Life from the StoryCorps Project* (2007). As anyone who has read Terkel's classic *Working* (1972) or listened to Isay's work knows, these direct personal reflections can be powerful.

Yet for all its power, I would argue that this kind of oral history as storytelling or journalism is just the starting point for a more rigorous interpretive social science research.[1] To explore this point in greater detail we need to step back and examine some of the basic principles of the interpretive approach.[2]

Interpretive social science rejects the positivist notion that our work as social scientists is based on counting the behavior of individuals in order to test hypotheses and theories. Instead, interpretive ways of knowing see the task as making sense of the complex webs of meaning that envelop human behavior. To complete this task it is not enough to skate across the surface of social life, counting behaviors; it requires what the American anthropologist Clifford Geertz has called "thick description" (1973).[3] Thus, the goal of interviewing in the interpretive tradition is not simply harvesting qualitative data from individuals to be either statistically coded or reported out in the form of colorful quotations and anecdotes. Instead, interviews are the windows through which we pass to begin the process of trying to make sense of complex social processes.

In many respects this approach to science turns positivism on its head. The philosopher Alfred Schutz (1967) and later Peter Winch (1958) suggest that the goal of the interpretive approach is not for social scientists to test *their* theories but instead to discover the theories that people use to make sense of their everyday lives and world. But, Paul Willis points out, "Social agents are not academic sociologists or organized into obedient seminar groupings, so their practices of sense-making require some digging out, some interpretation" (2000, xii).

Part of this excavation can happen in small pieces in individual interviews. I reject the idea, however, that an interview is just letting the tape roll, allowing us to glimpse some version of Rousseau's "noble savage" whose real thoughts and feelings emerge in some unmediated fashion in the interview process. With only modest input from an interviewer, interviewees often fall into stereotypical ways of expression. These often take the form of "the confession," "the testimonial," or "this is my life story," in part based on how they have seen interviews on television and in other media. These kinds of expression can provide insights, but we need to go deeper. More focused interviews provide the rich detail that propels ethnographic research. Interviews are all about chronicling the everyday and the ordinary, but in order to get there, those being interviewed must move to a more reflective space than we do in our daily lives. In part, this comes about as a product of the engagement of interviewer and interviewee.

For example, when I asked the Guatemalan workers to describe what they did, most responded, "I cut fish" (Tomás 2001, 3). I'm sure that is what they tell their friends or family members when asked. But because I wanted to know more about the intimate details of the labor process, we needed to elevate the conversation out of the everyday. I remember one interview in particular where despite all my follow-up questions—"Tell me more," "I don't understand"—a young man said little until I showed him a photograph from the newspaper of the inside of a fish house. He then spent quite some time describing the various operations in great detail. Together we had reached this reflective space.

Some people go to this reflective place naturally, some will never get there, and others need a bit of midwifery. Therefore, the role of the interviewer is not just to operate the recording machine but to coax, pull, nudge, and sometimes follow people into places they were not planning to go, to get into this reflective space. And if we're lucky, sometimes people tell us much more than just the details of cutting fish. The great interviewers are masters at knowing when to push, when to prod, and when to just be quiet.

The uncovering of how the people we interview make sense of their work and lives largely happens not in individual interviews but in comparing and connecting interviews. We collect bits and pieces—scraps of insight from individuals—but it was the whole I was searching for as I drove around Massachusetts listening to interview after interview in my car. It is at this intersection of interviews that the process of understanding and explanation takes place. It is not about enumerating or evaluating discrete pieces of data but all about making a whole out of disparate parts—no matter how complicated. In this way the interpretive approach is about more than just collecting individual oral histories.

For example, after my initial interviews with call center workers at Verizon I was confused. In several early interviews I had been struck by how angry they were about their working conditions and how they were being treated. Yet in other interviews the customer service reps went on about how much they cared about their work and their customers. These seemed like very contradictory findings. From a positivist perspective the question was which position was the correct one, or what percentage of people fall into which position. As my interviewing continued and as I compared interviews, however, it became clear that these were not, in fact, contradictory positions. The workers were upset about how the working conditions affected them personally, but they also found that poor working conditions were obstacles to their doing good work and serving their customers. So they both cared about their customer *and* resented how they were treated.

This was the connection I was looking for, and something I would have missed entirely if I had just done a few interviews or taken them individually at face value. In contrast to positivism, the goal of this interpretive approach is not to find out which interviewee is telling the truth but to develop a broader framework that can include and make sense of all truths.

The work of interpretation isn't bounded by the interviews themselves. Throughout the process it is critical to engage with theory, concepts, and specific literatures. We are not looking for some overarching theory to explain all our findings, as in the positivist tradition; as Paul Willis suggests "These concepts I throw at the data are not about scientifically understanding how human atoms respond to general laws" (2000 xii). Instead, we are looking for concepts and theoretical frameworks, writ small, to help us extend, deepen, or refine our analysis.

For example, I struggled with the interviews from the closing of Jones Beloit, particularly with regard to workers' self-worth after being laid off. My analysis would have been considerably thinner without Michele Lamont's (2000) insights about morality and working-class values, and Kathryn Dudley's (1994) discussions of the new social Darwinism. From an interpretive perspective we do not turn to the theorists to authenticate or make sense of what workers say, as some final authority. Instead, the interpretive process combines insights we gain from interviews with those that come from engaging with theory.

Finally, as Michael Burawoy has cautioned, it is very easy for ethnography to be inward looking, as he suggests happened to the "Chicago school" of sociology. Describing William Kornblum's *Blue Collar Community* (1974), he writes, "Kornblum did not reach beyond the workplace to the imminent collapse of the steel industry nor beyond the neighborhood to the eclipse of machine politics" (Burawoy et al. 2000, 22).

We need to expand the context for our ethnographic study of work, especially in this global era. For example, it was impossible for me to make sense of the dynamics of the labor process in the call center at Verizon without considering how the workers there are enmeshed in an emerging global industry. Similarly, it was not possible to understand the work of the Guatemalan workers without taking into account both the historical conditions in Guatemala that led to their migration and what it means to be an undocumented worker in the United States.

This is the general method that I used at each of the four research sites. Because of the very different types of workers and work, the challenges for each were very different. But my goal was to understand each set of workers on their own terms, from the inside out. Whenever possible, I use direct quotations from the interviews. I make no effort to quote equally from all interviews. Indeed, all the interviews contributed to my understanding and interpretation, but in each of the four chapters I focus on a handful of interviewees. Some of the people I interviewed stood out in their ability to reflect upon their work and their lives, and to articulate their thoughts and feelings. I use their words to propel the text. It is after all their story.

Taken by the power of the workers' words, I also wrote a series of songs based on the interviews I conducted for this book which proceed each chapter. Although I have been writing songs about work and labor for over two decades, these interviews provided insights into specific jobs and corporations. Their words, their expressions, and their turns of phrase were the raw materials that most songwriters only dream of.

I also wanted to allow readers to hear the voices of the people interviewed for this book. Reproducing full-length interviews was out of the question, but once I completed the songs, I realized that I could combine them with excerpts from the interviews to create a series of audio documentaries. For many years I have been a fan of the "Radio Ballads" produced by Ewan MacColl, Charles Parker, and Peggy Seeger for the BBC in the late 1950s and early 1960s, which pioneered the integration of music and interviews (MacColl 1981). Through this project I had the opportunity to explore and update this approach. My original songs and the audio documentaries are included on the CD in the back of the book and available on a project website: www.altarofthebottomline.com.

Finally, a few words about the photographs. They were shot by Paul Shoul, a Northampton, Massachusetts–based documentary photographer, in black and white with a large-format camera. Often in projects like this, photographs are an afterthought: once the research is completed, let's take some pictures to illustrate. We followed a very different course here. Paul joined this project a few months after it began and became deeply involved. Rather than just showing up to shoot pictures, Paul sat in on and participated in many of the interviews. Only after having spent time with people and building relationships with them did he photograph them. In this way, I believe, Paul was able to capture something genuine in the faces he has portrayed.

NOTES

Introduction

1   Recently concerns about workplace struggles have been reflected in the popular press, including Steven Greenhouse's *The Big Squeeze: Tough Times for the American Worker* (2008), Jared Bernstein's *Crunch: Why Do I Feel So Squeezed?* (2008), and David Kusnet's *Love the Work, Hate the Job: Why America's Best Workers Are More Unhappy Than Ever* (2008).

2   For a detailed discussion of my research methods, see the Appendix, "On Workplace Ethnography."

Chapter 1

1   For a more detailed discussion of worker agency and resistance in call centers, see Bain and Taylor 2000.

2   Charley Richardson (2008) argues that "working alone" also breaks down workers' solidarity and is an impediment to collective action.

3   For more on how both workers and managers engage and negotiate the various statistics generated in call centers, see Winiecki 2007.

4   Richard Edwards (1979, 101) suggests that the promise of Taylorism as a management practice in the United States was unfulfilled. "For one thing, the system was complicated and employers grew impatient long before the final elements were ready to be installed." This was particularly true in terms of ongoing monitoring (Juravich 1985).

5   It should be noted that Verizon is not the only telecommunications company with this approach to sick days; it was the policy in the old Bell system and has been adopted by most of the "Baby Bell" companies. The basic philosophy is to provide sick days as an entitlement but also to create a strong disincentive for using them by having them carry disciplinary action. In the smaller, community based call centers of the past, however, where there was more flexibility about time and scheduling, the use of sick days was less necessary.

6   Eaton and Rubinstein (2006) suggest that union involvement in managerial decision-making may be waning in general.

7   As Charley Richardson (2004) points out, the vast majority of recent technological changes that have taken place in the United States have seen little

intervention by unions, precisely because their contracts did not provide any mechanism to oppose or shape the use of technology. In the 1980s and 1990s, management in the telecommunications industry introduced employee-involvement programs, first QWL and later TQM. These programs were supposed to increase worker input in the work process—precisely what workers had lost in the postwar accord—and in doing so create better jobs. Virtually all these employee-involvement programs, however, came to be outside the collective bargaining framework; as management initiatives, they depended largely on the goodwill of management to continue. The vast majority of them were short-lived, and at AT&T, what had been a program with the participation of 100,000 union members was simply discontinued when the CEO changed (Bahr 2001). It is important to recognize that nothing was left institutionally for all these efforts by workers and their unions in employee-involvement programs to improve their jobs and their work life. No contractual floor was established for either worker participation or working conditions. One could argue that this is evidence that employers were not serious about really granting these rights to workers and that these programs were simply smoke screens to increase productivity and the speed of production. In the final analysis, workers were left with nothing to show for their efforts and no mechanisms to confront the rapidly changing workplaces.

Chapter 2

1   There is an ongoing debate about the impact of undocumented work on jobs and wages (Lowenstein 2006). Borjas (1999) and Briggs (2001) argue that undocumented workers take work away from native-born workers and in the process lower wages for low-skilled workers competing for these types of jobs. David Card (1999, 2005), however, suggests that the labor market is considerably more elastic, with immigration having little impact on job competition and workers' wages. For example, he examined the impact of the Mariel boat lift, when Cuban migration increased Miami's workforce by 7 percent, and found "no effect on the wages or unemployment rates of less skilled workers" (1990).

2   Maquiladoras are assembly plants located in an export processing zone, where national labor and environmental laws are not applied.

Chapter 3

1   For an excellent historical analysis of the restructuring of hospitals during this period, see S. Gordon 2005, 227–83.

2   In research on nurses with children, Scott, Hwang, and Rogers report what such nurses know all too well, that they have significantly higher fatigue and stress levels than nurses without children (2006, 86).

3   McIntosh, Palumbo, and Rambur (2007) suggest that the large number of nurses who have left the profession do not represent a "shadow workforce" that is willing or able to return to nursing, in part because of licensure issues. Because it is unlikely that nurses who have left the profession will return, it is even more important to create conditions that allow nurses how working to stay.

4   For more on the history of Filipino nurses, see Choy 2003.

Chapter 4

1   For more on the General Electric facilities and workers in Pittsfield, see Nash 1989.

2   Schuler and Jackson (1987) and Wright and McMahan (1992) discuss the alignment of human resources and larger corporate strategies.

Conclusion

1   This pegging of unionized auto workers' wages and benefits to their low-wage counterparts is not unlike what happened in the auto industry in Mexico in the 1980s and 1990s. In the midst of economic crisis, the Mexican government imposed wages and work rules in the unionized auto sector (Healy 2008).

Appendix

1   There is a great range of work that is considered oral history, from relatively simple journalistic accounts to much more complex work that approaches what I consider interpretive social science.

2   For an overview of interpretive social science, see Rabinow and Sullivan 1987.

3   Georg Von Wrights's *Explanation and Understanding* (1971) provides an excellent and very readable comparison of the positivist and interpretive traditions.

REFERENCES

Abraham, Yvonne. 2005. "Immigration Raids Empty New Bedford Fish Plant." *Boston Globe*, December 7: B1.

———. 2007a. "Patrick Says Promises Broken on Raid: Access Disputed on Immigrants." *Boston Globe*, March 15: 1.

———. 2007b. "As Immigration Raids Rise, Human Toll Decried." *Boston Globe*, March 20: A1.

Aiken, Linda H., et al. 2002. "Hospital Nurse Staffing and Patient Mortality, Nurse Burnout and Job Satisfaction." *Journal of the American Medical Association* 288 (16): 1987–93.

Allen, Everett S. 1973. *Children of the Light: The Rise and Fall of New Bedford Whaling and the Death of the Arctic Fleet.* Boston: Little, Brown.

Amatayakul, M. 2003. "Tough Questions? Scripts Provide Easy Answers." *Journal of the American Health Information Management Association* 74 (5): 16A–16D.

American Journal of Public Health. 2007. News release. March 29.

American Nurses Association. 2001. *Analysis of American Nurses Association Staffing Survey.* Atlanta, GA: Cornerstone Communication Group. February 6.

Anna (pseudonym). 2007. New Bedford Detainee Testimony. April 10. www.youtube.com/watch?v=2qG6FZbr9rM.

Annis, Sheldon. 1987. *God and Production in a Guatemalan Town* Austin: University of Texas Press.

Armstrong, Pat, Hugh Armstrong, Ivy Bourgeault, Jacqueline Choiniere, Eric Mykhalouskiy, and Jerry P White. 2000. *Heal Thyself: Managing Health Care Reform.* Aurora, ON: Garamond Press.

Associated Press. 2008. "Jobless Claims Data Paint Bleak Picture for 2009." *Yahoo! Finance*, December 31. biz.yahoo.com/ap/081231/economy.html.

AT&T. 1994. "AT&T Unit Is First U.S. Manufacturer to Capture Japan's Top Quality Prize." Press release. October 18.

Atkins, Judy. 2001. Interview. June 25.

Babson, Steve. 1995. *Lean Work: Empowerment and Exploitation in the Global Auto Industry.* Detroit: Wayne State University Press.

Bacon, David. 2007. "Who Killed the Immigration Bill, and Who Wants It to Come Back." *Truth Out Report.* www/truthout.org/docs_2006/061107T.shtml.

Baer, Ellen D., and Suzanne Gordon. 1996. "Money Managers Are Unravelling the Tapestry of Nursing." In Suzanne Gordon, Patricia Benner, and Nel Noddings, eds., *Caregiving: Readings in Knowledge, Practice, Ethics, and Politics*, 226–30. Philadelphia: University of Pennsylvania Press.

Bahr, Morton. 2001. "The Challenges to the Workplace in the Global Economy and the Opportunities Afforded by Labor-Management-Government Cooperation." Keynote address, 2nd Labor-Management-Government Symposium sponsored by APEC Human Resources Development Working Group, Mexico City, June 25.

Bain, Peter, and Phil Taylor. 2000. "Entrapped by the 'Electronic Panopticon'? Workers' Resistance in the Call Centre." *New Technology, Work and Employment* 15 (1): 2–18.

Bamberger, Bill, and Cathy N. Davidson. 1998. *Closing: The Life and Death of an American Factory*. New York: Norton.

Bartlett, Donald L., and James B. Steele. 1992. *America: What Went Wrong?* New York: Andrews and McMeel.

Batt, Rosemary. 1999. "Work Organization, Technology, and Performance in Customer Service and Sales." *Industrial and Labor Relations Review* 52 (4): 539–64.

———. 2001. "Explaining Intra-Occupational Wage Inequality in Telecommunications Services: Customer Segmentation, Human Resource Practices, and Union Decline." *Industrial and Labor Relations Review* 54 (2A): 425–49.

Batt, Rosemary, Virginia Doellgast, and Hyunji Kwon. 2005. U.S. Call Center Industry Report 2004 National Benchmarking Report. "Strategy, HR Practices, and Performance." Working Paper 05-06. School of Industrial and Labor Relations, Center for Advanced Human Resource Studies, Cornell University. digitalcommons.ilr.cornell.edu/cahrswp/6.

Batt, Rosemary, and Jeffrey Keefe. 1999. "Human Resource and Employment Practices in Telecommunications Service, 1980–1998." In Peter Capelli, ed., *Employment Practices and Business Strategy*, 107–52. New York: Oxford University Press.

Becker, Elizabeth. 2004. "Latin Migrants to U.S. Send $1 Billion Home." *New York Times*, May 19: section C.

Beloit Corporation. 1998a. Correspondence. August 20.

———. 1998b. Press release. August 20.

Bensman, David, and Roberta Lynch. 1988. *Rusted Dreams: Hard Times in a Steel Community*. Berkeley: University of California Press.

Bernstein, Jared. 2008. *Crunch: Why Do I Feel So Squeezed?* San Francisco: Berrett-Koehler.

Bieski, Tanya. 2007. "Foreign-Educated Nurses: An Overview of Migration and Credentialing Issues." *Nursing Economics* 25 (1): 20–23.

Blair, Mike. 2001a. Interview. June 21.

———. 2001b. Interview. December 7.

Bluestone, Barry, and Bennett Harrison. 1982. *The Deindustrialization of America: Plant Closings, Community Abandonment, and the Dismantling of Basic Industry*. New York: Basic Books.

Bob (pseudonym). 2003. Interview. June 11.

Boden, Glen. 2001a. Interview. June 7.

———. 2001b. Interview. December 16.

Borjas, George J. 1999. *Heaven's Door: Immigration Policy and the American Economy.* Princeton, NJ: Princeton University Press.

Boston City Hospital. Training School for Nurses. 1891. *The Thirteenth Year of the Boston City Hospital, Training School for Nurses.* Boston: Press of Rockwell and Churchill.

———. 1900. Pamphlet.

Boston Medical Center. 2002. *What Makes Boston Medical Center Special.*

———. 2007. *Annual Report.* www.bmc.org/about/Annual_2007.pdf.

Brannon, Robert L. 1994. *Intensifying Care: The Hospital Industry, Professionalization, and the Reorganization of the Nursing Labor Process.* Amityville, NY: Baywood.

Braverman, Harry. 1998. *Labor and Monopoly Capital: The Degradation of Work in the Twentieth Century.* 25th anniversary ed. New York: Monthly Review Press.

Briggs, Vernon. 2001. *Immigration and American Unionism.* Ithaca: Cornell University Press.

Bronfenbrenner, Kate. 2004. "Changing to Organize: A National Assessment of Union Organizing Strategies" (with Robert Hickey). In Ruth Milkman and Kim Voss, eds., *Organize or Die: Labor's Prospects in Neo-Liberal America,* 17–61. Ithaca: Cornell University Press, ILR Press, 2004.

———, ed. 2007. *Global Unions: Challenging Global Capital through Cross-Border Campaigns.* Ithaca: Cornell University Press.

Bronfenbrenner, Kate, and Robert Hickey. 2003. *Blueprint for Change: A National Assessment of Winning Union Organizing Strategies.* Ithaca: Cornell University Office of Labor Education Research.

Bronfenbrenner, Kate, and Stephanie Luce. 2004. "The Changing Nature of Corporate Global Restructuring: The Impact of Production Shifts on Jobs in the U.S., China, and around the Globe." Report submitted to the U.S.-China Economic and Security Review Commission. October 14.

Brush, B. L., J. Sochalski, and A. M. Berger. 2004. "Imported Care: Recruiting Foreign Nurses to U.S. Healthcare Facilities." *Health Affairs* 23 (3): 78–85.

Buchanan, Ruth. 2006. "1-800 New Brunswick: Economic Development Strategies, Firm Restructuring, and the Local Production of 'Global' Services." In Vivian Shalla, ed., *Working in a Global Era,* 177–97. Toronto: Canadian Scholars Press.

Burawoy, Michael, et al. 2000. *Global Ethnography: Forces, Connections, and Imaginations in a Postmodern World.* Berkeley: University of California Press.

Buss, Terry F., and F. Stevens Redburn. 1983. *Shutdown at Youngstown: Public Policy for Mass Unemployment.* Albany: State University of New York Press.

Calbreath, Dean. 2007. "Nursing Jobs Are Hot, but There's a Catch." *San Diego Union-Tribune,* September 9: F1.

California Nurses Association. 2005a. "RN-to-Patient Staffing Ratios and Patient Safety." www.calnurses.org/research.

———. 2005b. "RN-to-Patient Ratios Helping to Solve Nursing Shortage." www .calnurses.org/research.

Card, David. 1990. "The Impact of the Mariel Boatlift on the Miami Labor Market." *Industrial and Labor Relations Review* 43 (2): 245–57.

———. 2005. "Is the New Immigration Really So Bad?" *Economic Journal* 115 (507): 300–23.

Carl, Traci. 2008. "Village Fills with Deportees as US cracks Down," *Washington Post*, December 7.

Carmack, Robert M., ed. 1988. *Harvest of Violence: The Mayan Indians and the Guatemalan Crisis.* Norman: University of Oklahoma Press.

Centre for Education and Communication. 2006. "Bi-National Perspective on Offshore Outsourcing: Collaboration between Indian and U.S. Labour." October. www.jwj.org/campaigns/global/tools/outsourcing/us_india_report_2006.pdf.

Chacón, Justin Akers, and Mike Davis. 2006. *No One Is Illegal: Facing Racism and State Violence on the U.S.–Mexico Border.* Chicago: Haymarket Books.

Chase, Earl. 2001. Interview. May 5.

Chomsky, Aviva. 2007. *"They Take Our Jobs!" and Twenty Other Myths about Immigration.* Boston: Beacon Press.

Choy, Cather Ceniza. 2003. *Empire of Care: Nursing and Migration in Filipino American History.* Durham, NC: Duke University Press.

Chris (pseudonym). 2001. Interview. May 22.

Cohen, David. 2001. Interview. June 25.

Cole, Mark. 2001. Interview. June 21.

Compa, Lance. 2004. *Blood, Sweat, and Fear: Workers' Rights in Poultry Plants.* New York: Human Rights Watch.

Cowie, Jefferson. 1996. *Capital Moves: RCA's Seventy-Year Quest for Cheap Labor.* Ithaca: Cornell University Press.

Crandall, Robert W. 2005. *Competition and Chaos: U.S. Telecommunications since the 1996 Telecom Act.* Washington, DC: Brooking Institution Press.

Craypo, Charles. 1994. "Meatpacking: Industry Restructuring and Union Decline." In Paula Voos, ed., *Contemporary Collective Bargaining in the Private Sector,* 63–94. Madison, WI: Industrial Relations Research Association.

Cutler, Jonathan. 2004. *Labor's Time: Shorter Hours, the UAW, and the Struggle for American Unionism.* Philadelphia: Temple University Press.

CWA (Communications Workers of America). 2003. "Trouble on the Horizon: Verizon's Short-Sighted Strategy Spells Trouble for Workers, Consumers, Communities, and Shareholders." Spring.

———. 2006. "Bi-National Perspective on Offshore Outsourcing: Collaboration Between Indian and U.S. Labour." www.jwj.org/campaigns/global/tools/ outsourcing/us_india_report_2006.pdf.

Daley, Lauren, 2007. "DSS Wants at Least 10 Released From Prison." *New Bedford Standard Times*, March 12.

Dalton, Massachusetts. n.d. Department of Housing and Community Development. "Narrative." www.mass.gov/dhcd/iprofile/070.pdf.

De Janvry, Alain, et al. 1989. *Rural Development in Latin America: An Evaluation and a Proposal.* Program Paper / IICA, ISSN 1011-7741, no.12. San Jose, Costa Rica: Instituto Interameriacano de Cooperación para la Agricultura.

Department of Professional Employees. 2004. *Fact Sheet 2004: The Costs and Benefits of Safe Staffing Ratios.* Washington, DC: Department of Professional Employees.

Diego (pseudonym). 2001a. Interview. June 2.

———. 2001b. Interview. November 10.

———. 2007. Interview. June 30.

Don (pseudonym). 2003. Interview. June 11.

Doris (pseudonym). 2001a. Interview. April 16.

———. 2001b. Interview. May 23.

Dudley, Kathryn Marie. 1994. *The End of the Line: Lost Jobs, New Lives in Postindustrial America.* Chicago: University of Chicago Press.

Eaton, Adrienne E., and Saul A. Rubinstein. 2006. "Tracking Local Unions Involved in Managerial Decision-Making." *Labor Studies Journal* 31 (2): 1–29.

Economic and Financial Reporter. 2008. "Remittances to Guatemala Drop 2.9% in October." www.centralamericadata.com/en/article/home/Remittances_to_ Guatemala_drop_29_in_October.

Edwards, Richard. 1979. *Contested Terrain: The Transformation of the Workplace in the Twentieth Century.* New York: Basic Books.

Ehrenreich, Barbara. 2001. *Nickled and Dimed: On (Not) Getting By in America.* New York: Henry Holt.

Ellen (pseudonym). 2003. Interview. June 11.

Ellingwood. Ken. 2004. *Hard Line: Life and Death on the U.S.–Mexican Border.* New York: Vintage.

Esther (pseudonym). 2002. Interview. August 22.

Evans, Becky W. 2008 "Former Bianco Owners Settle Suit with Workers," *New Bedford Standard Times,* November 18.

Falla, Ricardo 1988. "Struggle for Survival in the Mountains: Hunger and Other Privations Inflicted on Internal Refugees from the Central Highlands." In Robert M. Carmack, ed., *Harvest of Violence: The Maya Indians and the Guatemalan Crisis,* 235–55. Norman: University of Oklahoma Press.

Fink, Leon. 2003. *The Maya of Morganton: Work and Community in the Nuevo New South.* Chapel Hill: University of North Carolina Press.

Folbre, Nancy. 2001. *The Invisible Heart: Economics and Family Values.* New York: New Press.

Fransman, Martin. 2002. *Telecoms in the Internet Age: from Boom to Bust to . . . ?* Oxford: Oxford University Press.

Frasch, Jill Andresky. 2001. *White-Collar Sweatshop: The Deterioration of Work and Its Rewards in Corporate America.* New York: Norton, 2001.

Freeman, Richard, and Joel Rogers. 1999. *What Workers Want*. Ithaca: Cornell University Press.

Gabriel, Jackie. 2006. "Organizing the Jungle: Industrial Restructuring and Immigrant Unionization in the American Meatpacking Industry." *Working USA* 9 (3): 337–59.

Garr, Emily. 2008. "As U.S. Construction Slows, Remittances to Families in Mexico Decline." *Economic Policy Institute*, July 9: 1–2. www.epi.org/content.cfm/webfeatures_snapshots_20080709.

Geertz, Clifford. 1973. *The Interpretation of Culture*. New York: Basic Books, 1973.

Georgianna, Daniel. 1993. *The Strike of '28*. New Bedford, MA: Spinner.

Gingras, Lawrence. 1998. Correspondence. September 24.

Golden, Lonnie, and Barbara Wien-Tuers. 2005. "Mandatory Overtime in the United States: Who, Where, and What?" *Labor Studies Journal* 30 (1): 1–26.

Goldman, Debbie. 2004. Interview. June 16.

Gordon, Jennifer. 2005. *Suburban Sweatshops: The Fight for Immigrant Rights*. Cambridge, MA: Harvard University Press, Belknap Press.

Gordon, Suzanne. 1997. *Life Support: Three Nurses on the Front Lines*. New York: Little, Brown.

———. 2005. *Nursing against the Odds*. Ithaca: Cornell University Press.

Gordon, Suzanne, John Buchanan, and Tanya Bretherton. 2008. *Safety in Numbers: Nurse-to-Patient Ratios and the Future of Health Care*. Ithaca: Cornell University Press.

Green, Hardy. 1990. *On Strike at Hormel: The Struggle for a Democratic Labor Movement*. Philadelphia: Temple University Press.

Greenhouse, Steven. 2009. "Fierce Lobbying Greets Bill to Help Workers Unionize." New York Times, March 11.

———. 2008. *The Big Squeeze: Tough Times for the American Worker*. New York: Alfred A. Knopf.

Griffin, Jean. 2001. Interview. May 25.

Gross, James A. 2003. *Broken Promise: The Subversion of U.S. Labor Relations Policy, 1947–1991*. Philadelphia: Temple University Press.

Grow, Brian. 2003. "How Much Do I Hear for This Nurse?" *Business Week*, December 8: 14.

Guskin, Jane, and David L Wilson. 2007. *The Politics of Immigration: Questions and Answers*. New York: Monthly Review Press.

Hall, Mike. 2008. "Nurses Take Campaign for Safe Staffing Levels to Capitol Hill." *AFL-CIO News*, July 14. blog.aflcio.org/2008/07/14/nurses-take-campaign-for-safe-staffing-levels-to-capitol-hill.

Hammer, Michael, and Steve A. Stanton. 1995. *The Reengineering Revolution: A Handbook*. New York: Harper Business.

Harris, Howell John. 1982. *The Right to Manage: Industrial Relations Policies of American Business in the 1940s*. Madison: University of Wisconsin Press.

Hartford, William F. 1996. *Where Is Our Responsibility? Unions and Economic Change in the New England Textile Industry, 1870–1960.* Amherst: University of Massachusetts Press.

Head, Simon. 2003. *The New Ruthless Economy: Work and Power in the Digital Age.* New York: Oxford University Press.

Healy, Teresa. 2008. *Gendered Struggles against Globalisation in Mexico.* Aldershot, UK: Ashgate.

Hector (pseudonym). 2001. Interview. May 5.

Hernandez, Juan. 2001. "All Things Considered." *National Public Radio.* Transcript. May 25.

Herrera, Yvette. 2004. Interview. June 17.

Heymann, Jody. 2000. *The Widening Gap: Why America's Working Families Are in Jeopardy—and What Can Be Done about It.* New York: Basic Books.

Hochschild, Arlie. 1983. *The Managed Heart.* Berkeley: University of California Press.

Hoerr, John. 1988, *And the Wolf Finally Came: The Decline and Fall of the American Steel Industry.* Pittsburgh: University of Pittsburgh Press.

Hoholik, Suzanne. 2005. "Shortage of Nurses Growing Nationwide," *Columbus Dispatch,* February 14: 1.

Holman, David. 2006. "Employee Well-being in Call Centres." *Human Resource Management Journal* 12 (4): 35–50.

Holtz, Jeff. 2007. "Severe Shortage Seen in the State by 2020." *New York Times,* May 27.

Hondagneu-Sotelo, Pierette. 1994. *Gendered Transitions: Mexican Experiences of Immigration.* Berkeley: University of California Press.

HRSA (Health Resources and Services Administration). 2007. *Severity of the RN Shortage.* bhpr.hrsa.gov/nursing/.

Hubban, Pat. 2001. Interview. June 7.

Hulse, Carl, and Robert Pear. 2007. "Immigration Bill, Short 15 Votes, Stalls in Senate." *New York Times,* June 8.

Human Rights Watch. 2000. *"Deck Is Stacked" against U.S. Workers.* hrw.org/english/docs/2000/08/31/usdom722_txt.htm.

Iadiapaolo, Janie. 2007. "Faster Food: Call Centers Transform Drive-Through Service." *Call Center Magazine.* July.

ICE (U.S. Immigration and Customs Enforcement). 2007a. Home page. www.ice.gov/about/index.htm.

———. 2007b. "New Bedford Manufacturer and Managers Arrested on Charges of Conspiring: ICE to Process Hundreds for Removal." March 6. www.ice.gov/pi/news/newsreleases/articles/070306boston.htm?searchstring=docking.

Isay, David. 2007. *Listening Is an Act of Love: A Celebration of American Life from the StoryCorps Project.* New York: Penguin Press.

Jacobs, Jerry A., and Kathleen Gerson. 2004. *The Time Divide: Work, Family, and Gender Inequality.* Cambridge, MA: Harvard University Press.

Jessica (pseudonym). 2002. Interview. August 15.

John (pseudonym). 2002. Interview. August 15.

Jones, Brent. 2007. "Illegal Workers Arrested: 69 Immigrants Held in Raids Targeting City Staffing Firm." *Baltimore Sun*, March 30.

Jones, LeAlan, and Lloyd Newman, with David Isay. 1997. *Our America: Life and Death in the South Side of Chicago*. New York: Scribner.

Juan (pseudonym). 2001a. Interview. May 6.

———. 2001b. Interview. May 26.

———. 2001c. Interview. November 10.

———. 2001d. Interview. November 18.

———. 2004. Interview. September 14.

———. 2007. Interview. June 30.

Juravich, Tom. 1985. *Chaos on the Shop Floor: A Workers' View of Quality, Productivity, and Management*. Philadelphia: Temple University Press.

———. 2007. "Beating Global Capital: A Framework and Method for Union Strategic Corporate Research and Campaigns." In Kate Bronfenbrenner, ed., *Global Unions: Challenging Global Capital through Cross-Border Campaigns*. Ithaca: Cornell University Press.

Juravich, Tom, and Kate Bronfenbrenner. 2004. "Out of the Ashes: The Steelworkers' Global Campaign at Bridgestone/Firestone." In William N. Cooke, ed., *Multinational Companies and Transnational Workplace Issues*. Westport, CT: Quorum Books.

Juravich, Tom, and Jeff Hilgert. 1999. "UNITE's Victory at Richmark: Community-Based Union Organizing in Communities of Color." *Labor Studies Journal* 24 (1): 27–41.

Kaiser Family Foundation. 2008. *Average Health Insurance Premiums and Worker Contributions for Family Coverage, 1999–2008*. facts.kff.org/chart.aspx?ch=706.

Katides, Mary. 2001. Interview. May 31.

Kay, Cristibal. 1997. "Latin American's Exclusionary Rural Development in a New-Liberal World." Paper presented at the 1997 meetings of the Latin American Studies Association, April 17–19.

Kennedy, Senator Edward M. 2007. "Making an Example of New Bedford Workers Doesn't Solve the Problem." *New Bedford Standard Times*, March 13.

Kesterton, Michael. 2008. "Verbatim." *Globe and Mail*, December 27.

Kibbe, David. 2008. "Former Bianco Owner Going to Prison," *New Bedford Standard Times*, November 4.

Kieffer, David, and Immanuel Ness. 1999. "Organizing Immigrant Workers in New York City: The LIUNA Asbestos Removal Workers Campaign." *Labor Studies Journal* 24 (1): 12–26.

Kilday, Anne Marie. 2007. "Opposing Groups Face Off over Immigration Sweep." *Houston Chronicle*, February 4.

Killarney, Janet. 2001. Interview. June 22.

Knowledge@Wharton. 2004. "Call Centers: How to Reduce Burnout, Increase Efficiency." June 16.

Knowlton, Peter. 2001. Interview. June 3.

Knox, Richard. 1996a. "City Expects 400 Layoffs with Merger of Hospitals." *Boston Globe*, April 12.

———. 1996b. "Firm Says Hospital Merger to Keep Deficits at $14m a Year." *Boston Globe*, May 1.

———. 1996c. "Mission Indisputable: As Merger Nears, BCH Clings to Culture of Caring." *Boston Globe*, June 11.

Kochan, Thomas A. 2006. "The American Worker: Disposable or Indispensable?" *Work and Occupations* 33 (4): 377–81.

Kogut, David H. 1981. "City Seafood Plant Workers Authorize Strike When Pact Expires Wednesday." *Standard Times*, July 27: 1.

Kornbluh, Joyce L., ed. 1964. *Rebel Voices: An I.W.W. Anthology*. Ann Arbor: University of Michigan Press.

Kornblum, William. 1974. *Blue Collar Community*. Chicago: University of Chicago Press.

Kowalczyk, Liz. 2001. "President of Struggling Boston Medical Center Resigns." *Boston Globe*, September 6.

Krugman, Paul. 2008a. "European Crass Warfare." *New York Times*, December 15.

———. 2008b. "Fifty Herbert Hoovers." *New York Times*, December 28.

Kusnet, David. 2008. *Love the Work, Hate the Job: Why America's Best Workers Are More Unhappy Than Ever*. Hoboken, NY: Wiley.

Kuttner, Robert. 2007. *The Squandering of America: How the Failure of Politics Undermines Our Prosperity*. New York: Knopf.

———. 2008. *Obama's Challenge: America's Economic Crisis and the Power of a Transformative Presidency*. White River Junction, VT: Chelsea Green.

Kwong, Peter. 1997. *Forbidden Workers: Illegal Immigrants and American Labor*. New York: New Press.

Kyler Workers. 2000. Testimony. September 16.

Lafer, Gordon. 2002. *The Job Training Charade*. Ithaca: Cornell University Press.

———. 2005. "Hospital Speedups and the Fiction of a Nursing Shortage." *Labor Studies Journal* 30 (1): 27–46.

Laing, Jonathan. 1999. "Grave Digger: How Harnischfeger's Flashy Chieftain Drove the Firm to Ruin." *Barron's*, July 12: 25–28.

Lambert, Josiah Bartlett. 2005. *If the Workers Took a Notion: The Right to Strike and American Political Development*. Ithaca: Cornell University Press.

Lamont, Michèle. 2000. *The Dignity of Working Men: Morality and the Boundaries of Race, Class, and Immigration*. New York: Russell Sage Foundation.

Latin American Economy and Business. 2007. "Guatemala. Heading of 5.6% Growth." September 27: 1.

Leidner, Robin. 1993. *Fast Food, Fast Talk: Service Work and the Routinization of Everyday Life*. Berkeley: University of California Press.

Leonhardt, David. 2008. "$73 an Hour: Adding It Up." *New York Times*, December 10.

Letvak, Susan. 2001. "Nurses as Working Women." *ACORN Journal* 73 (3): 675.

Lewensa, Ken. 2008. Interview. *As It Happens*, CBC. December 12.

Lichtenstein, Nelson. 1989. "From Corporatism to Collective Bargaining: Organized Labor and the Eclipse of Social Democracy in the Postwar Era." In Gary Gerstle and Steve Fraser, eds., *The Rise and Fall of the New Deal Order: 1930–1980*, 122–52. Princeton, NJ: Princeton University Press.

———. 2003. *State of the Union: A Century of American Labor*. Princeton, NJ: Princeton University Press.

Lorkin, Stuart. N.d. "Fish Processing in New Bedford." Report for the United Food and Commercial Workers, Local 328, Providence, RI.

Lowenstein, Roger. 2006. "What Is She Really Doing to American Jobs and Wages?" *New York Times Magazine*, July 10: 38–45.

MacColl, Ewan. 1981. *The Radio Ballads: How They Were Made, When, and by Whom*. www.pegseeger.com/html/radioballads.html.

MacDonald, Michael Patrick. 1999. *All Souls: A Family Story from Southie*. New York: Ballantine Books.

Maher, Kris. 2008. "Concessions Foreshadow a Tough Year for Unions." *Wall Street Journal*, January 4.

Marcelli, Erico A., and Phillip J. Granberry. 2006. "Latino in New England: An Emerging Demographic and Economic Portrait." In Andres Torres, ed., *Latinos in New England*, 25–51. Philadelphia: Temple University Press.

Margaret (pseudonym). 2001a. Interview. May 22.

———. 2001b. Interview. September 19.

Mark (pseudonym). 2001. Interview. May 23.

Marks, Alexandra, and Cristian Lupsa. 2007. "After New Bedford Immigration Raid, Voices Call for Mercy and Justice." *Christian Science Monitor*, March 16: 1.

Martinez, Ruben. 2001. *Crossing Over: A Mexican Family on the Migrant Trail*. New York: Picador.

Massachusetts Nurses Association. 2007. "The Latest Developments in the Massachusetts Nursing Environment." http://www.massnurse.org/News/2007/09/record_profits_2.htm.

McCammon, Holly J., and Larry J. Griffin. 2000. "Workers and Their Customers and Clients." *Work and Occupations* 27 (3): 278–93.

McIntosh, Barbara, Mary Val Palumbo, and Betty Rambur. 2007. "Does a 'Shadow Workforce' of Inactive Nurses Exist?" *Nursing Economics* 24 (5): 231–37.

McLean, Bethany, and Peter Elkind. 2004. *Smartest Guys in the Room: The Amazing Rise and Scandalous Fall of Enron*. New York: Penguin.

Meagan (pseudonym). 2002. Interview. August 22.

Melman, Seymour. 1983. *Profits without Production*. New York: Knopf.

Melville, Herman. 1967. *Moby Dick*. New York: Bantam.

Messina, Michael. 2002. Interview. January 25.

Migration Information Source. 2006. "Guatemalan: Economic Migrants Replace Political Refugees." April.

Milkman, Ruth. 1997. *Farewell to the Factory: Auto Workers in the Late Twentieth Century.* Berkeley: University of California Press.

———. 2006. *L.A. Story: Immigrant Workers and the Future of the U.S. Labor Movement.* New York: Russell Sage.

Milkman, Ruth, and Kim Voss, eds. 2004. *Rebuilding Labor: Organizing and Organizers in the New Union Movement.* Ithaca: Cornell University Press.

Milkman, Ruth, and Kent Wong. 2000. "Organizing the Wicked City: The 1992 Southern California Drywall Strike." In Ruth Milkman, ed., *Organizing Immigrants: The Challenge for Unions in Contemporary California,* 169–98. Ithaca: Cornell University Press.

Mining Journal. 2001. "Joy Global Inc.: Harnischfeger Industries Inc. Renamed after Financial Restructuring." July 20: 51.

Mishel, Lawrence, Jared Bernstein, and Sylvia Allegretto. 2006. *The State of Working America 2006/7.* Ithaca: Cornell University Press.

Molly (pseudonym). 2003. Interview. June 1.

Montgomery, David. 1979. *Workers' Control in America.* Cambridge: Cambridge University Press.

Moore, Michael. 1989. *Roger and Me.* Film. Directed by Michael Moore. Burbank, CA: Warner Bros., Inc.

Moore, Solomon. 2008. "Push on Immigration Crimes Is Said to Shift Focus." *New York Times,* January 12.

Mullenneaux, Lisa. 2007. "New Bedford Crackdown on Undocumented Workers: Early Morning Raid Triggers a Humanitarian Crisis." *Z Magazine* 20 (5): 1.

Munaiz, Claudia, and Alberto Mendoza. 2007. "Guatemala: The High Price of Violence." January 23. www.ipsnews.net/news.asp?idnews=36279.

Nalven, David S. 1998. Correspondence. September 14.

Nash, June C. 1989. *From Tank Town to High Tech: The Clash of Community and Industrial Cycles.* Albany: State University of New York Press.

National Public Radio. 2007. "U.S. Facing Critical Shortages of Nurses." *All Things Considered.* June 3.

Ness, Immanuel. 2005. *Immigrant, Unions, and the New U.S. Labor Market.* Philadelphia: Temple University Press.

Newsday. 2007. "ICE Breakers: Raids by Immigration Agents Were Hamfisted Attempts at Law Enforcement." October 5.

New York Times. 2007. Editorial. "Stop the Raids." October 4.

———. 2008. Editorial. "The Labor Agenda." December 29.

Nicodemus, Aaron. 2001. "Workers Followed Jobs Out of New Bedford." *South Coast Today.* March 22.

———. 2006. "Hundreds March on City." *New Bedford Standard Times,* April 11: A7.

Norwood, Stephen H. 1990. *Labor's Flaming Youth: Telephone Operators and Worker Militancy.* Urbana: University of Illinois Press.

Nurses Health Study. 2006a. "Night Work, Melatonin, and Breast Cancer Risk." *NHS News* 13: 4.

────. 2006b. "Sleep Patterns and Cognitive Function." *NHS News* 13: 4.

Olver, John. 1998. Correspondence. September 10.

Parker, Mike. 1985. *Inside the Circle: A Union Guide to Quality of Worklife*. Boston: South End Press.

Parker, Mike, and Jane Slaughter. 1985. *Choosing Sides: Unions and the Team Concept*. Boston: South End Press.

Parks, James. 2008. "UAW: Union Willing to Go Extra Mile to Save Auto Industry." *AFL-CIO News*, December 12. log.aflcio.org/2008/12/12/ UAW- Union-Willing-to-Go-Extra-Mile-to-Save-Auto-Industry/.

Passel, Jeffrey S. 2005. "Estimates of the Size and Characteristics of the Undocumented." *PEW Hispanic Center*, March 21.

Pavlo, Walter, Jr., and Neil Weinberg. 2007. *Stolen without a Gun: Confession from Inside History's Biggest Accounting Fraud, the Collapse of MCI Worldcom*. New York: Etika Books.

Pear, Robert. 2003. "Report Cites Danger in Long Nurses' Hours." *New York Times*, November 5.

Peras, Pete, and Kathryn Peras. 2001. Interview. December 7.

Pfeiler, Rudy, Tonio Acasio, John Sherman, Victor McCullough, and Jerry Riligan. 2001. Interview. December 17.

Phillips-Fein, Kim. 1998. "The Still-Industrial City: Why Cities Shouldn't Just Let Manufacturing Go." *American Prospect*, no. 40 (September–October): 28–36.

Pina, Tatiana. 2007. "Immigrant-Advocacy Groups Protest Money-Transfer Fees." *Providence Journal*, September 23: 1.

Piore, Michael. 1979. *Birds of Passage: Migrant Labor and Industrial Societies*. Cambridge: Cambridge University Press.

Plunkett, Chuck, and Anne C. Mulkern. 2007. "Raids Point to Push for Reform: Officials Say the Swift Roundup Advanced a Bush Goal." *Denver Post*, January 29: A1.

Popora, Douglas. 1990. *How Holocausts Happen: The United States in Central America*. Philadelphia: Temple University Press.

Porter, Eduardo. 2005. "Illegal Immigrants Are Bolstering Social Security with Billions." *New York Times*, April 5.

────. 2006. "Auto Bailout Seems Unlikely." *New York Times*, April 14.

Preston, Julia. 2007a. "Judge Voids Ordinance on Illegal Immigrants." *New York Times*, July 27.

────. 2007b. "Surge in Immigration Laws around U.S." *New York Times*, August 6.

────. 2007c. "Government Set for a Crackdown on Illegal Hiring." *New York Times*, August 8.

PR Newswire. 2000. "Results of Beloit Sale Hearing Announced." February 10: 7623.

————. 2007. "Change to Win Condemns ICE Raids in North Carolina: Calls for Immigration Reform That Gives All Workers a Chance to Achieve the American Dream." August 23.

Public Services International. 2007. *Nurses' Working Condition Are Fueling a Global Shortage.* May 12.

Quintalla, Carl. 1999. "Harnischfeger's CEO, Finance Chief Steps Down amid Pressure to Reorganize," *Wall Street Journal,* May 26: B8.

Rabinow, Paul, and William M. Sullivan, eds. 1987. *Interpretive Social Science: A Second Look.* Berkeley: University of California Press.

Ranalli, Ralph. 2001. "AG Aids Foreign Workers, Not INS." *Boston Globe,* April 1: A1.

Reich, Robert B. 1984. *The Next American Frontier: A Proactive Program for Economic Renewal.* New York: Penguin.

————. 1992. *The Work of Nations.* New York: Vintage.

Richardson, Charley. 2004. "Viewpoint: Surrendering the Shop Floor Means Surrendering the Future." *Labor Notes.* Spring.

————. 2008. "Working Alone: The Erosion of Solidarity in Today's Workplace." *New Labor Forum* 17 (3): 68–78.

Rising, David. 1999. "Worker Dies in Grisly Mishap." *New Bedford Standard Times,* July 32: 1.

Roberson, Jason. 2008. "Toyota Sweats U.S. Labor Costs." *Detroit Free Press,* December 12.

Roberto (pseudonym). 2001a. Interview. May 5.

————. 2001b. Interview. November 10.

Rodney (pseudonym). 2003. Interview. June 1.

Rogers, Ann E. 2005. Interview by *Healthcare 411.* Audio transcript. November 1.

Rogers Ann E., Wei-Ting Hwang, and Linda D. Scott. 2004. "The Effect of Work Breaks on Staff Nurse Performance." *Journal of Nursing Administration* 34 (11): 512–19.

Rones, Philip L., Randy E. Ilg, and Jennifer M. Gardner. 1997. "Trends in Hours of Work since the Mid-1970s." *Monthly Labor Review,* April: 304.

Rosa (pseudonym). 2001a. Interview. June 2.

————. 2001b. Interview. November 18.

Rosenbluth, Todd. 2007. "Telecommunications: Wireline." *Standard and Poor's Industry Surveys.* August 30.

Ross, Casey. 2007. "Gov Rips Feds on Treatment of Illegals." *Boston Herald,* March 9: 4.

Rubin, Lillian B. 1994. *Families on the Fault Line.* New York: HarperCollins.

Ruiz, Linda Barros. 2001. Interview. June 3.

Sally (pseudonym). 2001. Interview. May 22.

Sargent, Robert, and Gae Sargent. 2001a. Interview. June 6.

————. 2001b. Interview. December 17.

Satterly, Faye. 2004. *Where Have All the Nurses Gone? The Impact of the Nursing Short-age on American Healthcare.* Amherst, NY: Prometheus Books.

Savage, Mark. 2000a. "Valmet's Purchase of Beloit Corp. OK'd." *Milwaukee Journal Sentinel*, April 20: 1D.

———. 2000b. "Beloit Corp. Owes Workers Severance Pay, State Says." *Milwaukee Journal Sentinel*, April 20: 3D.

Schaffner, Julie W., and Patti Ludwig-Beymer. 2003. *RX for the Nursing Shortage.* Chicago: Health Administration Press.

Scharf, Adria. 2003. "Scripted Talk." *Dollars and Sense*, September–October: 1–3.

Scheve, Kenneth F., and Matthew J. Slaughter. 2007. "A New Deal for Globaliza-tion." *Foreign Affairs*, July–August: 1–2.

Schlesinger, Stephen, and Stephen Kinzer. 1999. *Bitter Fruit: The Story of the Ameri-can Coup in Guatemala.* Cambridge, MA: Harvard University Press.

Schuler, R., and S. Jackson. 1987. "Linking Competitive Strategies and Human Re-source Management." *Academy of Management Executive* 1 (3): 207–19.

Schutz, Alfred. 1967. *The Phenomenology of the Social World.* Trans. George Walsh and Fredrick Lehnert. Evanston, IL: Northwestern University Press.

Scott, Linda, Wei-Ting Hwang, and Ann E. Rogers. 2006. "The Impact of Multiple Care-Giving Roles on Fatigue, Stress, and Work Performance among Hospital Staff Nurses." *Journal of Nursing Administration* 36 (2): 86–95.

Seaman, Hank. 2004. "Young Mayan Bears Heavy Burden after His Father's Un-timely Death." *New Bedford Standard Times*, August 22.

Seidenberg, Ivan. 2003. Speech delivered to the Economic Club of Detroit. April 14.

SEIU (Service Employees International Union). 2001. *Agreement: Boston Medical Center and Local 285 SEIU.* October 1, 2000–September 30, 2001. Boston: Local 285 SEIU.

Shalla, Vivian. 2006. "Jettisoned by Design? The Truncated Employment Relation-ship of Customer Sales and Service Agents under Airline Restructuring." In Vivian Shalla, ed., *Working in a Global Era*, 120–48. Toronto: Canadian Scholars Press.

Sharon (pseudonym). 2002. Interview. August 22.

Shelly (pseudonym). 2003. Interview. June 1.

Shrader, Debra. 2001. Interview. June 3.

Silvers, Damon. 2008. "How We Got into This Mess." *American Prospect*, May 23–25.

Sochalski, Julie. 2002. "Nursing Shortage Redux: Turning the Corner on an Endur-ing Problem." *Health Affairs* 21 (5): 157–64.

Spalter-Roth, Roberta A., and Heidi Hartman. 1995. *Women and Minorities in Tele-communication: An Exception to the Rule 1995 National Study.* Washington, DC: Institute for Women's Policy Research.

Spang, Heather Radach, Gloria J. Bazzoli, and Richard J. Arnould. 2001. "Hospital Mergers and Savings for Consumers: Exploring New Evidence." *Health Affairs* 20 (4): 150–59.

Springsteen, Bruce. 1984. *Born in the USA*. New York: Columbia Records. June 4.

Stein, Theo. 1998. "Workers' Protest Idles Beloit Plant," *Berkshire Eagle*. October 1: A1, A4.

Stolberg, Sheryl Gay. 2009. "Signing Stimulus, Obama Doesn't Rule Out More." *New York Times*, February 17.

Stolberg, Sheryl, and Bill Vlasic. 2009. "U.S. Lay Down Terms for Auto Bailout. *New York Times*, March 30.

Suro, Roberto, Sergio Bendixen, B. Lindsay Lowell, and Dulce C. Benavides. 2003. *Billions in Motion: Latino Immigrants and Banking*. Washington, DC Report by PEW Hispanic Center and Multilateral Investment Fund.

Szaniszlo, Marie. 2007. "Judge: Don't Transport Any More Detainees." *Boston Herald*, March 10: 4.

Tastad, Ann. 1999. "In Dalton, Mass., They Understand," *Beloit Daily News*, September 2. www.beloitdailynews.com/99/jones2.htm.

Taylor, Frederick. 1911. *The Principles of Scientific Management*. New York: Norton.

Taylor, Phil, and Peter Bain. 1999. "An Assembly Line in the Head: Work and Employee Relations in the Call Centre." *Industrial Relations Journal* 30 (2): 101–17.

Telesco, Pat. 2004. Interview. August 18.

Terkel, Studs. 1972. *Working*. New York: Pantheon.

Time. 1979. "Chrysler's Crisis Bailout." August 20.

Tomás (pseudonym). 2001. Interview. May 6.

Uchitelle, Louis. 2006. *The Disposable American: Layoffs and Their Consequences*. New York: Knopf.

Uriate, Miren, Phillip J. Granberry, and Megan Halloran. 2006. "Immigration Status, Employment, and Eligibility for Public Benefits among Latin American Immigrants in Massachusetts." In Andres Torres, ed., *Latinos in New England*, 53–78. Philadelphia: Temple University Press.

U. S. Census Bureau. 1990. *United States Census of the Population*.

———. 2000. *United States Census of the Population*.

Useem, Michael. 1996. *Investor Capitalism: How Money Managers Are Changing the Face of Corporate America*. New York: Basic Books.

U.S. Department of Health, Education, and Welfare. 1973. *Work in America: Report of a Special Task Force to the Secretary of Health, Education, and Welfare*. Cambridge, MA: MIT Press.

U.S. Department of Labor. 2009 "Employment and Training Administration Fact Sheet: The Worker Adjustment and Retraining Act." www.doleta.gov/programs/factsht/warn.htm.

U.S. Department of the Treasury. 2008. *Indicative Summary of Terms for Secured Term Loan Facility*. December 19. www.ustreas.gov/press/releases/reports/gm%20final%20term%20&%20appendix.pdf.

U.S. House of Representatives. 2007. "Hearing of the Subcommittee on the Western Hemisphere of the House Committee on Foreign Affairs." *Federal News Service*, October 2.

U.S. Senate. 2007. "News Conference." *Federal News Service*, June 29.

Verizon. 2001. "About Verizon Careers: Meet the People That Are on the Verizon." www.verizon.com/about/careers/testimonials.html.

———. 2004. *Annual Report*. investor.verizon.com/financial/quarterly/pdf/04VZ_AR.pdf.

———. 2007. *Annual Report*. investor.verizon.com/financial/annual/2007/downloads/07_vz_ar.pdf.

Vogel, Norris J. 1980. *The Invention of the Modern Hospital: Boston 1870–1930*. Chicago: University of Chicago Press.

Von Wright, Georg Henrik. 1971. *Explanation and Understanding*. Ithaca: Cornell University Press.

Waldinger, Roger, and Claudia Der-Martirosian. 2000. "Immigrant Workers and American Labor: Challenge . . . or Disaster?" In Ruth Milkman, ed., *Organizing Immigrants: The Challenge for Unions in Contemporary California*, 49–80. Ithaca: Cornell University Press.

Wallace, Patricia. 2004. *The Internet in the Workplace: How New Technology Is Transforming Work*. New York: Cambridge University Press.

Wcislo, Celia. 2002. Interview. January 30.

Weber, Max. 2002. *The Protestant Ethic and the Spirit of Capitalism: and Other Writings*. Ed. Peter Baehr. Trans. Gordon C. Wells. Penguin Classics.

Weinberg, Ari. 2003. "Verizon and Its Unions Begin Contract Talk." *Forbes*. June 16: 17.

Weinberg, Dana Beth. 2003. *Code Green: Money-Driven Hospitals and the Dismantling of Nursing*. Ithaca: Cornell University Press.

Wells, Donald M. 1987. *Empty Promises: Quality of Worklife Programs and the Labor Movement*. New York: Monthly Review Press.

Williams, Corinn. 2001a. Interview. April 20.

———. 2001b. Interview. May 5.

———. 2004a. Interview. June 30.

———. 2004b. Interview. September 14.

———. 2007. Interview. June 30.

Williams, Henry (Terry), III. 1995. *From E. D. Jones and Sons to Beloit Fiber Systems, 1845–1995*. Dalton, MA: Jones Beloit..

———. 2001. Interview. December 16.

Willis, Paul. 2000. *The Ethnographic Imagination*. Cambridge: Polity Press.

Winch, Peter. 1958. *The Idea of a Social Science and Its Relationship to Philosophy*. London: Routledge and Kegan Paul.

Winiecki, Donald J. 2007. "Subject, Subjectivity, and Subjectification in Call Center Work: The Doings of Doings." *Journal of Contemporary Ethnography* 36 (4): 351–77.

Wolman, William, and Anne Colamosca. 1997. *The Judas Economy: The Triumph of Capital and the Betrayal of Work*. New York: Da Capo Press.

Wotapka, Dawn. 2008. "Home Value Decline by More Than $2 Trillion, New Report Says." *Wall Street Journal*, December 15. blogs.wsj.com/developments/2008/12/15/home-val.

Wright, P. M., and G. C. McMahan. 1992. "Theoretical Perspectives for Strategic Human Resource Management." *Journal of Management* 18 (2): 295–320.

Zatorski, Joe. 2001. Interview. June 21.

ACKNOWLEDGMENTS

I WISH to begin by thanking all the people who were interviewed for this book. Given how precious time is for all of them, the hours they took at kitchen tables, in living rooms, and in coffee shops to share their lives with me was a gift.

Corrine Williams, who has worked with the Guatemalan community for many years in New Bedford, not only coordinated interviews and acted as an interpreter but brought tremendous knowledge and insight to the project. Kim Wilson from the Labor Center at UMass Dartmouth first suggested I focus on Guatemalan workers. At Boston Medical, Celica Wsiclo, president of SEIU Local 285 (which is now part of SEIU 1199), Hal Ruddick, Joanie Parker, and Jean Griffin assisted in identifying interviewees. Dave Cohen and Judy Atkins of the United Electrical Workers first introduced me to the story of Jones Beloit and shared their archives with me. At Verizon, Steve Early of the Communication Workers and local union representatives Debbie McCarthy and Madeline Shields assisted in setting up interviews

This research was funded by an appropriation of the Massachusetts legislature. I would like to thank former senate president Thomas Birmingham and Massachusetts AFL-CIO president Robert Haynes for their efforts in securing funding that will also allow a copy of this book to be placed in every public library and every public and parochial school in Massachusetts.

I am grateful to Bruce Wilcox, director of the University of Massachusetts Press. From his enthusiastic first reading of the manuscript, Bruce has championed this project. Managing editor Carol Betsch skillfully shepherded the text through to final copy, and associate production manager Sally Nichols and designer Dennis Anderson created an evocative context for these words. Paul Shoul's photographs are the centerpiece of the design, and they so beautifully capture faces and moments that I will never forget.

The manuscript was copyedited by Patricia Sterling, Deborah Smith, and Beth Berry. I am grateful to them for the care they took with these pages. Eugenie Harvey, Beth Berry, Janice Webster, Kathy San Antonio, and Virginia Voudren transcribed the original interviews, and Mike Taber provided the index. At the Labor Center at UMass Amherst graduate students John Donahoue, Cassandra Engman, Carolyn Meadows, Amanda Plumb, Heysoll Rodriguez, and Heidi Zwicker provided research assistance. I also wish to thank Kate Bronfenbrenner, Dan Clawson, Harris Freeman, and Eve Weinbaum, who read and commented on earlier drafts of the manuscript. I am grateful for the comments of the two anonymous reviewers who read closely and captured the spirit of the project.

On the CD, Dave Mattacks, Duke Levine, and Richard Gates brought my songs to life with musical parts I could only have imagined. Mark Thayer deftly captured these moments as the recording engineer. In the mastering process David Cain's artistry wove the project together. Bob Carty was a wonderful adviser and mentor on the audio documentaries. James Stephens brought his skills as a sound engineer and his good humor to the project.

To my children, Nick, Mary, and Guy, who are ever-present. Finally I want to acknowledge Teresa Healy. From very early on Teresa knew the place this project occupied in my heart and joined me there. I am grateful for every breath.

INDEX